THE KAREN RE/

CW01311115

# STORM OF SUSPICION

THE 'TRIALS OF THE DECADE' AS EXAMINED BY COURT TV EXPERT

KEVIN LENIHAN

WILDBLUE
PRESS

WildBluePress.com

*STORM OF SUSPICION published by:*
*WILDBLUE PRESS*
*P.O. Box 102440*
*Denver, Colorado 80250*

*Publisher Disclaimer: Any opinions, statements of fact or fiction, descriptions, dialogue, and citations found in this book were provided by the author, and are solely those of the author. The publisher makes no claim as to their veracity or accuracy, and assumes no liability for the content.*



*ISBN 978-1-964730-44-8 Hardcover*
*ISBN 978-1-964730-45-5 Trade Paperback*
*ISBN 978-1-964730-43-1 eBook*



*Interior Formatting and Book Cover Design by Elijah Toten*
*www.totencreative.com*

THE KAREN READ MURDER TRIALS

# STORM OF SUSPICION

# CONTENTS

# PROLOGUE

**April 17, 2023**

I woke up to a text from author Dave McGrath: "Take a look at this... multiple police agencies involved... biggest story in the country!"

He included a link to a blog article about a corrupt State Trooper covering up the murder of a Boston cop by another Boston cop and the framing of the innocent girlfriend.

I had only known Dave for about a month, though we had already become friends who spoke daily. He worked for a Massachusetts sheriff's department, dividing his time between working as a correctional officer at the county prison and serving warrants alongside State Troopers in armpit cities like Fall River.

I immediately grasped what Dave saw in this story: opportunity.

But I hesitated.

A sense of foreboding? Hard to say now with so much water under the bridge, but I had deep reservations about covering the story, perhaps because it involved the kind of big conspiracy that seldom proves to be real. My misgivings were strong enough that I did something I had never done before in calling my friend and channel moderator, Tom Fleming, to see if I should take on this wild tale for my YouTube channel. I sensed hazards on the road ahead but couldn't quite articulate them. It was almost like I wanted him to talk me out of it.

He didn't.

### Desperate Search

In the early hours of a historic blizzard, an hour before sunrise, three women in an SUV searched for Boston Police Officer John O'Keefe. Hunched over the steering wheel, Kerry Roberts, a close friend of John's since they went to Homecoming together in high school almost three decades earlier, strained to see through the impenetrable dark. In the passenger seat, Jen McCabe, another close friend of John's, checked her phone to see if he had replied to any texts.

Perched on the back seat, leaning forward between the two women, was Karen Read. John's girlfriend of the last two years, now hysterical, she occasionally screamed and asked if John was dead.

Kerry and Jen, neither known as a shrinking violet, rode in stunned silence, scanning the suburban streets of Canton, Massachusetts. They didn't really understand why Karen thought John was in any danger or that any harm had come to him. He had probably just crashed on someone's couch after a night of drinking.

As they turned onto Fairview Road, headlights cutting through the near-zero visibility, they approached the home of another Boston cop, Brian Albert, married to Jen's sister. Reaching the edge of the property, windshield wipers straining to keep the heavy snow at bay, Karen sent a call to John. In yet another in a long string of seeming coincidences and odd events, that call would capture the heart-wrenching moment of finding John on his voicemail.

In this book, I'm going to go over the peculiar circumstances and wild claims that have made this perhaps one of the most talked-about and divisive cases in many years. I'll go over the best evidence and logical analysis to determine what really happened… not with certainty, but perhaps beyond a reasonable doubt.

And I'll zoom in on the big mystery that remains and the danger it presents to justice in this country.

**Odd Things**

As Karen was sending that call from Kerry's SUV, which was slowly cutting through the blizzard, John lay on the frozen lawn about six feet from the street, buried under several inches of snow. Clinging to the thinnest tendrils of life, he was no longer breathing. Temperatures had hovered around 18 degrees all night. The sound of Kerry's coming SUV barely broke through the howling wind. Rescue was finally arriving.

The prosecution tells us that Karen struck John with her SUV while traveling at high speed in reverse and then left the scene of the accident. The defense claims that John was lured into an ambush inside the house, where several men and a large German shepherd attacked him, and was then later carried out and deposited on the lawn so the cold could finish him off.

Assuming the prosecution is correct, when did Karen know she had struck John? Had she actually returned to the scene of the crime BEFORE finding John with the two other women? Kerry and Jen believe this, and Kerry gave compelling testimony in this regard.

Or, if the defense conspiracy theory is correct and the real killers used Karen as a mere patsy, was it, in fact, Jen who now returned to a scene where she EXPECTED to find her friend dead in the yard?

As we explore the case together, one thing we must state from the outset is that the Karen Read case is a two-sided coin. Either she fatally struck John with her Lexus SUV, or there was a comprehensive effort to plant evidence and manufacture the case against her. Either/or, heads or tails. Both the prosecution and the defense agree on this.

There ARE a lot of seemingly odd things in the Karen Read case that grab people's attention. Here's a sample.

At the scene outside 34 Fairview Road, with Karen hysterical and the first responders arriving, the residents inside the house never woke up and came outside. Police cars, an ambulance, fire truck, flashing lights, loud engines, and a screaming woman… all were right outside Brian and Nicole Albert's window, about 70 feet away. Brian is a combat veteran, someone who worked many years on the Boston Police's elite Fugitive Task Force. He had spent much of his life on call and ready for action. But that morning, nothing woke him.

In fact, from the scene, Jen called Brian's wife Nicole (Jen's sister) twice, and Brian himself once, but those calls didn't wake these parents of five.

Other mysteries center on John's injuries. The fatal wound came to the back of his head, a blow which left a horizontal gash and which crushed bones in the rear of his skull. Few other visible wounds existed. Eyes badly swollen, a couple of scratches on his face, but beyond that, practically no injuries showed anywhere else on his body, other than a bruise on his right hand, a minor contusion on his right knee, and some odd abrasions on his right arm.

Those abrasions on John's right arm have been the focus of great public debate. The State argues that it was his elbow that broke the taillight, and parts of the housing caused the shallow abrasions in linear patterns on his upper arm and forearm and shattered pieces. However, the defense argues that these arm wounds resulted from an attack by a large dog inside the house. They point to the fact that the dog was re-homed only a couple of months after John's death; an effort, they claim, that was intended to hide evidence. Indeed, a retired emergency room doctor materialized in odd circumstances during the middle of the trial to testify that the wounds on John's arm were from a large dog.

And in a stunning development, the defense actually enlisted the federal government to dig into whether the investigation into John's death was on the level. They subpoenaed the communications data of the witnesses inside the house and their family members, as well as investigators and their family. Incredibly, the powerful US Attorney from Boston handled the federal inquiry, even questioning witnesses in the grand jury himself, something unprecedented. To seemingly refute that a vehicle killed John, the Feds hired an elite accident reconstruction company to test the plausibility of the prosecution's claim; these experts then testified that John's injuries were inconsistent with being struck by a vehicle.

That *should* be game over, right? It not only establishes reasonable doubt, but it shows that John was, in fact, murdered in some other kind of attack, doesn't it? Which means a massive conspiracy took place to frame an innocent woman.

Well, I'll examine whether that testimony is credible. And I'll do it with extensive sources closely connected to the events.

Here's more of a taste of some of the odd mysteries.

How did glass pieces, some of which the criminologist couldn't identify, end up on the bumper of the SUV?

Why did Bureau of Alcohol, Tobacco, Firearms, and Explosives (ATF) Agent Brian Higgins, who had been at the house, and with whom Karen had recently been flirting by text, strangely report to work at the Canton Police Station around 1:30 A.M.?

Why did Brian Albert call him at 2:23 in the morning, in what he now calls a butt dial? Why did Higgins reply with his own "butt dial"?

What about the morning calls from Higgins to Canton Police Chief Kenneth Berkowitz, another close friend of the Alberts?

Why did Berkowitz try to keep the Alberts' name out of the media reports? Was it odd that he found evidence on the road when he drove by six days later?

Why didn't police ever investigate the home at 34 Fairview? Why did they collect blood samples from the scene, storing them in plastic party cups?

Why didn't local police find any pieces of taillight in the morning? The large, red pieces remained undiscovered until over an hour after sunset, more than half a day later.

But the evidence most driving the conspiracy theory involves data.

According to the defense's forensic data expert, who analyzed the extracted information from John's phone, John "ascended/descended" three flights of stairs after being dropped off by Karen. The data also says he traveled 116 steps on foot, which contradicts the evidence showing John never went far from where Karen dropped him off at the edge of the property.

And it's simply beyond the pale to think that John went inside the house, walked up and down stairs, and eluded all nine guests, only to come back outside and be struck by Karen's high-speed car. So if John indeed went inside the house and up and down stairs, that's where the fatal attack occurred.

But the data that really launched the Free Karen Read armies is summed up in this number: 2:27.

The defense's expert also analyzed the extraction of the phone of Jen McCabe, who had voluntarily turned it in to police. And what they found was shocking.

According to the most updated version of Cellebrite, the extraction software used by police the world over, McCabe, from her home, searched at 2:27 A.M. for "Hos long to die in cold." If she did make that search at that time, there's no innocent explanation. Because her friend of eight years, John O'Keefe, according to the defense, soon would be doing just that, when the killers put him out onto their own lawn to let the cold finish him off.

## Yellow Cottage Tales

While John lay in the snow, incapacitated and fiercely struggling to live, I was in the middle of a different kind of battle 35 miles away. I had a 104-degree temperature and my oxygen had dropped to an alarming level, which the outstanding staff at Mass General Hospital was monitoring because they had been treating me for stage IV lung cancer since 2018. Their hallways were stacked with COVID-19 patients, so they decided it was best to keep me at home.

That night the fever rendered me completely unable to sleep, so I went onto HBO and looked for documentaries. True crime rarely held much interest for me, but I found one that had a personal connection. Melanie Perkins McLaughlin's *Have You Seen Andy?* investigates the disappearance of her 10-year-old friend in 1976.

In 1976, I was nine years old and growing up in Lawrence, Massachusetts, a fading mill town racked by poverty and high crime, when a tragedy happened that remained seared in my memory. Ten-year-old Andy Puglisi, a kid from the projects who lived about a mile from me, went missing. He had last been seen at a public pool. To this day, his fate remains unknown.

While I didn't know Andy, the event shocked the city for a week, as news crews descended and a massive search took place involving the National Guard and even the Green Berets. I still remember the helicopters thundering overhead, the anxious headlines, and the tension in the faces of parents everywhere. They were different times, when people were unaware of the danger to children that lurked in the shadows.

Even in the first grade, I walked to school alone and could go wherever I wanted, as long as I was home for supper.

After six days, the tension finally drained from the city when headlines reported the police believed Andy was actually safe with relatives somewhere. Life went back to normal. Kids ventured wherever they dared, unsupervised and unprotected.

But not unwatched—because monsters were, in fact, still watching. And the calming headline put out by the Lawrence Police had actually been a lie.

Andy wasn't safe with relatives. To soothe the nerves of the city, police had falsely reported this to the media, something that became apparent as months and years went by and Andy never turned up.

A lesson learned: we can't just sit back and trust that authorities will take care of things.

Whether it's police or prosecutors… or the media… we can't just sit back and assume that someone doing their job somewhere will make sure that justice is served or our loved ones are protected.

Or that the truth comes out.

These professionals do have a vital and primary role, of course. But can we citizens be mere passive players? Or is there a role for us?

As I watched *Have You Seen Andy?*, Melanie's personal search for answers about her missing friend, the need for each of us to get involved in some way awakened within me.

As a result, my new YouTube channel, Yellow Cottage Tales, took its first turn into true crime.

# PART ONE: SETTING THE STAGE

# 1. INTO THE STORM

John O'Keefe and Karen Read had been dating for two years, but from John's point of view, the relationship had "run its course." His family liked Karen and approved of the match for the lifelong bachelor. Karen, described by lead investigator Michael Proctor as a "babe," taught as an adjunct professor of finance at Bentley University in Waltham.

Both Karen and John were in their forties, and neither had ever had a problem finding dates. John, a natural flirt with an enormous heart, had stepped up in a crisis to take on the role of father to his niece and nephew. Neither Karen nor John had ever married or had kids of their own, so both families looked at it as a good match.

However, some of John's friends referred to Karen as a "babysitter with benefits." And while Karen wanted to settle down, that didn't seem to be at all in his plans.

The reason John would have use for a babysitter is both a heart-wrenching and heartwarming story, and it tells us a lot about John's character.

Canton, Massachusetts, a pleasant suburban town with a population of around 24,000 and a median home value of $700,000, is about 20 miles southwest of Boston. To understand its culture, it helps to have a sense of Boston's history, particularly that of the heavily Irish district known as Southie.

Irish descendants make up more than a quarter of Canton's population, and many of these families trace their roots back to Southie or Dorchester just a generation or two ago. These are blue-collar people taking the next step in upward mobility, grabbing their share of the American dream. The children of people who grew up in the projects of Southie found middle-class success in Canton, some owning their own small businesses, some working as cops or firefighters. And their children continue that progress. Where their grandparents played street hockey on glass-littered parking lots and baseball on fields of dirt, the grandkids got daily rides to soccer practice at landscaped playing fields and discovered their "R"s as they slowly lost the Boston accent.

However, some of the old Boston culture remained. Highly patriotic, many still signed up during times of war to serve their country. They worked hard and could still stand up for themselves in a bar fight if provoked. Closely involved with the lives of their kids, they became youth sports coaches and raised money to sponsor the teams. A Yankee Tom Petty might say they loved the Red Sox and America too.

However, another aspect of that Southie Irish culture remained: hard drinking.

John O'Keefe grew up in nearby Braintree, another enclave of descendants from Boston. His dream had always been to follow in the footsteps of his grandfather and become a Boston Police officer. The middle child, he had an older sister, Kristen, and a kid brother, Paul. All three were tight. His parents remained together and would be a daily presence at Karen's trial.

John had a way of drawing people to him, forging friendships that lasted a lifetime. Brendan Kane, his friend since first grade, became a pallbearer, as did John Jackson, whom he met on his first day at Bridgewater State University. He had attended a high school dance with Kerry Roberts decades earlier, and she remained a close friend not only to John but also of his family. Even his ex-girlfriend, Tara Kerrigan Hayes, continued to support the family in court and in the media.

Graduating from Northeastern University with a degree in criminal justice, John dauntlessly pursued the dream of becoming a police officer, working as a summer cop with the Falmouth Police on Cape Cod, then with the Duxbury Police for a few years, before finally getting on the Boston force at the age of 29.

A bachelor living in the Boston neighborhood of Dorchester, John finally had the life he wanted: a promising career in law enforcement and a hard-partying lifestyle in his off hours.

But then doctors diagnosed Kristen with terminal cancer. And she had two young children.

John spent every day in the hospital at her bedside as brain cancer ate away his beautiful, outgoing sister.

The Irish have a unique sense of tragedy, born from the centuries of oppression and misery that seemingly ever lurked in the shadows. For some, the so-called "Black Irish," this gloom creates a defense mechanism; expecting disaster lessens its sting when it arrives. But this isn't the O'Keefes. Kristen maintained her sunny optimism even through the long ordeal of her dying. John's mother, Peg, always arrived in court infused with energy and ready for battle. Paul generously offers emotional support to the very people the defense accuses of killing his brother. Gloom isn't their way.

And John very much carried this spark of vitality. These are the Irish who raise a pint in the face of tragedy and carry on with a song. They embody the spirit expressed in the old Irish saying, "May you be in heaven a half hour before the devil knows you're dead." In other words, always one step ahead of the darkness and full of mischief till the end.

He had an expression that his brother Paul now carries with him in his heart: "It's only a movie."

But Tragedy, not satisfied with Kristen's gut-wrenching death, would put that all to the test for the O'Keefes. Months after her passing, John was in New Orleans with friends when his father called him to report that Kristen's husband had suffered a heart attack and had passed away. Now their two children were orphans.

John jumped on the next flight home, and with the family debating how to care for the kids, he stepped up. Saying "I got this," the next day he moved in with the children. He went from being a lifelong bachelor to becoming an instant father of a six-year-old girl and a three-year-old boy. As Paul said at John's eulogy, most dads have nine months to prepare for fatherhood, but John had to jump right in. He bought a house in Canton so the kids could remain in the same town and continue their lives with as much normalcy as could be managed.

The town of Canton also rose to the occasion, embracing the family and doing everything they could to support them. Prominent within this circle was Jen McCabe, who had a daughter who was already friends with John's niece in the first grade.

Karen Read, who had briefly dated John long ago when they were in their 20s, came back into his life two years before his death. Attractive and intelligent, she had always been the kind of woman who had a boyfriend, the kind who doesn't maintain a cluster of close female friends. She's a guy's gal, comfortable around men, used to hanging out in bars and drinking at a rate that men do, even as she reached her 40s.

She also had a long history of jealous rages with boyfriends who broke up with her and possessive behavior that made them uncomfortable.

On the afternoon of January 28, 2022, with the region preparing for a blizzard, John took his nephew to D&E

Pizza in downtown Canton. The owner, Chris Albert, Brian's brother, had until recently lived a couple of houses down from John. Enjoying warm relations with his old neighbor, Chris invited John out for drinks later that night. Chris would be meeting friends and family at the Waterfall Pub, a short way up the street from D&E Pizza.

During the afternoon, Karen hounded John with text messages, beginning to feel unappreciated. Sensing that John was in his gentle way ending things, she didn't want to let the relationship go. After all, she had invested two years in it. As he ignored some of her texts and calls, she doggedly persisted in trying to get through. He remained politely unmoved. He did, however, feel slightly guilty over being sharp with her that morning when he accused her of spoiling the kids. Karen didn't technically live with John, but she had been spending most nights there for some time. She owned her own homes in Mansfield and Medfield, though most of the time she rented them out.

Throughout January of 2022, for much of the population, the dam was about to burst. People had endured a year and a half of lockdowns and social isolation. In December, as the president kept insisting that the virus would be defeated if everyone just got the vax, the Omicron variant of COVID-19 spread like wildfire. It hit vaccinated and unvaccinated people equally hard, so the public ignored both the administration and the state government in Boston. This wasn't China, so when the people had had it with the lockdowns, they rebelled.

By the weekend of January 29, that meant going out for drinks.

John made plans to go out drinking with Michael Camerano and Curt Roberts at C.F. McCarthy's, an upscale pub next to D&E. Before leaving home with Camerano, John, ever the gentleman, moved his Chevy Traverse out of the garage so that, with the impending storm, Karen could park there. It's a two-door garage, but one that normally didn't have space for Karen's SUV, the other bay being filled with John's hobby car.

At C.F. McCarthy's, O'Keefe, Camerano, and Roberts drank beers and talked about their kids. Camerano's daughter and John's niece, Kayley, had both just been accepted into an elite high school, so it was a celebration of sorts. Eventually, Karen started texting him.

She wanted to join them.

## Night Out

Karen's routine was to start drinking vodka at home at five, so she could certainly handle her booze. It's not known whether she drank before reaching C.F. McCarthy's to join John and his friends, but while there, she downed multiple drinks and ordered shots of vodka on the side to amp them up, consuming a total of seven shots. She would have two more at the next pub. No one, however, testified that she appeared intoxicated.

At 9:45 P.M., Chris Albert texted John to join them at the Waterfall, and he and Karen left five minutes later. The Waterfall is a short walk from C.F. McCarthy's. With the approaching blizzard, and with Canton being too close to Boston to attract a younger crowd, the establishment was dead that night, despite it being a Saturday and despite there being a band. No other customer is visible on the surveillance tape other than those with the group of friends.

Brian Albert, part of the Boston Police's elite Fugitive Task Force, was somewhat of a legend, the cop who had collared the Craigslist Killer. He had appeared as a regular on the reality show *Boston's Finest*, where he stepped into the fighting ring to train as a boxer. Chris Albert described his brother as "the toughest guy I know… but also the smartest." A former Marine, Brian was a veteran of the Gulf War. We'll take a closer look shortly.

**Canton Noir**

Hours earlier, Albert had driven from New York with ATF Agent Brian Higgins, where they had attended the funeral of a cop killed in the line of duty. Higgins had an office at the Canton Police headquarters. Weeks before John's death, Karen had initiated a flirtatious text relationship, despite barely knowing him, saying she found him "hot." The flirtation lasted only a couple of weeks, and it included a kiss planted on his lips by Karen and a visit to Brian's house. But it had ended just as suddenly about 10 days before that night everyone met at the Waterfall. During that encounter, she would avoid him, and he would text her: "Umm, well?"

There are no indications that John ever learned of her text romance with Agent Higgins. By the time of the get together on January 29, Karen had ended those texts, but Higgins likely remained interested, though also conflicted, because he considered John a friend and didn't like the image of himself moving in on a buddy's girlfriend. But for Higgins, someone like Karen—attractive and somewhat sophisticated—represented a rare catch that was hard for him to resist.

In surveillance video from the Waterfall, Higgins and Albert are seen play fighting, something the defense focused on in the trial, trying to suggest they were actually *planning* an attack on John. Subsequent viewing of the surveillance by fans of Karen suggests that, as he was leaving, Higgins was angry and shouting at John, who was sitting quietly with Karen.

But no one testified to such an incident, and Karen has never claimed that Higgins ever showed any anger at John that night. There's simply no doubt that Karen would have exploited this and talked about it in her many media interviews if it had happened.

Other guests at the Waterfall:

Nicole Albert, Brian's wife, a tall, motherly figure.

Their 26-year-old daughter Caitlin, who lived in Southie with her boyfriend and worked for the Attorney General in Boston.

Chris Albert and his wife Julie, close friends with the sister of the eventual lead investigator, Trooper Michael Proctor.

Matt and Jen McCabe, later the focus of the conspiracy theory put out by the defense.

And another couple whose kid played in the basketball game that night.

This was the occasion for meeting: most of these parents had kids in a local game that evening.

With the bar's kitchen closed, Karen tried to talk Chris into opening D&E so they could grab some pizza for a late-night snack. Chris might normally accommodate that kind of request, but he was trying to lose weight, part of a New Year's resolution.

Instead, the group decided to head over to Brian Albert's house for a little after-hours party. Most of them were in their 40s, so the other couple declined the offer, and Chris and Julie walked home, but the McCabes eagerly accepted. Higgins agreed to join them. Caitlin, whose boyfriend Tristan would drive from Southie to pick her up around 1:30, also decided to go.

As did John O'Keefe.

It's only a movie.

**After Hours**

A small party had already been underway for several hours at 34 Fairview. Brian Albert Jr. is a towering and intelligent young man, but a gentle giant who, at the time, suffered from anxiety, a physical condition due to the subtle chemistry of the brain, something very common and controllable in young adults. It was his birthday, but the anxiety made him more comfortable celebrating at home with a small group of friends.

By the time his parents and their guests for the after-hours party were heading over, most of Brian Jr.'s friends had gone home for the night. But Sarah Levinson, a 23-year-old nurse, and Julie Nagel, also 23, remained.

Also present was Colin Albert, who had arrived late to pay his respects to his cousin. Decades earlier, his father Chris had been convicted of a deadly hit-and-run accident, so one thing Chris made sure his children didn't do was drink and drive. The drinking age in Massachusetts is 21, but it's not uncommon for high school kids in this area to drink alcohol, and indeed it's a strong part of the culture for these descendants of Southie. So, Colin, a senior in high school, got dropped off and picked up an hour or so later.

What time he actually left the house was key information hotly debated at the first trial and likely to be argued over in the second. In fact, attempts to point the finger at Colin would take an even more bizarre turn in the summer of 2023, when allies of Karen would try to use me—the humble reporter at the Yellow Cottage—to put out a false and defamatory story about the 17-year-old high school football star.

After leaving the Waterfall, John called Jen McCabe to get Brian Albert's address and entered it into Waze for directions. Minutes later, they arrived at the same time as a pickup truck, which was there to collect Julie Nagel, one of Brian Jr.'s guests.

Karen seems to have decided not to go to the after-hours party, though she tells very contradictory versions of the story. On *Dateline*, she says she was waiting for John's signal from the house to say it was cool to go inside. In other versions, she had an upset stomach and needed to go home. She told the troopers "grown-ass" people don't go to after-hours parties. It's likely that she and John were in a heated argument, as they had been fighting a lot the last few weeks, and hours of drinking now fueled the tension.

They pulled up just past the driveway, then she moved up to park at the edge of the property, about 80 feet away. She remained there for several minutes before going home.

## Cover-Up?

Exactly where and when John got out of the car remains in dispute. On two national TV interviews, Karen said she dropped John off at the "foot of the driveway" and watched him walk across the threshold into the house. When exactly she first recovered that memory or made that claim is part of the dispute, since she had never said this before. And she didn't explain why, in this scenario, she pulled over to the far edge of the property and waited for six or seven minutes. She also claimed that she called and texted John before leaving, but there were no texts from her at that time, and the first call comes when she was likely on the road.

The prosecution says that John didn't get out of the car at the driveway and never went inside the house, a claim backed by all the witnesses, including Julie Nagel, who went out to the pickup truck to tell her brother that she had decided to stay at the party and get another ride home, and who then returned inside the house. None of the three passengers in the truck saw anyone get out of Karen's Lexus SUV. And none of the other eight people in the house saw John.

The defense, however, charges that these witnesses are lying in order to protect the *real* killers, whom they propose were inside the house.

Hundreds of thousands of people, probably even the vast majority who follow the case, believe the defense theory. They feel, based on their understanding of the evidence, that not only was there a systematic attempt to cover up the crime by the killers, but that this conspiracy includes a powerful network of local and state cops, medical officials, and perhaps even the District Attorney himself.

Many things drive these beliefs, but certainly among them *are* the odd things, or at least seemingly odd things. We've discussed a few, but there are many more, and I'll hit them all.

This actually is a good time to introduce one of the Yellow Cottage Tales rules I've developed along the way. The Yellow Cottage is my YouTube home. Ready?

**YCT Rule #6: Odd things can add up to UNreasonable doubt.**

Sure, they can certainly add up to *reasonable* doubt. We all know that. But there are odd things in EVERY case. No exception. Dig long enough... and with the resources of a good defense team, digging isn't a problem... and odd things will be found.

But if the prosecution's evidence of a case is compelling enough, then odd things are just that... odd things. If that evidence is indeed compelling, then the doubt that the odd things create is actually *unreasonable.*

What we're going to do is go over whether the prosecution's evidence is compelling enough to render the odd things as merely odd things.

But we're also going to examine whether any of the odd things actually have reasonable explanations. To the extent that the State's case isn't compelling, explaining the odd things becomes more important, and if we can't explain them, that could lead to reasonable doubt.

It might even add up to a cover-up.

### Different Paths

That Friday afternoon, as Brian Albert and Agent Higgins were driving back from New York and John was making plans to go out drinking, low pressure gathered steam off the coast. Flights were already being canceled. Arctic air swept down from the north while the warmer Atlantic Ocean pumped moisture into the spinning cauldron that slowly descended over the region.

While events unfolded in Canton that weekend, Dave McGrath anxiously awaited the self-publication of his first book, to be released that Monday. He had long dreamed of becoming a published writer, but his journey had been long and winding, taking him from the Dorchester projects to the battlefields of Afghanistan and Iraq… and finally, to walking in the footsteps of predators and their victims.

Two things had driven Dave to write *OBSESSED: A Survivor's Quest to Find Justice for the Lost Boys of New England*. For one thing, he had always been obsessed with true crime—every book he could find, every documentary. And he stored the details in his mind like an encyclopedia of modern misery. To understand his interest, it helps to know that as a child, he himself became a victim of a long period of predatory sexual abuse, so he felt a kinship with other victims.

When he retired from the military, he began pursuing writing gigs for any journal involved in topics that interested him, from sports to politics. But it was only a matter of time before he began putting his developing skills to work in hunting monsters like the ones who had preyed on him.

He focused on a predator from the '70s from the city he had settled in: Providence, Rhode Island. Wayne Chapman had been bringing little boys into the woods to rape them throughout the decade, until 1976, when he was pulled over in New York driving a converted bread truck filled with kiddie porn, handcuffs, a starter's pistol… and a pair of socks that would later be identified by Andy Puglisi's mother. So, at the same moment I was watching *Have You Seen Andy?* and John O'Keefe was lying unconscious in the snow, Dave was sweating out the reception to his first book, the product of seven years of obsessive work.

I tell you this because through most of this journey covering Karen Read, Dave was a close partner. He remains a very close friend. But this journey would eventually take us down different paths and to different destinations.

# 2. A TALL, DARK MAN

ATF Agent Brian Higgins seems like the kind of guy you would want to sit next to at the bar and at the same time, the kind you would avoid if it was too late at night, depending on how deep he was into his Jameson and gingers. A burly guy with tattooed arms, he was also a man who came to tears several times on the stand when talking about family members or John O'Keefe's nephew, with whom he had played video games. The impression is of the kind of man whose quick emotions might make him capable of warmth to a stranger or sudden anger with an acquaintance.

It's important to take a moment to point out that these aren't characters in a TV series. Whether it's Karen, Jen McCabe, or Brian Higgins, these are real human beings who have lived full lives… and in the case of Higgins, an extraordinary one.

Brian Higgins comes from a line of firefighters for the town of Cambridge, all the way back four generations, a tradition that meant a lot to Brian growing up. He was very close to both his father and grandfather, retired Cambridge Jakes. His eyes moisten when he talks about them, but besides love, he carries tremendous respect for the lives they led. And they were all extremely proud when he made lieutenant of the Cambridge Fire Department.

But he felt a call to duty. In the '90s, he had been in the Army National Guard, and his former commander had been in touch with him as the occupation of Iraq heated up and hundreds of American soldiers were dying. They needed all the help they could get.

The commander offered him the chance to go to Officer Candidate School, but he refused and instead chose direct deployment to Iraq, where his superiors assigned him to a security detail for supply convoys. This was very dangerous work, where his skills as an EMT came in handy as the lines of trucks came under attack.

He returned home, like every combat veteran, a changed man. He went back to the fire department for a couple of years, but for some reason, the work no longer satisfied him. When one of his oldest friends, who had made a successful career at the Bureau of Alcohol, Tobacco, Firearms, and Explosives, recruited him to join federal law enforcement, he decided to at least take the interview. When they eagerly offered him a job, he had a dilemma: take on this new challenge, one which promised intense work and high adrenaline, or stay with the family tradition in Cambridge.

Brian's father hadn't approved the decision to go to Iraq. His father had been in the Navy during the Vietnam War, and his grandfather had fought during World War II. But Americans were dying in Iraq, and as much as his dad valued the military tradition in their family, no one wants to risk losing a son. Brian wasn't a young man; his career would get no boost from this service. He was already a lieutenant, so it wasn't worth the risk.

Now, with this new choice, Higgins consulted his grandfather instead. Even on the stand, when discussing his family, Brian's emotion was palpable. The older man didn't wish to see his grandson leave the cherished institution the family had been so much a part of. But wisdom allowed him to see what even Brian couldn't: that he had pretty much already made up his mind.

Higgins told the ATF that he would take the job on one condition: he had to be assigned to the Boston area.

The ATF had understandable reluctance. They intended to use Higgins for undercover work, and the risk of being recognized was much greater locally. But Brian's unique skill set made him too valuable for the agency to pass up. So, he became a Fed.

It didn't take long for him to get another baptism under fire. In 2010, he was working with a partner from the Somerville Police, Mario Oliveira, assigned to work with the ATF in order to put a dent in the heavy gun traffic afflicting the city. A gunrunner who had been cooperating with the government had gone AWOL, so there was a warrant out for him. Higgins and Oliveira decided to swing by his apartment in the Broadway area of Somerville. They pulled into a parking lot where they could see his car and the apartment door and called for backup.

But before backup could arrive, the target was on the move, heading from the apartment to his car, wearing a backpack that the cops suspected was filled with weapons. Not knowing if they had been made, Oliveira ducked into the bushes while Higgins went for their vehicle so he could attempt to block in the target's car. With their unmarked car blocking the front of the target's car, Higgins joined his partner, who was now making a move.

The target made it to his car and got in just as Oliveira arrived, weapon drawn, and yanked the door open. Higgins was right behind his shoulder and felt the bullets fly by when gunfire quickly erupted.

By then, backup was finally arriving, and a shootout took place. Oliveira was struck six times and immediately entered a fight for his life. Higgins pulled his partner to safety as the gunfight raged around them. The target was eventually hit and killed, while Higgins found his medical bag and applied his many years of training to keep Oliveira alive.

For Higgins, there was nothing heroic about it. He was just reacting without thinking, doing what years of experience had conditioned him to do. He would later receive several medals for his performance in the line of duty.

Higgins clearly isn't comfortable talking about his achievements. We Massachusetts Irish squirm even when someone else says something nice about us. The highest compliment we hope for is "he stood his watch and did his job," or depending on where you grew up, "he kept his mouth shut." Anyone seeking more praise than that tends to be mistrusted as someone trying to rise above their station, and there's no sin around here greater than that.

However, whether you're Karen or one of the witnesses, it's difficult to ignore the smears about you flooding through social media and on TV. You become a caricature, all of the decent things you've done in your life get ignored or forgotten, and what's left is an image that owes more to popular imagination than reality.

Higgins had married as a young man, but it ended without offspring. His beloved sister died from a drug overdose in a hotel where the rates are hourly and, like John, he tried to fill in the gap by helping to raise the children of a sibling who had left the world too early. It was through this difficult period that he became close to Chief Berkowitz, because Higgins was trying to arrange it so his nephews and nieces could remain in the Canton schools. The chief gave him an office so he could work out of the Canton Police station and allowed him to store government vehicles in the CPD parking lot.

Why would he have government vehicles? Because he did undercover work. That's essentially what he had joined the ATF to do.

Adrenaline had been the reason he took that job. Did combat in Iraq create a need for working on the edge? That would be understandable.

It wasn't adrenaline. What Higgins had developed a taste for was mission planning. With the fire department, there could be plenty of danger and adrenaline, but it was reactive. Something happens and you respond. But in a war zone, protecting convoys that are under constant attack, there's less waiting and little down time. And there's constant intellectual challenge as you plan missions and then execute them. Undercover work is very much that way.

However, there's a downside to such work. You lead a double life, and during working hours, you're socializing with criminals with whom you will not maintain any connection after the case. You also have to be very self-contained. Loose lips can get you killed, so you can't talk about your workday with anyone, even those closest to you.

Higgins met Karen and John at the neighborhood bar called the Hillside Pub, where all of them were regulars. What led to Karen initiating a flirtatious text relationship?

He told the story in court. One fall afternoon, he was driving by O'Keefe's house and saw Karen out there blowing leaves. When he waved, she chucked him the bird, so he pulled around to see why. Not recognizing him out in the daylight of the non-pub world, she got nervous and told him her husband was a cop. He then explained where they knew each other from.

A few weeks before the tragedy, out of nowhere, she texted him, saying he was hot. He wondered where she had gotten his number and whether she was still with John. John and Higgins weren't old friends or close friends. They mostly knew each other from the Hillside Pub, but Higgins is old school and wouldn't want to get involved with the girlfriend of any friend, no matter how close. He tried to feel her out. Or "sus" her out, as he said. Were they breaking up? He was very interested but also very hesitant. Karen explained that if John was having an affair, she wouldn't want to know, and they weren't married, so they were free to do whatever they wanted.

Was Karen really interested, or was there some other game?

In January of 2022, just weeks before John's death, multiple people from the group took a joint vacation to the Caribbean island of Aruba. Karen, John, and his niece and nephew went along, as did Laura Sullivan and her sister Marietta, who also had become close friends with John.

Laura Sullivan had a deeply personal connection to John. One of his best friends on the force was Patrick Rose, who was engaged to Laura, five months pregnant with their child. Inexplicably, Patrick committed suicide in 2021. O'Keefe, ever dutiful to his friend, stayed with Laura throughout her pregnancy and became a kind of godfather. Yet another example of John stepping up whenever needed.

But there was an incident in Aruba that resulted in an explosive argument witnessed by the kids. After a long day of drinking, Karen got off the elevator in time to see John staggering from the bar and bumping into the beautiful Marietta. Karen misinterpreted this contact as flirting and flew into a rage. The anger of that continued even after they went home. Did it drive her to flirt with Agent Higgins? Karen would tell *Vanity Fair*, "I knew Higgins found me attractive. It helped me emotionally validate myself, which is embarrassing to admit."

However, before the messages became public during the first trial, Karen, trying to explain these messages to her minions, since there were 56 pages of messages between them in discovery, lied. She told them that she was merely acting as a go-between for John and Higgins. But not only was she texting him, she walked him to his car at John's, planted a kiss on his mouth, and arranged to see him at his house.

Of course, it's no more surprising that Karen might be less than forthcoming on this stuff than Higgins. It's embarrassing. All human beings do embarrassing things from time to time. No one expects it to come out in a trial watched by millions. From the prosecution's POV, all of this tells the jury something important about Karen's mindset.

From the defense's POV, it turns Higgins into a possible third-party culprit.

Higgins had arrived first at the after-hours party, even before Brian and Nicole Albert, but he didn't go into the house until they got home a moment later with their daughter Caitlin. Driving a Jeep Wrangler rigged with a snowplow, he pretended to make a sweep of the dusting of snow, then parked on the street at the foot of the driveway by the mailbox. He then went inside the house with the Alberts. The McCabes would soon arrive.

As this group was getting there, Colin Albert, who had come to pay his respects to his cousin, Brian Jr., on his birthday, was just leaving.

Or so say the witnesses.

Let's introduce a new character: 17-year-old Allie McCabe, the oldest of Matt and Jen's four girls, a senior in high school, a good student and athlete. It was a Saturday night, when most kids this age are either getting into a bit of trouble, playing video games, or lying on the couch binge watching TV. Not this kid. She spent her night giving other teens rides, even stopping to rescue a stray dog. Canton is a drinking town, and a lot of the seniors in high school, the "cool kids" if you will, were out at small parties. Allie made sure they didn't need to drink and drive.

She had known Colin all her life. Their moms were close friends, and Colin's uncle was married to Jen's sister, Nicole. Colin had already had a couple of beers when Allie dropped him off at 34 Fairview. When he was ready to leave at 11:54, he texted her: "U can get me now… if easier." She replied: "OK, I am driving people home now."

She reached 34 Fairview at 12:10 and texted: "here," to which he immediately texted back: "OK."

Brian and Nicole recalled seeing Colin briefly as they got home, essentially in passing. He brushed past Nicole as she was taking off her shoes inside the door. Caitlin had tagged along with her parents and also saw Colin as he was leaving. Allie's parents arrived minutes later but didn't see Colin or their daughter.

Not in his initial testimony, but in later grand jury testimony, Higgins would say he saw a tall, dark man in the house. This excited Karen's supporters into claiming this was John. But Higgins was friends with John, and he would testify he never saw him in the house. Karen's supporters would claim, somewhat absurdly, that Higgins was merely trying to navigate a perjury trap, since he had already testified that John didn't come into the house.

While Higgins knew John, he had never met Colin. So almost certainly, that's who he saw, since he walked in with the Alberts, which is exactly when Colin was leaving.

Aspects of Higgins's testimony remain mysterious, or at the very least not fully explained. We'll get into more of it later, but for now, let's focus on this: where did he park and when exactly did he leave?

He claims he parked along the street near the mailbox. Well…

Karen and John turned onto Fairview just after 12:24. Right behind them came the pickup truck carrying Ryan Nagel, there to pick up his sister. But none of the three people in the pickup would remember seeing Higgins's Jeep with the plow, which would have been parked right in front of them on the other side of the driveway.

Higgins testified he left between 12:30 and 1:00 A.M. He punched into work at the Canton Police station, only a five-minute drive away, at 1:27. Did he go somewhere else and not report it?

Did he, in fact, leave before Karen and John, and the pickup truck arrived at 12:24? This would create an even longer time gap from when he left and then logged in at the station.

All of this would become more interesting when we learned, during the trial, that weeks before John's death, Karen had initiated a series of flirtatious texts with Agent

Higgins, getting his number from someone at the Hillside Pub and contacting him out of the blue, telling him he was hot. Karen had stopped the brief text romance only 10 days before the tragedy.

But that night, when Karen and John arrived at the Waterfall, while John greeted him with a hug, she ignored the ATF agent.

And the jilted Higgins did notice, texting her while there: "Umm, well?"

## Chloe

The Alberts owned a six-year-old German shepherd named Chloe. A couple of months after John's death, the dog would send a woman to the emergency room with a significant bite. There's no evidence the dog had ever been aggressive with humans, and in this biting incident, the dog had escaped the front door and attacked a dog it saw being walked on the street. When the owner tried to defend her dog, she was bitten.

Chloe slept in the room with Brian and Nicole. When they got home that night, one of the first things Brian did was go up to the bedroom to get the dog and bring her out to go to the bathroom in the fenced-in back yard. Then he returned her to the bedroom.

At trial, the defense would suggest that at 1:30 A.M., Caitlin called Tristan, her boyfriend in Southie, to not only pick her up… but to remove Chloe, who *they* believed had just been involved in the attack on John.

After the incident a couple of months later, when Chloe bit the neighbor, the Alberts re-homed their dog. These are things that make many people go "hmmm."

## Yellow Cottage Tales: True Crime

The first true crime case I dug into was the disappearance of Andy Puglisi, but when it came time to create a video on the subject, I scripted it and got a professional narrator. The truth is I didn't feel like I had the voice for narration or the camera presence.

But it's not easy narrating someone else's work because you don't have the same understanding of the subject as the writer. And my narrator unsurprisingly struggled with the pronunciation of Massachusetts towns, such as Worcester or Haverhill, so it lacked a certain authenticity.

And the truth is, I still didn't know what I wanted to do with the channel. I had launched it in January of 2022, around the same time John O'Keefe traveled to Aruba with a group of friends and Karen Read, a perhaps fateful trip since it seemed to be where their troubles began.

***"I have been through some terrible things in my life, some of which actually happened."* - Mark Twain**

I would have to do a whole lot more coloring between the lines than Mark Twain to make my personal story interesting, so let's boil it down: I went to college, hated the corporate world, went back to tend bar at the old bucket of blood, eventually bought my own bucket of blood. For many years, the joint was packed, then yada, yada, yada, I lost it all, break out the world's smallest violin.

There, biography done; we survived it.

I tell you this because understanding the trajectory of my life will give context to just how much things eventually came to a head in my coverage of the Karen Read case.

By the time I had COVID that January and John was lying alone in 18-degree temps, desperate for someone to find him, I had been attempting a new career as a writer for ten years. But how does a writer in his 50s get the interest of a publisher?

Short answer: he doesn't.

Not unless he's famous, and the only way someone like me was going to get famous was by being notorious. And I didn't want to do anything notorious.

So I launched YCT with a vague idea of using it to hopefully get just a bit more exposure for my fiction.

The process of creating a story is a weirdly immersive one where you inhabit the characters and are consumed by them. You learn the ability to jump into the shoes of everyone in the story, and this is something that only comes with years of practice. When you read work by writers who haven't learned this yet, it immediately stands out, because the side characters often make choices and do things that make no sense. In stories like this, the author knows the main character inside out but hasn't yet learned the lesson that EVERY character is the hero in their own story.

This ability to jump into a character's shoes would actually be very helpful in my true crime analysis. But at the time I began this, I was only exploring ways to get my fictional work out there.

My early thinking was that the channel might dabble in stories that have elements of truth. Urban legends, creepypastas… things that might have a basis in reality but where the real purpose is just entertainment. True crime was low on the list. It's not a genre that has ever interested me because it's a little, well, depressing, and because the good guys seldom triumph in the end… at least not in time to save the victims.

It also involved homework: digging into documents, watching trials, interviews, and surveillance. Don't get me wrong; I'm a confirmed document diver, a researcher, but with most of my time committed to writing fiction, I didn't want to take on things that would distract too much.

Were it not for that COVID-fever night, I never would have discovered *Have You Seen Andy?* and never taken the plunge into the deeper depths of a criminal case.

However, I went in as a babe in the woods. I knew nothing about forensic data, autopsies, court motions, accident reconstructions, or federal proffers. Most of my experience of criminal trials came from *My Cousin Vinny.* I had no training as a journalist, nor did I ever aspire to be one. I never had any interest in being a podcaster or doing live shows. The notion of going on Court TV or being in documentaries wouldn't have interested me even a little. All I wanted was a vehicle to get some of my stories out.

One more thing before we get back to Canton. August of 2023 would become a watershed time for me personally and also for what became a growing team at the Yellow Cottage: new friends, talented people, interesting projects.

And something new for me to learn how to deal with: sources.

Not being a journalist, I had never had a source. Like the geek whom the prom queen asks to dance, I didn't know what to do. And I really never sought sources in the Karen Read case, but they started reaching out. Even Karen's celebrity attorney, Alan Jackson, reached out to me at this time.

I had a lot to learn.

How do you handle these people who come to you with info?

When do you know what to report?

How can you establish the veracity of a source?

In one incident, I was in the car with a new team member, Erica, returning from an unrelated documentary shoot with co-author Dave McGrath at the prison called Bridgewater State Hospital. The three of us had a conference call with a man who would later launch his own channel and become a member of Karen Read's inner circle, covering the case daily from outside court. But at this time, he was just one of so many people for some reason trying to insert himself into the case.

He had called us to say he had tracked down an ex-girlfriend of ATF Agent Brian Higgins, who had become a focus of the defense team's third-party culprit theory. Rumor had it that Higgins had texted her early on the morning of John's death, and she might know something. The woman worked as an oncology nurse, and this guy… let's call him 3PCO… had learned where she worked and what she drove, and as we all spoke on speakerphone, he was waiting in ambush at her car at the hospital! He was hoping to get a word out of her.

As I drove, Erica holding up her phone, I told this guy that he needed to leave that parking lot. Ambushing this woman was wrong and, well, creepy.

He refused and even began considering a way to win her confidence by helping her change a flat tire… supposing that tire should, he hinted, for some reason go flat.

I told Erica to hang up.

Both she and Dave immediately agreed, and we permanently cut communications with this clown who, months later, would have thousands of people watching his daily coverage of the case outside court, and who would become a close confidante of Karen's inner team.

When Alan Jackson had reached out to me, I told him that while I was happy to talk to him, I would always cover the case from both sides.

All of this would build to a breaking point in August of 2023, something more clearly visible in hindsight. As I covered the case from both sides, my questions threatened the Free Karen Readers and her social media allies. The others on the Yellow Cottage team didn't like the questioning either.

In the summer of '23, virtually no one else was challenging the Free Karen Read mob. So my channel was, in its small way, reaching the pinnacle of its success.

But it was also on the precipice of disaster.

# 3. FINDING JOHN

Around 12:30 A.M., John got out of Karen's SUV. His health app would show him "ascending/descending" three flights of stairs minutes earlier, and it would suggest he took 116 steps, but according to his phone's GPS, he never went inside the house or even in the direction of it. In fact, the final GPS coordinates were reached at 12:24:40, only 22 seconds after they had taken the right onto Fairview. Those coordinates were right where Karen pulled up to at the far edge of the property. Still parked several car lengths behind this position was the pickup truck carrying Julie Nagel's brother and two others. No one saw John get out of the SUV.

Karen would attempt 53 calls to John in those early hours of the morning, and the first of a rapid string came at 12:33. It came from the road as she raced home on traffic-less streets. Between 12:36 and 12:37, she pulled into John's driveway and parked, her phone connecting to John's Wi-Fi. Video of her arriving home was mysteriously deleted. And there, in the driveway, she left her first of five voicemails, telling John, *"I fucking hate you!"* At 12:42 comes the next voicemail, in which she can be heard pulling into John's garage, warning sounds chirping in her SUV, the garage door closing, and then her heels clicking on the cement. No message.

In the next three voicemails, the last of which comes at 1:18 A.M., she tried to force John to come home by threatening to go to her parents' house, thus leaving John's nephew and niece alone (she forgot the nephew was at a sleepover), and she accused John of being a "pervert" who was cheating on her. In one message, she vaguely said, *"No one knows where you are."*

In the middle of this string, she tried to call her parents at 1:10, but the call went unanswered.

The phone activity stops at 1:18, and the next call comes at 4:38 when she tried John again. She has said she took a nap on the couch, and this seems consistent with the evidence. But something had drastically changed in her mindset after 4:30. Where earlier she thought John was cheating on her, for some reason she was now in a state of panic and hysteria, believing John was possibly dead.

What had led to that change?

The damage to her SUV was much more significant than a broken taillight. A palm-sized dent sat about a forearm's length away on the lift. Above the taillight ran a long, jagged scar. And the taillight itself was missing pieces, especially along its side.

At 4:40, she called her parents; no answer again, and then at 4:42, same result. Around that time, she woke up John's 14-year-old niece, Kayley, screaming that something had happened to John. She called Katie Camerano, a nurse working the late shift at a local hospital, to see if she had heard anything, since Katie's husband Mike had been drinking with John at C.F. McCarthy's.

Just before 5:00 A.M., Karen called Jen McCabe, using Kayley's phone. Kayley and Jen's daughter were best buds. Karen told Jen her taillight was busted, and that she had left John at the Waterfall, a conversation witnessed by the niece. One shouldn't be too quick to say Karen was lying to Jen in this moment; after all she had just woken up and was still loaded, but it wasn't true, of course, that she had left him there. She had taken John to 34 Fairview.

Next, she called Kerry Roberts, exclaimed, "John's dead!" and hung up. Calling back a moment later, she told Kerry that maybe John had been hit by a plow.

Roberts called the police and the hospital to see if anyone with injuries like that had been found.

Shortly after this, Karen left to search for John. RING video shows her backing out into heavy snowfall, lightly bumping John's Chevy Traverse, parked in the driveway, and then driving off. Two inches of fresh, fluffy snow is visible coating the pavement, snow which remains unbroken around the Traverse as she pulls away. There is no sign of fallen taillight pieces, but the defense claims this is when the taillight was broken. Sources tell us that testing done after the first trial may prove that the taillight couldn't have been damaged in this way. We'll see.

Surveillance video from the library in downtown Canton shows Karen's black SUV a few minutes later heading in the direction of the Waterfall. A short time later, the Lexus retraces its path and heads possibly in the direction of Fairview. Her phone's GPS had been off since before these events, so it was no help, and it can't be said whether she reached Fairview, or even remembered how to. It also will be hard to show, even if they can prove she drove by the house, that Karen saw John buried in the snow.

### A New Hero?

For the second trial, the County hired elite Boston defense lawyer Hank Brennan to prosecute the case. Brennan had come to prominence from his work in many cases, but most notably as the defense attorney for organized crime boss James "Whitey" Bulger. Bulger and Brennan had a unique goal in that case. They recognized that there was essentially no chance of escaping the many charges against Bulger, including several for murder, so what they wanted to do was put the federal government on trial. They wanted to make clear to the public that the US Attorney's Office, and especially the FBI, had essentially been business partners with Whitey.

Bulger hoped to prove that he hadn't been a rat, but rather, instead of giving information to the government, he was getting information in exchange for cash.

The Bulger experience may have contributed to Brennan's willingness to take on the Karen Read case. He had grown suspicious of the machinations of federal law enforcement. These agencies are extremely powerful, driven by the desire for headlines and not at all inclined to police themselves. In fact, because of their immense power, they're very difficult to investigate by any other authority. Any serious investigation into their actions can really only by done by themselves, such as by an inspector general. But if the Feds are deflating footballs before the game, are they likely to rat on themselves?

A major development for the second trial is the possibility of critical new vehicle data. In December of 2024, in the presence of Karen's team, the State performed another "chip off" on the vehicle. Trooper Nicholas Guarino had performed the first chip off the previous year, but he encountered problems and couldn't complete it. So, he asked Karen's data expert to help. She was able to get it partly done, but much data remained uncollected.

Under Brennan's direction, using an independent expert, the State withdrew three motherboards from the Lexus, sent them to a lab in Texas to have the software updated, then returned them to the SUV. The new chip off produced what seems to be an enormous trove of new data, eight gigabytes. But reading that data has turned out to be a challenge, and whether any useful information was obtained remains to be seen. Even video remains a possibility.

I'll go more into the data later (it will be painless, I promise!), but we might learn things like more GPS points for the trips taken by the Lexus, timestamps, objects detected, doors opening, and passengers detected. This data could be either inculpable or exculpable to Karen.

For example, the data could show that the Lexus was close to where John was found when GPS shows he last moved. That would be crushing to the defense. And it could show that Karen returned to the scene before John was found, as the State charges. However, it could also show that the passenger seat was empty while Karen sat there waiting. It could show Karen was on the way home minutes before John's phone had last moved.

**Witness**

Around 5:30 A.M., several minutes after driving around looking for John, Karen arrived at the McCabes' house. The scene was tense.

The McCabes had already gotten out of bed after Karen's 5:00 call and were making coffee, trying to figure out what to do next. Matt, a local business owner, is an amiable figure, slow to anger, ready to give someone who has had too much to drink a ride home from the pub. The McCabes have four kids, all athletic daughters, and while Jen coached all of their junior basketball teams, Matt coached them in soccer and lacrosse.

Karen's attorney would try to exploit his congenial nature in the first trial, asking him on the stand if he found this all funny. He didn't, of course, but it's just not his nature to be confrontational.

Jen McCabe used to teach a fifth-grade class but now was a full-time soccer mom. Voted most attractive in her high school class, she remains very petite into her 40s, though being the mom of four very active girls means she knows how to take charge if needed, and if necessary, become a mama bear. We all know that type of mom: organizing trips to buy sneakers, planning sleepovers, getting all the moms together to watch the games, making sure no one is left out. It's a full-time job, and there's no tougher one.

She would put those skills to work eight years earlier when her daughter's best friend, Kayley, lost both her parents and became the custody of Kayley's uncle, John O'Keefe. Jen helped lead the community response to support the O'Keefe family, becoming a surrogate mom to the six-year-old girl.

When Karen arrived in their driveway in the middle of the blizzard, it wasn't quietly. She got out of her Lexus screaming. Matt and Jen, worried that their girls would wake up, hurried out to quiet her.

Braving the blizzard, Kerry Roberts soon followed. Her husband Curt had been drinking with John the night before, and Kerry had been extremely close to the O'Keefes since high school. Her husband hadn't wanted her going out into the storm, but after Karen's alarming phone call, Kerry was determined to help. She arrived at the McCabes' minutes after Karen.

Karen showed them her broken taillight and insisted they travel to 34 Fairview to look for John. This confused the other women, especially Jen, who knew John had never shown up at the after-hours party, though she remembered seeing Karen's SUV parked outside, engine running and lights on.

With Karen still drunk and behaving hysterically, she allowed Jen to drive her Lexus while Kerry followed them back to John's house. They thought maybe John had returned, or possibly had been there all along, and Karen just hadn't noticed him crashed somewhere.

The way the defense tries to portray it, Jen McCabe must be one of the most diabolical villains in true crime history, because they suggest that she was trying to steer the group away from 34 Fairview so the killers would have time to place the unconscious O'Keefe onto the lawn.

Arriving at John's house on 1 Meadows Avenue, Kerry and Jen took their shoes off upon entering the house, knowing that John, anal about neatness, would have insisted. Karen didn't take hers off, something the prosecutor would later make a big deal of in the trial, implying that Karen understood John would never know.

Inside the house, Kayley waited nervously for word.

After a quick search of the home, they went back into the storm to look for John, piling into Kerry's SUV. But before they did, according to Gretchen Voss, who interviewed Karen in the presence of her lawyers in the summer of 2023, Karen again examined the taillight with the women. This time, she actually pulled a piece of taillight plastic out and dropped it on the driveway. Recording of this interview is in discovery and could be crucial evidence in the second trial, because it actually refutes the theory Karen's lawyer, Alan Jackson, told the jury in the first trial. Jackson would show an image from RING video taken at 5:08 and tell the jury that the taillight was intact. But if Karen was plucking pieces from it a half hour later, that obviously wasn't the case. More on this later.

Strangely, the RING video of this inspection, which took place around 5:45, was also deleted, just as the video showing Karen getting back to 1 Meadows around 12:36 A.M. is missing, and possibly one of her pulling into the garage at 12:42.

As they drove in the pitch dark, slammed by wind and heavy snow, Karen's hysteria rendered the two other women silent. Screaming frequently, she wondered out loud if she had hit John with her vehicle.

The streets were in an early stage of being plowed, paths running up the center of main roads, lesser streets untouched. Brian "Lucky" Loughran, who would become a key player in the conspiracy theory, would testify for the defense that he had last plowed Fairview at 5:30 A.M. This matches what is seen in police dashcam video showing a small plow bank along the sides of the road.

As the women were searching, John had been unconscious and outside long enough to show signs of hypothermia in his pancreas and stomach. No one can say what his final experience was, but hopefully he suffered little.

Coming from the direction of Chapman, 34 Fairview is on the left, two houses from the corner with Cedarcrest. About 80 feet before the driveway is the property line, where there is a mulched area that divides the yards. It contains bushes, trees, and boulders. Just past that mulched area, on the Albert side, is a flagpole, a fire hydrant, and a disused telecommunications box.

With Karen perched on the back seat leaning forward between Jen and Kerry, as they neared this property line, she sent a call to John. And right at that moment, with the call sending, she spotted his figure buried in the snow about six feet from the curb. Tossing her phone, she screamed, "I see him!" and started banging on the door to get out. Not seeing anything, and therefore confused, Kerry slowed to a crawl but didn't stop, so Karen kicked open the door and jumped out, leaving her phone on the seat, with the call to John still sending.

She fell when she landed, sprang to her feet, and ran to the figure buried in the snow, which she knew must be John.

Jen and Kerry would testify that they couldn't understand how Karen could see John at all. Even after Karen jumped out of the car, Kerry believed she was just running to a "mound of snow" until Karen cleared enough away to reveal John. To them, this eventually became the basis for their belief that Karen had been back to the scene BEFORE she went to the McCabes'.

Karen's phone, still sitting on the back seat of the car, recorded everything that happened in the next few minutes into John's voicemail.

As Jen called 911, Karen and Kerry attempted CPR on John. His eyes were badly swollen, blood trickled from his nose, and he wasn't breathing. But he didn't look dead, just unconscious.

Karen repeatedly screamed Kerry's name and asked if John was dead. The anguish of it all is difficult to listen to.

Jen, ever the mama bear, kept her composure with the 911 dispatcher, something Free Karen Readers strangely take as a sign of her guilt. She referred to John as a "guy," which bothers those thinking she should have said "my friend" or "John O'Keefe," or "Boston police officer." But of course, the dispatcher wasn't conducting an interview. He was just trying to obtain the essential information needed to dispatch first responders, and at that point, Jen only knew someone was buried in the snow. She certainly suspected it might be John, but at the time of the call, she hadn't seen identifying features.

After the call, Jen joined the women outside trying to warm John and administer CPR. Minutes later, the first squad car arrived, driven by Officer Steven Saraf, and the dashcam video of that event was shown in court. Another cruiser reached them moments later, and then finally the ambulance and a rescue vehicle.

But inside the home, nothing stirred.

### Yellow Cottage Tales: Fever

The night of John's death, when fever kept me up watching the documentary about Andy Puglisi, the whole story really got into my blood. It made me angry. Monsters were out there hunting kids in the 1970s, and the police had kept it hidden from the public. Melanie Perkins McLaughlin reported that Lawrence police had learned that at least five known child predators were lurking around the public pool that August afternoon. Some of the suspects Melanie would investigate had indicated to police that they hunted children in places like Lawrence because of easy access to the highways and because the police in those cities were already stretched thin.

A fire had been lit inside me by Melanie's documentary, and I was starting to shift my views on how to approach the genre of true crime. I felt torn and still do. Discussing these subjects isn't enjoyable for me. It's much more fun to watch old episodes of *Hogan's Heroes*.

But could my YouTube channel also be used in some very tiny way to make a difference?

I was following my instincts. Nothing in my life included any relevant experience. I had never been in law enforcement and had no training in forensics, data, or research. To be honest, I really brought little to the table unless there was a need for a good Bloody Mary.

Doing a deep dive into the Puglisi case, I employed one of the few talents I do have: logical analysis.

Sorry, yeah, I could be that annoying cold-water guy at the party debunking things… though to be fair to myself, I was also the guy who brought the beer funnel!

So what does logical analysis actually mean? Well, exploring that is a theme not only of this book but a constant approach on YCT. A couple of quick thoughts:

Money might not grow on trees, but logic actually does. It has branches. You follow them until you get to a dead end, then try another branch. So, think of yourself as a squirrel. This might seem obvious, but there is actually a key that unlocks it all: asking questions.

You have to get really good at continuously generating questions and using them to explore new branches. We've already discussed the need to weigh why Karen returned to the crime scene—or Jen McCabe—if you consider it from that side. There are many questions people should be able to quickly generate as soon as they begin thinking about this case.

What are the chances that the nine people inside the house would all remain silent, even in the face of an FBI investigation?

Why would killers deposit the victim on their own front lawn?

Why would they leave him unconscious instead of finishing him off to make sure he never talked?

What motive would multiple cops and investigators have to actively participate in a murder cover-up that, if caught—which was somewhat likely—would put them in prison for a very long time?

On the other hand, if Jen McCabe had searched at 2:27 A.M. for "Hos long to die in cold?" then something certainly had happened, right? After all, wasn't data just data?

Could a vehicle strike even actually explain John's wounds?

Was he, in fact, attacked by a large dog?

Did the many other strange things—Higgins logging into work at 1:30 A.M. at the police station, the Alberts not coming out, abrasions still visible on Colin's knuckles a few weeks later, the police chief stepping in, data that showed John "ascending/descending" stairs, and lead investigator Trooper Michael Proctor's connections to the Alberts—all have explanations?

The fire that *Have You Seen Andy?* lit within me was based on an idea that had never occurred to me before: that true crime could be more than just entertainment. Maybe collective attention that resulted from interest in true crime could actually be useful. Sure, instances of amateurs helping to solve cases are rare. But in helping to bring hidden things to light, wasn't it possible that in some very tiny but real way, the public—both content creators and fans of true crime—could perhaps help move the needle in the direction of truth?

# PART TWO: INVESTIGATION

# 1. FIRST RESPONDERS

The black-and-white dashcam video from Officer Saraf's cruiser shows him cautiously traversing the partially plowed streets to respond to a call about a man found in the snow on Fairview Road. Street lights cast a pall in the morning blackness. He passes plows, perhaps one driven by Lucky Loughran, on a machine they called the Frankenbeast. The cruiser seat squeaks from his ample weight. The 53-year-old Steven Saraf isn't the kind of cop who would be useful in a foot chase, but whose size does give him a certain presence. On the stand, he would remain calm and unflustered, just as he was at the crime scene. He had been on duty since midnight and was nearing the end of his shift.

Turning onto Fairview from Chapman, the tension mounted: where were they? He knew women were on scene, struggling to save the man's life. Conditions didn't allow him to drive fast. Visibility made seeing people in a yard unlikely. He switched on his spotlight.

At last, ahead in the middle of the street, the image of an open SUV emerged from the darkness. On the left, he made out figures bent over someone in the yard. They waved anxiously at him.

Coming from the opposite direction, from Cedarcrest, Saraf could make out the flashing blues of another cruiser. Not until this moment did he put on his own blue lights. None of them had on their sirens, which is consistent with the protocol in most towns when it comes to responding on empty streets at night.

Officer Saraf joined a chaotic and desperate scene. A woman he would soon come to know as the victim's girlfriend had blood smeared on her face. Three women in total were attempting CPR and trying to warm the six-foot-two-inch man lying unconscious in the snow wearing no coat or gloves, missing one shoe. He looked like he had been beaten up, with eyes badly swollen, a couple of scratches and smeared with blood.

Karen could be heard screaming John's name and yelling, "Nooo!" The cops took over CPR efforts until the paramedics arrived just minutes later. Karen kept repeating the question, "Is he dead?" Several other first responders would hear her shout, "I hit him!" multiple times. In the car she had been asking if she could have hit him, so it's not unreasonable to wonder if she was just asking the same thing at the scene. However, no one there remembered it as a question.

As the paramedics were desperately trying to revive John, an officer put Karen into a cruiser to warm her up. Jen and Kerry squeezed in with her. Karen seized their hands, begging them to pray, but at that moment noticed something that puzzled her: blood on her hands.

In perhaps a revealing moment, studying her hands, she actually asked if she had her period. Kerry and Jen explained that the blood was John's.

So, Karen's mind stood on the brink of becoming unhinged. She made them promise to take care of the kids, John's nephew and niece. Then, seeing them moving John to the ambulance, she told Kerry to go look and see if he was dead. Engaging in the odd repetitive behavior she had been exhibiting all morning, she cried it out rapidly over and over, so Kerry got out of the cruiser to check on John.

At that very moment, Karen had another request. With her hands bloody and her phone inside Kerry's SUV, she asked Jen to make a search on her phone: How long does it take to die from hypothermia?

### Central Casting

Sergeant Sean Goode, an 18-year veteran of the Canton Police Force, still appeared fresh-faced and youthful, a cop from central casting to play Officer Friendly. This is how suburban towns want their police officers to look and behave. Not street hardened, but competent, diligent, approachable by citizens… the kind of cop who says "righto" on 911 calls.

In Canton, the officers double as dispatchers, manning the 911 desk, and that morning, Goode was at the helm. Around 5:00 A.M., he received a call from a woman wanting to know if the police had transported an injured man to a hospital. This was Kerry Roberts, having just been told by Karen that John might have been hit by a plow. She informed Goode that the man's girlfriend had dropped him off at a party. He hadn't come home and therefore might be hurt.

An hour later, it would again be Goode who took the 911 call from Jen McCabe, who reported a man found unconscious in the snow. After dispatching the first responders, Sergeant Goode had one of the patrol cops return to the station in order to man the 911 desk so he himself could respond to the call. On the way, he called Lieutenant Paul Gallagher and Detective Lieutenant Michael Lank at their homes to alert them because of the seriousness of the situation.

He arrived at a chaotic scene blanketed by whiteout snow. Officer Saraf, a tall ski hat adding to his height, stood like a bear. The ambulance with John had already left. Karen, unable to remain within the squad car, paced franticly, confused and muttering, shouting through the howling wind, "Is he dead?" Goode became the next to try to warm and calm her by putting her in his cruiser, leaving the door open.

Meanwhile, an officer asked Jen to go into the house and wake up her sister and brother-in-law. She had tried calling both of them, to no avail. Finding the front door unlocked, she entered the house and went up to Brian and Nicole's second-floor bedroom. Pushing open the bedroom door, she found them sound asleep. The German shepherd, Chloe, slept in the bedroom, but Jen wouldn't remember noticing the dog.

Karen Read has described Brian as someone you don't expect to be at social events because he seems like he doesn't want to really be there, and that actually seems to capture him to some degree. He wears a guarded aloofness not uncommon in street-hardened cops, someone quietly observing and continuously taking mental notes. A combat veteran of the Gulf War, Brian had been conditioned through his experiences to be cautious in social settings, gathering information instead of giving it.

His brother Chris has a very different personality, engaging, approachable, active socially. He described Brian as the toughest and smartest guy he knew, but not someone who maintained a large circle of friends.

The Massachusetts Irish tend to come in two flavors: the Dancer and the Quiet Observer. In Ireland, for centuries going back into the boggy mists of time, the main entertainment consisted of the *céilís* (pronounced kaylees). Villagers would get together at a road juncture, tell stories and dance to traditional Irish music. Of course, there would be plenty of drink, mostly the moonshine called *poitín*, made, of course, from potatoes.

And this type of socializing continued in Massachusetts. Instead of at roadsides, however, they would move the furniture out of the way in the living rooms of their three-decker apartments and kick up a storm. My grandparents met at such an event.

There were those who sought the center of the circle at a *céilís*, dancing with all comers or spinning yarns at speeds too fast for their American grandchildren to follow. These survivors of impoverished Irish farms, who filled the ranks of factories, rail yards, and police departments, worked hard all week… and let off steam on the weekend. Hardened by the rock-strewn farms of Ireland and the less-than-welcoming streets of America, these guys were all tough.

But the toughest among them were the Quiet Observers. They became, for some reason, an archetype more typical of Boston than anywhere else. Where the New York Irish tough guy has to be ready to do combat with language, the toughest guys in Boston display an unusual economy of words. Except for those times when they let down their guard with their closest friends after a handful of beers, they mostly just stand at the edge of the *céilís* and observe.

Brian Albert grew up in Canton, not Southie or Dorchester, but he was mostly old school and would have fit right in with the very hardest of the Boston Irish.

His wife Nicole, tall and strong, also conveys quiet strength, whereas her sister Jen is tiny and petite but assertive. Reserved and quiet, Nicole is described as sweet, and her face suggests the deep depths of motherly fortitude common to the survivors of generations of Irish poverty. These women know how to bear suffering.

They woke up groggy and confused when Jen burst into their room with news of the tragedy unfolding below. When told O'Keefe had been found outside his window, Brian replied, "John who?" They hurried to get dressed and descended the stairs to find Detective Lieutenant Michael Lank already waiting inside the house.

Like most of the characters in this drama, Lank grew up in Canton, his family having moved there when he was five. Also, like many of the characters, he was an athlete who starred in high school sports and then went on to coach youth sports as a father. We'll meet many police officers in this narrative, and some of them seem like guys who look as though becoming a cop was almost an inevitable destiny, predictable from an early age. Lank is such a guy: tall, broad-boned, square-jawed.

Of course, he knew the Alberts, who also played sports and had kids playing sports. The average high school class in Canton is only 225 kids, so pretty much everyone who grew up there knows everyone who grew up there. And certainly a Canton badge would be as familiar as a Boston badge, especially given that Kevin Albert, Brian's brother, was also a detective on the Canton force.

That didn't make Brian Albert and Michael Lank social. In court, Lank described their relationship as "civil."

With the Alberts rubbing sleep from their eyes, Lank talked to them and Jen for about 20 minutes. At some point, Jen's husband Matt arrived. Then Lank returned outside to assist with the about-to-begin investigation, led by Lieutenant Gallagher.

The question that dogs many people is this: should Lank have investigated inside the house?

It's understandable why people think it's obvious the Canton Police should have.

Multiple legal experts have reported that there was insufficient evidence to obtain a warrant, but to be honest, I find this dubious. John had been dropped off at the house to attend a small party within, and he was found on the lawn looking like he had been in a fight. A broken cocktail glass found beside John on the lawn *could* have come from the house. And the witnesses Lank spoke with *could* have been hiding something. Had the detective applied for a warrant on these grounds, was it really likely a clerk magistrate would have denied it?

The easier way to search the house, of course, would have been to ask the owner for permission. But was this ever really likely?

Consensus about what had happened to John was in the very early stages of forming, but it wasn't moving in a direction that would lead Detective Lank to think something had happened inside the house. The door had been unlocked, and no one stopped him from entering. The Alberts weren't behaving suspiciously, instead seeming confused, having just woken up. All four witnesses present said John had never come inside the house. Finally, there were possibly already early reports of a broken taillight, strange behavior by the girlfriend, and statements that sounded like confessions.

The detective didn't ask for permission to search the house, but he also didn't send a cruiser out to examine Karen's vehicle. It's worth noting this, because we in the public probably have very unrealistic expectations about how police investigations work, and we'll see it again when the troopers take over. We imagine these things proceed with dramatic urgency and speed. But they don't. Investigations are generally more cautious and plodding, probably out of a desire to avoid mistakes. It might even be true that there's a kind of institutional inertia that results from a desire to not appear too energized, to look like a rookie. You know… been there, done that.

Is it fair to wonder whether Lank might have been more reluctant to ask permission to search the home of a fellow law enforcement officer?

Of course!

But the truth is, whatever people think in hindsight, the notion of asking Brian if he could go through his house probably never entered Lank's mind, because he was able to walk right in through an unlocked door, and his instincts told him these people had just woken up and didn't know anything.

If we consider the angle of John having been attacked inside the house, then it's certainly possible Lank was duped, or that he passively assisted the cover-up by looking the other way.

However, if John was, in fact, killed in a hit-and-run, there's no reason to call a lack of search here a failure by the Canton Police. They had no reason to think John ever went into the house, and no reason to believe anyone was lying to them. So, whether they did their job well really depends on the rest of the evidence.

### Crime Scene

Lank left the Alberts and McCabes inside the house to go back into the storm, where a very unusual investigation was about to begin. But while he was inside the house, another drama unfolded.

It's important to keep reminding ourselves just how much events of that day were impacted by the seventh largest blizzard in New England's history, one that was particularly powerful in Canton, which is close enough to Boston that the rain/snow line often reduces accumulations. However, it was unusually frigid, and that rain/snow line stayed off the shore, so the snow piled up and winds blew at 50 to 60 MPH.

Officer Goode, worried not only about Karen's state of mind but about the impact of the cold, sent the women off, Kerry driving Karen to the hospital in the warm vehicle. But they didn't get far. On the phone with her father, Karen expressed a desire to kill herself, so her anxious parents called the Canton Police and had her taken into custody for her own safety. Dispatch called Sergeant Goode at the scene. Goode, who now had Kerry Roberts's contact information, called her as she drove Karen. They had only left minutes before, so they quickly returned to 34 Fairview, where the Canton Police put Karen into an ambulance to be Section 12'd: sent to the hospital in custody for observation.

While in the ambulance, she actually questioned the paramedic on the same thing she had asked Jen to google: how long can someone survive in the cold?

Her blood alcohol level was even then still close to the legal limit, which is .08% in Massachusetts. It's estimated that her level reached between .135% and .292% by the time they left the Waterfall. That estimate aligns with her body weight and the number of drinks she consumed in the surveillance footage, which would mean she was at least at twice the legal intoxication limit when driving John to the after-hours party. A daily drinker, Karen IS able to handle her booze and function at a high level.

While Karen was on her way back to the crime scene, Lieutenant Gallagher arrived and brought with him a very unexpected tool: a leaf blower.

Rescuers found John about six to eight feet from the plowed portion of the street. Snow around had him hadn't accumulated during the night, as it had only snowed lightly for most of those hours. By the time Karen left John's house at 5:08, there was perhaps a couple of inches of accumulation, but now it was coming down hard. By the time they found John an hour later, there was about four inches of snow on him, but the grass beneath and immediately around him remained exposed. However, in the brief time since they transported John, snow had really built up in the space where they had found him.

Only two solid pieces of evidence were collected by the Canton Police: John's phone, found beneath him, and a shattered cocktail glass, which he had taken from the Waterfall Pub. Much later, investigators detected taillight pieces, but the Canton Police didn't find these at that time. This supports the theory, held by many, that someone planted the pieces later.

But as the Canton Police were documenting the crime scene, taking photos, and inspecting the ground, they discovered something else: blood drops.

The drops were in the area right where John had been found, and with snow piling up, they wouldn't be visible for very long. Knowing the evidence was perishable, Gallagher,

Lank, and Goode determined they needed to find a way to collect it. However, they had no evidence kits. So, when a neighbor produced some red, plastic solo cups—the kind you might see at a keg party—having no other options and snow falling hard, they put the bloody snow in the cups.

One thing we have to realize is WHY they wanted to collect this blood in the first place. Normally, there's no reason to collect blood at a hit-and-run. The only purpose for collecting blood is identification. So, the only plausible reason the Canton Police collected this blood was that they at least entertained the notion that it belonged to someone else. In other words, maybe John had been in a fight.

Why didn't the prosecution ask why the Canton cops collected the blood? Because they didn't want Lieutenant Gallagher to explain that they thought maybe John had been in a fight, since that would further fuel the question of why they didn't search the house.

For some reason, the defense team neglected to spot this opening, which brings me to the next rule from the Yellow Cottage:

**YCT Rule #1: There are no geniuses.**

I'll come back to it a lot, since this rule is kind of my Golden Rule. While there are plenty of talented, intelligent individuals in any crime case, certainly in this one, there are no geniuses. Whether on the defense team or the prosecution, whether the witnesses or the defendant, good guys, bad guys, cops, robbers... or the author of this book... don't expect to find any.

So, if your theory about what happened requires a genius, it probably needs a re-think.

The Canton Police placed the blood in storage back at the police station and took it out later when the Massachusetts State Police arrived to gather the evidence. With somewhat poor judgment, they took a photo of the open cups with bloody snow sitting inside an open paper bag situated near Karen's Lexus in the police station sally port, raising concerns of biological evidence transfer.

In any case, the State Police disposed of the evidence without testing it because by that time, they had concluded that Karen's Lexus struck John. So, no need to test the blood.

The leaf blower was used to expose the blood drops layer by layer. Many people have laughed at this, and many other law enforcement officers have criticized it, but because they filmed their work, it actually proved to be a brilliant approach. Not something that added to our knowledge in this case, as it turned out, but the film shows not only the precise location of where each drop was found, and thus the spray pattern, but also the level, giving an idea of the time the drops fell.

The blood certainly belonged to John. When the women began attempting CPR, it forced blood out of John's mouth. Karen ended up with blood on her face and hands. Likely some of that dripped into the snow, and one to two inches had fallen by the time Gallagher began gently melting layers of snow with the leaf blower.

I want to emphasize something, though: the very fact that these local cops were filming their use of the leaf blower, and that they collected bloody snow in party cups, suggests a *very high level of motivation*. Had these officers suspected John was attacked inside the house, and had they been inclined to look the other way because it involved a fellow cop from Boston, they would NOT have gone the extra mile. They would have done nothing more than what was required, and then they would have washed their hands of it. So…

A) These cops were extremely motivated and even creative;

B) Yet they saw no need to search the house.

Brian Albert would later say in court he wished they had. The defense, of course, would fire back, "So do we!" But the high level of motivation displayed by these officers isn't at all what one would expect if they were trying to protect the homeowners by looking the other way.

### Yellow Cottage Tales: Lizzie

In the summer of 2022, blissfully unaware of events slowly unfolding in Canton, I completed a seven-part series on Lizzie Borden for the channel. The crime had long fascinated me, and this was the kind of case I could get into for two reasons: one, there was a big unsolved puzzle; and two, it happened long enough ago that no one from the events was still alive. No victims, no suspects, no family members. This created enough distance that it didn't flood me with uncomfortable feelings of empathy. All that remained was the puzzle, and I like puzzles.

See, for me, empathy isn't enjoyable. I don't want to experience the suffering of others in a personal way. Women dominate the true crime community, which seems ironic, because women are much more empathetic than men, and you would think that this empathy would drive them away from true crime. Not only is that not the case, but the women I talk to who are passionate about true crime are actually extra high on the empathy scale. They identify very much with not only the victims, but the families.

This only seems ironic on the surface, that the people who most enjoy true crime are the ones who share the experience of vicarious suffering most acutely. But digging a little deeper, we realize that people who enter nursing and health care tend to have a higher capacity for empathy, or that those who love animals often become veterinarians. Their ability to put themselves into the shoes (or paws) of others is what drives them into these professions in the first place, and it's very similar to those interested in true crime.

But for me, Lizzie Borden was safe territory, something that happened a long time ago.

The Borden case remains an intriguing puzzle because the evidence, in many ways, says it was only Lizzie who could have done it… and yet it also says she couldn't have. Without going into the whole case, I want to touch on it just a bit so we can explore how to use logical analysis to eliminate possibilities.

Or… let's restate this more carefully. Usually what we do is eliminate things that are highly improbable—not impossible, but improbable—because it's seldom the case that something can be eliminated with certainty.

Abby Borden was killed around 9:30 A.M. and Andrew around 11:00 on August 4, 1892. The house was small, with only three ways in or out, two of them locked. Only two people were home—Lizzie and the Irish maid, Bridget Sullivan. Neither of them heard anything unusual.

Wait… let's pause a moment.

I smell smoke burning, so either I've had a thought or there's a new rule being cooked up in the cottage. Okay, let's put it on the table.

**YCT Rule #15: When you come to a fork in the road, take it.**

Come on, you say, that's Yogi Berra's rule.

True, but we're re-purposing it. When you come to an either/or situation, a spot where the logic tree splits into two, even if this fork is one where BOTH paths are unlikely, you still have to choose one branch. Unfortunately, this means sometimes you actually have to choose something unlikely. But this will come up frequently in cases, and the important thing is to choose the MORE likely branch, even if they're both somewhat unlikely.

The real challenge is actually to recognize the fork in the first place; to identify those either/ors. For example, in the Karen Read case, either someone planted evidence or Karen struck John with her SUV.

But we often miss some of these essential either/ors. What happens is that often, once we see something that is somewhat unlikely, we stop exploring other paths. Consequently, we don't even see those forks in the road.

This is the situation in the Borden case. You have a small house, mostly locked up, and murders separated by an hour and a half. This is understandably the primary reason people then and now believe Lizzie killed her parents. It's unlikely that an intruder killed Abby, hid in that small house for an hour and a half, leaving the young women alone, then sprang out and killed Andrew minutes after he arrived, managing all this without being seen or heard.

But now let's send in that monkey with the wrench: no one ever found the murder weapon.

Stop the presses.

Andrew was killed some time after 11:00 A.M., and Lizzie started shouting for help no later than 11:08. Bridget came down, the neighbor came over, and minutes later, the police and the doctor arrived. They sat Lizzie in a chair in the kitchen, comforting her, and didn't notice any blood in her hair, on her hands, or in her layers of Victorian clothing. And these had been truly bloody killings, with blood, bone, and brains splattered everywhere.

Now maybe by some miracle she managed to clean up in the minutes she had. But where was the murder weapon? She didn't have time to go anywhere.

By that afternoon, police had decided they had their man… eh, woman. And over the next several days, they performed multiple searches of the house for the weapon they were sure was there, each search more rigorous than the last. They brought in masons to plumb the chimney, carpenters to look through the walls, and whoever drew the unlucky straw had to comb through the septic pit. They knew it had to be there, but they just couldn't find it. Desperate, they eventually submitted a rusty old broken hatchet found in a toolbox, but scientists proved it didn't match the wounds.

This is what I mean by coming to the fork in the road and taking it. There are two highly unlikely scenarios here: first, one where an intruder hides in the house; and second, one where Lizzie hides the murder weapon. One of these unlikely things happened, but most Borden experts completely ignore the near impossibility of hiding that weapon. Why? Because they had already decided Lizzie did it because they concluded it was impossible for an intruder to hide in the house.

Hey, if I just sent your head spinning with all that, sorry. I don't own a pub anymore, so I can't do that the fun way.

But this is something that will come up in a lot of cases. People decide something is unlikely, so they stop exploring the possibilities more thoroughly.

What I want you to take from it is this: in a lot of cases, something that seems rather unlikely to happen DID actually happen. The important thing is to choose the road that is LEAST unlikely.

At the end of the day, gun to my head, I would say Lizzie likely committed the crimes. But it's not even close to proven beyond a reasonable doubt, and there is plenty of justification for arguing she's innocent. My series on the Bordens was more an exercise in how to apply logic than anything else. If Lizzie didn't leave the house, and the police left no stone unturned looking for the murder weapon, it remains at least somewhat unlikely she actually committed the crimes. And unlike other female killers who do these kinds of vicious slaughters, there's nothing else in her personal history that points to her having this potential. No mental illness, no substance abuse, no history of violence. There are other brutal female killers in history, but Lizzie's profile stands out as unique.

A year after doing the Lizzie series, I took the same approach to the Karen Read case: time lines, impossibilities, improbabilities, and contradictory evidence.

And we also saw in the Borden murders something else we can recognize: these high-profile cases draw strange witnesses like teens to TikTok.

Everything stopped in Fall River when the Bordens were hacked to death. Factories emptied out, businesses closed, and thousands gathered outside the house. This was the biggest event of their drab lives. And almost all of us have relatively drab lives. By that, I mean we play no role in momentous events. We're just spectators. For many of us, that's preferable, but for a percentage of the population, the chance to step onto the stage, even if for just a moment, is hard to resist. That leads, inevitably, to a certain number of unreliable witnesses.

And in the age of social media, it can lead to much more than that—especially if a savvy defendant and her team are willing to use it.

# 2. MASSACHUSETTS STATE POLICE

Trooper Michael Proctor got the call from his partner, Sergeant Yuri Bukhenik, a little before 7:00 A.M. as the blizzard raged. An injured man had been found outside in Canton in grave condition. If the man died, this would automatically become an investigation led by the State Police, who take lead on all "unattended death" cases, except in the large cities of Boston, Springfield, and Worcester, which have their own homicide units. Proctor had been assigned, in a schedule posted at the beginning of the month, as the on-call case officer for January 29 from 7:00 P.M. to 7:00 A.M. With snow piling up and streets only partially plowed, it was time to get dressed and shovel his way out.

Proctor had been a State Trooper for 10 years, assigned to the homicide unit at Norfolk County for five. He had handled some big cases, including eventually Brian Walshe, charged with killing his wife and disposing of the body so that it would never be found.

Being assigned to homicide was Proctor's dream job. Having obtained a degree in criminal justice from Anna Maria College, he was accepted into law school. But law enforcement had always been in his heart and, as we said, there are some guys who, if you know them in high school, you're already thinking "this guy's gonna be a cop." Proctor was definitely that guy. Nicknamed "Bear," and having played Division 3 baseball in college, he no doubt would be a valuable power hitter on a slow-pitch softball team.

Like most of the characters in this tragedy, he grew up in Canton, a guy's guy who likes beers and barbecues, the Patriots and the Red Sox. He's tight with his two golden retrievers, especially Penny, with whom he has a special bond. While he loves to ski and golf, downtime for Proctor usually involves knocking back a couple of IPAs around a fire pit.

But Proctor would also become notorious in this case because of extremely inappropriate text messages about Karen discovered by the Feds on his personal phone. Suspended for this behavior, his status with the State Police remains in doubt as of this writing.

Even before these texts emerged, the trooper had been in the crosshairs of a defense team claiming, despite no evidence for it, that he had planted evidence to frame Read. Motive was said to be either his sister's friendship to Julie Albert or some kind of "thin blue line" thing, where cops protect cops.

Human beings are complicated and flawed. Proctor has one sibling, a younger sister named Courtney, whom he described in court as his best friend.

Defense attorney David Yannetti, in a stunning and disreputable attempt to throw off Proctor's testimony, met a witness in the parking lot of the elementary school where Courtney worked. The appearance of three men in the schoolyard had the intended effect, causing disruption within the school, and seeming to rattle Proctor on the stand a couple of days later.

Yeah, it's been that kind of circus.

But after receiving the call from Bukhenik at 6:48 that Sunday morning, Proctor had no idea what lay in the future. No idea this involved the death of a Boston Police officer. And no idea it involved the Alberts.

Proctor had never met Brian Albert, but his sister Courtney went to school with Chris Albert's wife's sister and remained very good friends. She also had become friends with Chris's wife Julie.

That's a lot to remember, so let's sum it up for you. Chris Albert is Brian's brother. His wife Julie and her sister are close friends with Proctor's sister.

In fact, at some point a pool party took place at the home of Proctor's parents, and Julie attended with the kids. One of those kids was Colin, whom the defense would later try to propose as John O'Keefe's actual killer.

Rubbing sleep from his eyes, Proctor's first call was to Canton Police Detective Lank on the scene at 34 Fairview. This suggests that Proctor already had Lank's cell phone number, which isn't surprising, since Proctor is a detective assigned to the Norfolk DA's Office in the same town, Canton. Lank would testify that Proctor told him they wouldn't be coming. It's unclear what Proctor meant, but he might have simply said they weren't going to the crime scene, or perhaps they were waiting for John's death to be declared, which didn't occur until 7:50.

Proctor's next call was to firefighter Anthony Flematti to get more information on the injured man. The firefighter informed him that the victim had a 10% chance of survival, so the trooper began making preparations to head out into the storm. They got permission to use their personal vehicles because of the weather.

Next stop: the Canton Police station.

Yuri Bukhenik immigrated from Ukraine as a boy and served with distinction as a US Marine, obtaining Top Security "Yankee White" clearance so he could work on the Presidential Helicopter Squadron. Built rugged like an aging warrior, his demeanor more suggests that of a medic. He's patient, meticulous, non-confrontational, the kind of person who not only stays cool in a crisis, but keeps everyone else calm.

After his stint as a Marine, he worked law enforcement for the town of Attleboro, where he was on the SWAT team, before joining the Massachusetts State Police in 2012. By 2015, he had been assigned to homicide at the Norfolk County District Attorney's Office.

About 9:15 A.M., Proctor and Bukhenik arrived separately at the station. They walked in together, but before they did, Proctor told Yuri, his supervising officer, about his family's connections to Chris Albert's family. So by this time, he understood who owned the home where John was found. Whether that knowledge came from a personal call or through police channels isn't known.

Sergeant Bukhenik didn't believe this created enough conflict for Proctor to recuse himself. With the biased perspective of hindsight, it's easy to be critical of this decision, but we have to understand that the number of homicide investigators assigned to Norfolk County at the time was only four, all with full case loads. And getting someone transferred from another county would be difficult at any time, but realistically not possible on a Saturday morning in the middle of a historic blizzard. So, as they weighed this, their decision wasn't surprising. Proctor barely knew the Alberts and didn't know Brian at all, and by the time they arrived at the police station, Karen had been Section 12'd at the hospital, and Lank had had a second meeting at 34 Fairview, where a picture was just starting to emerge. They didn't see this so much as a who-done-it murder investigation as an ordinary hit-and-run. Given that understanding, the Monday morning quarterbacking going on seems unfair and unreasonable.

Inside the Canton Police station, they spent about 20 minutes gathering more facts from the detectives and Sergeant Goode. From there, they climbed into Bukhenik's large truck and would travel together the rest of the day. First stop would be the McCabe home. There, perhaps oddly, they would also eventually find Brian Albert.

Why not make 34 Fairview the first stop?

Logic suggests the reason is that the McCabes had younger kids that they had to get back to. They had four daughters, the oldest being 17 at the time, but also the unfolding tragedy would have been hard on those kids, who knew John well and who were close to his niece Kayley. By contrast, the only Albert kid in the house at the time, Brian Jr., was 23. So it's quite understandable why the McCabes needed to get home, and they probably communicated this somehow to the troopers. Brian made it easier on them by meeting them there. This looks suspicious to many people now, but from their point of view, it was very reasonable.

Proctor and Bukhenik interviewed both McCabes and Albert, each separately and by themselves. Their next stop would be Good Samaritan Medical Center to view John's remains, collect evidence, speak to staff, and visit with the person emerging as the suspect, Karen Read.

But they would never visit the crime scene that day— at least according to them and the District Attorney. He would, under intense pressure from witnesses, make a special press statement eight months before the trial, insisting that the troopers never went to the scene that day.

Therefore, they couldn't have planted evidence.

### State Police

At this point, we should discuss further how this is all structured in Massachusetts. Those of us outside the system imagine that homicide detectives… and all of the other investigators working the cases… work out of a State Police barracks.

Nope.

We think they're a completely independent entity that, once assigned a case, work on their own, doing their own thing, using all of their own facilities and manpower.

Nope.

Homicide investigations are generally run at the County level in cooperation with local police. The TV show *Law and Order* highlights the fact that police detectives work hand in hand with prosecutors, and the same logic applies with investigations run by the State Police in towns and smaller cities. The State Police work in collaboration with local police to do the grunt work of the investigation, and the prosecutors they're working hand in hand with are at the County level, which is the District Attorney's Office.

Each District Attorney's Office has a State Police Detectives Unit (SPDU) permanently assigned to it. Those troopers don't report to work at a barracks. They report every day to offices assigned to them inside the DA's office, which in Norfolk County happens to be in Canton. Remember that, because it will impact a key decision in the case.

Thirteen troopers were assigned to SPDU Norfolk County in January of 2022, two of them being Proctor and Bukhenik, and they were two of only four homicide detectives.

Other TV shows may have given us a very false impression of how homicide investigations work. We imagine a couple of detectives heading out to solve the puzzle by sniffing out clues, but it's more like a large team, where each member has certain tasks for which they're trained. They rely far less on instincts and hunches, and far more on the routine actions they've been taught, each performing their specialized role.

Individual investigators performing their delegated parts of the job make decisions on their own or collectively. Ultimately, the buck stops with the commander, who in Norfolk County was Lieutenant Brian Tully. Any decisions where the investigators weren't sure what to do, they would go to him, but they don't need to go to him for every decision, as each member of the team has enough autonomy to perform their task.

So, an investigation is very bureaucratic and compartmentalized. There are many people, each doing their part, and no single trooper needs to know everything the others are doing. At the end of the day, the only ones who need to oversee the investigation and put it all together are the prosecutors.

Therefore, it's more accurate to call Trooper Proctor the "case manager" rather than "lead detective," since his job is more one of a "facilitator" who organizes witness interviews, evidence collection, record keeping, and report generation. Any decision where there might be a question, he consults his supervisor, Bukhenik, who in turn can consult his supervisors if needed.

**CSI Effect**

It's only a movie.

But is it a TV show?

Is it strange that the lead investigators never went to the crime scene that day? It sure seems it to us civilians, right?

On a TV show, the crime scene would be the first stop, crawling with all kinds of activity, a couple of grizzled detectives taking it all in. Maybe they would spot some critical clue that the other characters missed. Cue the dramatic music. Maybe they talk to some witness who has a really innocent explanation, but who our main character, with an eye for subtlety, would spot doing or saying something a little suspicious, some minor inconsistency or subtle tick within their body language. And eventually, through detective ingenuity, the riddle of what REALLY happened would be solved.

But that's a TV show. Remember YCT Rule #1? In real life, there are no geniuses.

But how can a crime be solved without a genius?

Well, in the real world, it's done by a team of highly specialized investigators routinely performing their own tasks.

That time you find a genius in a criminal case, whether with the good guys or the bad guys, will be the first.

And when you think about it, isn't that how we want it? Do we want homicide detectives sitting around saying, "Where do we start? Anyone got any ideas?" No, we want them proceeding methodically in the way they were trained.

So, the first step is to interview the local police to find out what happened.

Proctor and Bukhenik began that process before leaving the house and continued it at the Canton Police station, talking to cops who had been to the crime scene.

Then you talk to witnesses.

They did that at the McCabes' house.

At this early stage, the need isn't to be thorough and talk to every witness. It's gathering an overview so they can take necessary actions to do things like identify suspects, determine if there's public danger, and secure evidence before it can be erased.

After Proctor and Bukhenik left the McCabes, it was time to talk to the suspect, whom they had been told was at the hospital, which was convenient, since that's also where John's remains were.

Here's where the troopers made, it seems, their first big mistake… *though ironically, this mistake actually renders the idea of planting evidence as illogical.* By the time they left the McCabes' house, they certainly knew this case likely involved a hit-and-run. Yet they made absolutely no effort to secure the vehicle! They either knew, from the Canton Police, where it was, or should have known. Right?

Why didn't they secure it? Why didn't they make THAT the next stop?

The answer is most likely the need for probable cause, though that seems a little weak. Did they have more probable cause when they left the hospital and finally went to visit Karen and confiscate the Lexus? A little. They had learned there was a missing shoe, which is a common signature for a hit-and-run.

But probably by the time they left the Canton Police station, and certainly by the time they left the McCabes, they had heard talk of Karen's statements, strange behavior, and a broken taillight. They believed she was the suspect. They understood her to be at the hospital, but they also knew that the murder weapon wasn't.

However, it's important to ask: if the troopers had the corrupt goal of tampering with the vehicle, wouldn't they want to secure it as soon as possible before anyone took any photos?

If someone had enlisted the troopers in a conspiracy to frame someone for murder, wouldn't they be acting with extreme urgency at this moment? The conspirators had so much to do: gain access to the vehicle, remove parts, plant them at the scene undetected, and ensure the parts were found at street level.

Snow was piling up. And at some point, that scene would be crawling with State Police investigators digging for evidence. The clock was ticking.

But the evidence suggests their behavior was the opposite, that they were a little too casual.

It's possible that their normal routine was thrown off by the fact that they had lost their usual partners, the local police, who had been conflicted out because of Kevin Albert. Maybe the task of securing the vehicle would have normally been assigned to them, or at least they would have been ordered to send a cruiser to guard it in place until the troopers arrived.

Not securing the vehicle is a blunder. What if there was evidence inside it? Perhaps signs of a fight, such as blood, or of alcohol consumption, such as empty beer bottles?

This might be a good time to introduce you to… drum roll, please…

### YCT Rule #7: Don't just ask why someone did something. Ask why they DIDN'T do something.

This rule is probably important enough to be listed number one, but eurekas come when they come!

In a nutshell, when you look at the actions of everyone involved—suspects, witnesses, victims, investigators—don't just ask why they did something. Ask why they DIDN'T do something. Don't just look at actions they took; look at actions they DIDN'T take.

Great movie dialogue writers like Quentin Tarantino understand that when creating a script, the writer has to be able to put themself into the shoes of every character in the scene they're crafting. To know what the character might say in that moment, you have to *become* that character. *Think* like they do. *Imagine* how they would act given their array of choices.

Analyzing a case involves playing out virtually endless hypotheticals about the actions of people we don't know. But we CAN put ourselves in their shoes and consider a range of possibilities.

### Applying YCT Rule #7 to Lizzie Borden

With the Lizzie Borden murders, let's say we entertain the possibility of an intruder in the house being the culprit. Abby was killed around 9:30, Andrew at 11:00. In the meantime, Bridget and Lizzie were in and about the small house. An intruder would have to have hidden inside after killing Abby and waited until Andrew got home.

Let's apply Rule #7 to that case: why DIDN'T the killer murder Lizzie and Bridget?

A possible answer is that they were harder targets. Not that he couldn't kill them, but the neighborhood's houses were closely packed together, every one of them with windows open in August, and a lot of people on the streets. A scream would be heard. Harder to sneak up on younger women than the elderly parents, and Andrew was killed while napping on the couch.

So that particular question—why the killer didn't kill Lizzie and Bridget?—might not produce a definitive answer. But if we keep asking enough questions, we can hopefully narrow things down considerably. Insights can be gained.

If we're entertaining the hypothetical of Proctor planting taillight pieces that he pried from Karen's SUV, don't we have to ask why he didn't hurry over to get to Karen's car that morning? Why WASN'T he acting with any urgency to plant evidence before the Special Emergency Response Team (SERT) arrived to search the crime scene?

Asking these questions will start to reveal branches on the logic tree that are more… and less likely.

**Escape**

While the troopers were on their way to the hospital, Karen Read was actually on her way back to John's house. She had been released to the custody of her father and brother. And while the troopers viewed John's body, talked to staff, and collected his clothing, Karen bagged her belongings at John's, then went home with her father to the town of Dighton, forty-five minutes away… taking with them the alleged murder weapon.

# 3. BROTHER

Paul O'Keefe's phone woke him at 6:40 in the morning, making his heart skip a beat when he saw it was his mother. *Shit. Something wrong with Dad? Or maybe her?* The early hour of the call alarmed him.

"It's your brother," she told him as he sat up. "Something's happened. They found him in the snow."

He tried to process it. John? Snow? Maybe he had a heart attack while shoveling. The poor kids must have found him. He couldn't have been out there long, and he was in excellent shape.

In bed beside him, his wife Erin studied his face. He touched her hand. Erin was his strength. Through all the tragedy, she had remained his haven. She had become very good friends with Karen, John's most recent girlfriend. Paul liked her too. Educated, classy, Karen was good for John and for the kids. John had become a great father to them, but they really needed a mother figure in their lives, especially 14-year-old Kayley, already becoming a young woman.

"Where is he?" Paul whispered.

"Good Samaritan. Kerry's on her way to pick up me and Dad."

Paul's mother Peg served as a tower of strength through the tragedies of his sister and then her husband, but Paul could hear the worry in her voice. This was bad.

After hanging up, he took a deep breath. He wasn't sure how to proceed. Get dressed, get in the car. So simple, but everything seemed a blur. Just out of habit, he went to brush his teeth. Erin, sensing something terrible had happened, followed him. He explained what his mother had said.

Not remembering having gotten dressed, he found himself in his Toyota Forerunner, pulling out onto the street, icy hands gripping the steering wheel, the white fog of his breath hitting the windshield and creating a swirling storm inside the vehicle to match the one outside.

*Good Samaritan.*

*John.*

*Something happened.*

The snow crunched beneath the wheels. He had never seen it come down like this, and the wind rocked the big SUV, its engines growling as he punched through snow banks. Because only one lane was plowed, he drove down the center of the streets.

Kerry Roberts was braving *this* to pick up his parents? God, it had to be bad. A flurry of beats. He had already lost Kristen eight years ago… *No, don't go there.*

The journey to Brocton felt like it took forever. Curtains of snow rendered even stoplights almost invisible. Finally, he pulled into the parking lot of Good Samaritan Medical Center. He fought his way through the wind into the ER. A cousin who worked as a 911 dispatcher in Brocton, a city of a hundred thousand, met him there, telling him they were trying to warm John up. But the look on her face said more than words.

Minutes ticked by with cruel slowness. He updated Erin, saying he had no update, hoping their daughters were still asleep.

At last, Kerry ushered in his parents. He hugged his mom, tried to reassure her that the doctors were working on him. *John's a fighter. John's tough.*

The staff now brought them to a private room to wait. His heart sank. Not a good sign.

The expressions on the doctor's face said it all when he came in, the words sounding a mile away and almost unnecessary. All efforts to save him were unsuccessful.

He felt numb, like this was happening to someone else. It couldn't be true. He would be the only one left now, both siblings gone.

What would he tell the kids?

The doctor asked the family if they wanted to see him. Numb. This wasn't happening. He didn't want to see John like this.

The doctor led them into the hallway and past more rooms. From one of the rooms, a woman was screaming. Turning, he recognized her: Karen Read. The staff was struggling to restrain her. She spotted them and screamed her question, "Is he alive? Is he alive?!"

Paul felt a rush of sympathy. Why weren't they telling her?

They entered the room with John. Paul gasped. A sheet covered him from the waist down. His gaze went right to his brother's face, covered in a breathing mask. The swelling above his eyes was jarring, the size of ping-pong balls. He looked beat up. Some kind of scratches were on one arm. A sob escaped his mother. His dad, a quiet man who looked like an older version of Paul, wiped a tear.

When they left, the staff in the next room were still struggling with Karen. Poor woman, still screaming, asking whether John was dead. In a gesture meant to comfort her, he blew a kiss.

They met Kerry in the ER waiting room. She hugged them and wept. There were no words, only a moment of confusion about what to do next. Should they just leave? It felt wrong leaving his brother behind.

*What the hell had happened to him? How did he end up looking like that? Shouldn't there be police here?*

Arm around her, Paul ushered his mother into the Forerunner while Kerry drove his father, all of them heading to John's house. Streets remained practically impassable.

How did John get those injuries?

When they finally arrived at 1 Meadows, around 10:30, his heart sank once more. John would never enter his own home again. Never help the kids with their homework, never fuss over his lawn, never have guys over to watch a Patriots game.

At the moment, the kids weren't home. Patrick, 11, was at a sleepover, and this morning someone had picked up Kayley to prevent her from being home alone. They would be coming home now to learn once again that they were orphans. After making sure his parents got inside okay, he shoveled the relentless snow while waiting for them.

As expected, Kayley took it hard when she arrived. They huddled in the kitchen, sometimes almost in denial that John wouldn't be coming home, sometimes angry, but since they had no idea what had happened, they had no target for their anger.

And Paul had never been someone quick to anger anyway—he knew that about himself. He had even once or twice wished he had more rage he could tap into if needed, but his instincts were always to try to get along.

Then his phone rang. Karen Read.

"Is it okay if I come over to see the kids?" she asked.

"Of course," he told her.

She was in the car and only a few minutes away.

A short time later, with everyone still huddled in the kitchen, Karen came in with her father, brother, and sister-in-law. To Paul's surprise, she didn't rush to embrace Kayley, with whom she had always seemed so close. Instead, it was awkward.

What the hell had happened last night?

Ever non-confrontational, Paul didn't ask. Always tending to see the goodness in people, his mind never went to the possibility that Karen had some blame.

But then Patrick came in. From his face, they knew he suspected something terrible. But watching the boy being told was the most heart-wrenching thing he had ever seen in his life, and he could see they all felt that way, each of them wanting to comfort the inconsolable kid.

Except for Karen.

Karen stood quietly in the corner, no emotional reaction at all. Was she in shock? Paul didn't understand it. She had said she wanted to be here to hug the kids, but she had completely stayed away from them.

Instead, she took her father up to the bedroom to collect some things. Paul made a phone call… all the endless details that had to be taken care of in these situations… while Karen and her dad spent 15 or 20 minutes alone in the bedroom.

Later, if Paul could change one thing about what he had done that day, it would be not letting them go alone to the bedroom.

Where there was a computer.

Then the Reads came down, and along with Karen's brother and his wife, they braved the storm to make the trip to her parents' home in Dighton, 45 minutes away in normal weather.

Paul went back to trying to comfort the kids, reassuring them that the family would stay strong and life for them would go on as close to normal as possible. But his thoughts went more and more to Karen's strange behavior in the house.

Just what the hell had happened last night?

# PART THREE: THIRD-PARTY CULPRIT

# 1. A STORM BREWS

I'm going to bring you back in time not only to the very beginnings of the third-party culprit defense, but to Ground Zero. I'll put you right there so you can feel the first gusts of wind that would eventually swirl into the great storm that became Free Karen Read.

The movement has become a global phenomenon, with pink-shirted armies from coast to coast, national media coverage, and a slew of major documentaries. For many, it has almost become a kind of religion, something that resonates at a very personal level, moving them to not only show up daily at court to cheer Karen but also to boo the family and friends of the victim, to persecute those accused of being part of the conspiracy and, stunningly, to accuse John's best friends—and even his brother—of being part of the cover-up. Indeed, the primary voice of Free Karen Read has actually called for John's family to "burn in hell."

What led to such passions?

Well, it's complicated. But all the conditions came together at just the right time and place, with just the right circumstances, in order to create a perfect storm. Contributing to these conditions were the many odd and even unique elements. For some of these things, it turns out there's a perfectly good explanation, and for some there's at least a reasonable one. But for others, things remain mysterious.

A great source on how this unfolded was an investigative piece by *Boston Magazine* writer Gretchen Voss, who spoke with Karen, her defense team, and many of the people at the eye of the storm. Building on her work, we've managed to zoom in even closer. Like an old *Star Trek* episode, we'll beam you onto the ground in the first days after the tragedy so you can see it all take shape.

## It Begins

Curled up on the couch at her parents' house in Dighton, snow piling up around her Lexus in the driveway, Karen hadn't been home long—doctors had pronounced John dead only five hours earlier—when her cell phone rang. Trooper Proctor. They were on the way.

After hanging up, with her life on the line, she googled "DUI lawyer."

What did she discuss with her parents and brother at this time? They certainly knew about the broken taillight.

Bill Read, her dad, was the dean of Bentley College, a business school. He had been a professor of accounting for his entire adult life. Certainly, he must know some defense lawyers, or at least powerful people who did know such lawyers. Did Karen wish to avoid the subject with him? It strikes us as somewhat surprising that the Reads would find Karen's lawyer through a Google search.

Do the specifics of her search tell us anything about her mindset at the time? Remember YCT Rule #7: Ask what she didn't do. And she didn't google "*criminal* defense attorney."

## Yannetti

David Yannetti grew up in the plush Boston suburb of Newton and graduated cum laude at Bowdoin College, one of the hardest-to-get-into liberal arts schools in the country. He majored in government and legal studies. While there, he played varsity baseball and even now, in his early 60s, he looks fit.

Right out of Bowdoin, he went to Boston College Law School, graduating in three years, and then headed straight to work for the Suffolk County District Attorney's Office in Boston. All of this portrays a hard-working and disciplined man who has been that way all his life.

In court, he presents a confident figure, though his voice frequently becomes high-pitched whenever he switches gears. While he's an effective communicator, his oratory skills are well short of spellbinding.

Like many defense attorneys, Yannetti got his trial experience working as an assistant prosecutor, toiling there ten long years, handling several major cases, until finally came the one that would prompt him to put out his own shingle. This last case, which he successfully prosecuted in 1998, was the notorious and horrific trial of two pedophiles who abducted and killed a 10-year-old boy named Jeffrey Curley.

It's hard to know what goes through the minds of prosecutors who have to spend so much time pouring over the gruesome details of a case like that. The effort and the emotional turmoil are grueling. We don't know if the Curley case pushed Yannetti to move into the private sector, or whether he just felt that 10 years was enough and it was time to open his own office, but in 1999, he set out into the private sector as a defense attorney.

We'll take a much closer look at Yannetti, whose earlier work on another so-called "dream case" sheds a lot of light on his future handling of Karen Read.

John died on Saturday, January 29. Police arrested Karen Tuesday night; she spent a night in jail and was arraigned Wednesday, February 2. If you have a highlighter handy, mark these dates, because they serve as a kind of Mason-Dixon line when it comes to understanding the origins of the third-party culprit theory.

Just before her arraignment, Karen met Yannetti over prison bars, their first meeting. Reading from the charging document, he went over what the State had: how a contributing cause of death was hypothermia; how Karen had showed Kerry Roberts and Jen McCabe her broken taillight that morning; how she had said, "I hit him, I hit him," at the scene; how taillight pieces from her car had been found buried in the snow.

Then guards whisked her to court to be arraigned.

Yannetti told the court that his client had "no criminal intent" and that she loved the victim. He repeated this to the media minutes later on the courthouse steps.

So, up to that point, neither Karen nor her defense lawyer had any notion that John had been killed in some other way than being struck by Karen's Lexus.

However, on the way home from court, Yannetti returned the call of a man with a gravelly voice who had left a message under an assumed name. The man now told him he had reason to believe that John had been attacked inside the house by Brian Albert, Brian's nephew, and an ATF agent!

Drop the mic, right?

This marks, in Yannetti's explanation of it, the beginning of the third-party culprit theory. In fact, at various times in the year-long run up to the first trial, the man with the gravelly voice, whom we'll soon introduce you to in detail, was presented to the public as a whistleblower who had spoken to a secret witness who had been in the house and seen the attack. In fact, even now, Yannetti coyly tries to suggest this is the truth.

Was this how Karen's team managed to convince the Feds that there was a conspiracy to kill John? That's right, the powerful US Attorney and the FBI would soon join forces with the defense!

Pick up the mic just so you can drop it again.

Yet another thing that sets this case apart from virtually any other is the alliance between the defendant and one of the most powerful justice officials in the country. And it was rumored that Gravelly Voice might have given that unusual federal probe its predication.

Gravelly Voice would tell a different version of events. But in our view, one thing is almost certain: Karen Read didn't originate the third-party culprit theory. She has been more actively involved in her own defense than just about any other defendant. Sure, Ted Bundy defended himself and was extremely savvy in handling the media, but Karen has far more tools at her disposal because of social media, which she uses to aggressively push the conspiracy narrative and also to research the witnesses and investigators. And she did, in fact, find interesting material on her own.

But she had more resources than that. People who had become close friends of hers in Canton during the two years she dated John, and who believed in her innocence, became a vital source of information, because they knew all the players.

And one of these sources knew something else: that the Alberts owned a German shepherd.

## 2. HARD-TO-EXPLAIN INJURIES

The biggest problem with the State's case against Karen Read is explaining John's injuries. The state says Karen's SUV struck John. However, not only have the defense produced experts who say a dog attacked John, but other experts hired by the federal government itself actually agreed that John was likely not struck by a vehicle. Indeed, the State's own medical examiner testified that these were "not classic pedestrian collision injuries."

At a glance, the prosecution's argument does seem weird. John had no significant injuries below the neck, but they claim the traumatic injury to the head was the result of being struck hard enough to launch him backward with enough force that he crushed bones in his skull when he landed. This, they argue, knocked him out and left him to die in the cold. The damage to the car, mostly a shattered taillight, was caused by his arm.

But the only visible injuries below John's neck were shallow abrasions on his right arm and a small contusion on his right knee.

You no doubt see the problem. A 6000-lb. vehicle hit John hard enough to throw him onto his head, yet it left no significant injuries. That is weird.

During the year before the trial, as I began digging hard into this case, I reached out to many contacts in law enforcement who had experience with accident fatalities.

What I heard from all of them was how odd the injuries often appeared, and how much variance there is from one scene to another. One friend who had worked as a local cop in North Carolina before moving into federal law enforcement said that so often was it the case that injuries like this were baffling and mysterious that this was practically the norm. The reason is that these are collisions involving high speeds with steel machines much larger than the human body.

But each of the cops assured us that what appeared mysterious to them, and of course to us, wouldn't puzzle accident reconstruction experts. With their training and their experience, they can generally figure out exactly what happened and how each injury occurred.

So I awaited the State's argument from their experts during the trial and expected we would get a satisfying explanation when it came to John O'Keefe's seemingly mysterious injuries.

We didn't.

At least, not convincingly. Some things were explained. For example, many people in the public wondered why John's extremities didn't show any signs of frostbite. But the medical examiner, Dr. Irini Scordi-Bello, gave a convincing explanation in her testimony. She explained that she didn't see the body until Monday, two days later, and by then John had been warmed and given fluids in the effort to save him, and his body had then been stored for 48 hours. If there were any questions about why ER doctors didn't note any signs of frostbite, the defense didn't raise them with those doctors, and if it wasn't an issue the defense could exploit, it's not an issue.

So let's run down John's injuries and see how they fit into the third-party culprit theory developed by the defense team and Karen's agitators.

## Medical Examination

First, let's dispel a myth. Medical examiners don't perform autopsies independently from investigators. We, the public, with our suspicious minds, think investigators must keep it sealed off and independent, otherwise the police might influence the doctors' conclusions. That would be logical if… if… performing an autopsy was an exact science. Turns out it's not. It's not actually the case that doctors can scientifically examine the remains, knowing nothing about the circumstances of the death, and then automatically form specific conclusions about what happened.

Scordi-Bello gave a great example. Hypothermia is actually difficult to determine in an autopsy. In John O'Keefe's case, she observed small hemorrhages on his stomach and pancreas; these commonly occur in bodies experiencing hypothermia, although the reason remains unclear. As we said, medicine isn't always an exact science. Therefore, as the medical examiner makes her determinations, she needs to know more about the circumstances surrounding the victim's death. Scordi-Bello contacted Trooper Proctor twice with questions, and of course she learned that John had been unconscious outside in 18 degree weather for hours.

The medical examiner makes the final decision about anything that goes into the autopsy report… the buck stops there. But she does need information from the investigators in order to do her job. Knowing the conditions John faced before dying—namely, hours of exposure to extreme cold while wearing light clothing—helped her reach her conclusions.

So it's not only not suspicious that Trooper Proctor was involved with the autopsy process but, in fact, it's the norm. Whether he corruptly influenced her in any way, we'll have to look at the totality of the evidence and draw conclusions later.

Here's what the medical examiner found:

John had a three-centimeter laceration on the back of the skull that resulted from blunt force trauma. That kind of trauma can come from a blow to the frozen ground, a baseball bat, or a stair… many things. The force of the impact caused a radiating pattern of fractures that began in the back of the head and spread to the front. This created the swelling known as "raccoon eyes."

In addition to the laceration, there was a scrape right above it on the back of his head. The defense tried, somewhat weakly, to suggest this could have come from being dragged on the ground. But the scrape was immediately above the laceration and perfectly matched it in width, so obviously, whatever caused the laceration also caused the scrape.

Two small, superficial lacerations were on John's face: one near his eye and the other on his nose.

There was also a tongue laceration, and though the medical examiner didn't explain this, it seems that this was likely the source of the blood coming from his mouth when the women found him.

A small abrasion showed on his right knee. Other than that, no injuries were located below the waist. And nothing on his back, shoulders, chest, or left arm.

Adjacent to the sternum, there were fractures to the fourth and fifth ribs consistent with and commonly seen in patients who have undergone CPR.

There were no significant signs that he had been in an altercation.

Scordi-Bello concluded that the blow to John's head hadn't been immediately lethal, but it would have knocked him out, and hypothermia then combined with the head injury to cause the fatality.

She admitted under oath that he didn't display "classic pedestrian collision injuries." She stated that it was "likely and unlikely at the same time" that a vehicle had struck him.

More usually in a hit-and-run, one sees injuries to the legs, depending on the height of the bumper, but the medical examiner noted that Karen's Lexus had a higher taillight and bumper. To that point, we have documented that if John, who was six foot two, was standing beside that vehicle, his elbow matched perfectly to the height of the taillight. Not only that, but a palm-sized dent on the front of the car also matched perfectly to where John's hand, likely holding the cocktail glass, would have hit a forearm's length from the taillight.

But what does the prosecution say about the position he was in when hit? Most pedestrian strikes are from the front of the car, thus explaining the leg injuries. But if John's elbow made contact with the taillight, shattering it, wouldn't there be significant injuries somewhere else, such as on his shoulder?

Not necessarily. The prosecution's theory is that the Lexus swept past John at nearly 25 MPH without stopping. John instinctively raised his arm to shield himself. The taillight hit his elbow, and then his arm snapped in the direction of the car, his hand creating the dent as it zipped past. Other than perhaps slightly nicking his knee, there was no other contact between his body and the vehicle. The impact launched him backward at an angle onto the frozen lawn, perhaps even spinning him a little, and he landed on the back of his head with enough force to create the skull fractures.

Dr. Renee Stonebridge, assisting with the medical examination, showed up in court with a sleeveless shirt, its green floral pattern blending in seamlessly with the black-inked jungle design covering her left arm. Prominent within that jungle was a gigantic skull, which faced the jury only feet away in the tiny courtroom, its skeletal face distorting when she flexed her arm. And working with skulls is actually her specialty. Feeling the pressure of having the eyes of millions on her, Dr. Stonebridge seemed just slightly nervous but very competent in her craft. She knew her shit. It was she who examined John's removed brain and the skull that previously contained it.

She explained that John's head trauma and radiating skull fractures caused brain hemorrhages; the swelling had nowhere to go because the brain is encased, resulting in numerous contusions and further swelling. What she observed was "consistent" with John being struck by a vehicle and then falling to the ground.

So there seems to be no question that frozen ground *could* have caused the head injury.

The right arm, however, has been the major source of the conspiracy theory.

## Dog Bites?

The way Karen told the story to *Boston Magazine*'s Gretchen Voss, she and her father had just made their first visit to Yannetti's office, where they looked at the autopsy pics. On the drive home, Karen called her mother, and when she explained the strange wounds on John's right arm, her mom wondered if it could be from an animal attack.

Karen then asked her friend Tom Beatty, a larger-than-life Canton resident we'll introduce you to soon, if a dog had been in the house at 34 Fairview. He looked into it and came back with yes, they owned a German shepherd named Chloe.

The dog had been acquired from Texas by one of the Albert sons and was six years old. They had fenced in the house's back yard, and Chloe had access to it. She slept in the master bedroom with Brian and Nicole.

A year before the trial, the defense team would bring a blown-up photo to court of the wounds on John's arm. Defense attorney Alan Jackson risked the ire of the judge by angling the blow-up to the camera so that everyone watching at home could see it. It shows several areas of wounds on the forearm and the upper arm, wounds consisting of parallel lines and possibly punctures. The defense told the court—and of course, the public—that the wounds were the result of a dog attack. When we're shown the image while at the same time being told that's what it is, it creates a powerful impression that's hard to erase from your mind. Remember, we see the world in narratives, and we can easily imagine that teeth or nails might create parallel lines.

So, as we look at that photo, it's not hard to imagine incisor teeth chomping down and leaving punctures, or scratch lines forming as the victim tries to pull away.

Indeed, in somewhat strange circumstances, a retired emergency room physician, Dr. Marie Russell, who had previously published peer-reviewed work on dog bites, emerged during the middle of the trial to testify that these were, in fact, wounds from an attack by a large dog.

If they were dog bites, then almost certainly John went inside the house, Karen is innocent, and this involves one of the more memorable true-crime conspiracies of our time.

Interestingly, two months after the tragedy, the Alberts actually re-homed their dog, which they'd had for six years.

# 3. FEELING LUCKY

Brian "Lucky" Loughran plows snow for the town of Canton. Each one of us human beings is a unique blend of talents and weaknesses, and Lucky's blend is something one quickly recognizes as different. "Learning disabled" might be the words that come to mind, but given his special interest in cars and his above average knowledge in that area, it's fairest to just say Lucky has a unique blend.

In his 50s, a bit chubby and square-faced, Lucky had lost his beloved wife about a year before the trial, a void which pains him every day. A simple, child-like man who would never try to stand out in a crowd, for many years he had actually delivered orders for Chris Albert's D&E Pizza. Though he would never seek the spotlight, it found him during the trial, and he did enjoy the aftermath of his moment, as the Free Karen Read crowd celebrated him like a returning hero.

Why? Because Lucky would testify that on the night of John's death, driving his city plow known as the Frankenbeast, a six-wheel dump truck with a nine-foot plow, he would pass by 34 Fairview around 2:30 A.M.… and not see a body on the lawn.

He claimed to have spotted a mysterious SUV at the location where John was found around 3:30. Parked with the lights out.

If these observations are meaningful, they're explosive. If John wasn't lying unconscious in the yard at 2:30, where was he?

And why did someone park an SUV where John was found, around 3:30?

We have to go back to how this theory emerged. In the days after Karen's arraignment, Gravelly Voice met in Yannetti's office. Present was a tall, roly-poly private investigator named Paul Mackowski. To make this story seem more intriguing, I would like to be able to tell you that Mackowski was a shady operator working in the shadows like Mike Ehrmantraut from *Breaking Bad*, but I found no evidence of that. A retired Medford cop who had worked a long time as a police detective, everything I found about him suggested a man of good reputation. He gladly took a call and spoke at length, though he could, of course, not talk about the Karen Read case. By the time these three men left that meeting, a good chunk of the third-party culprit theory had formed. They sent Gravelly Voice out with a $1500 check to find what he could, and they sent Mackowski to canvas the town—only now, he wasn't just blindly looking for anything they could use. He had a working alternative theory: the beginnings of third-party culprit.

With John O'Keefe lying unconscious in the yard, only feet from the street, in the early stages of a blizzard, it's common sense that investigators needed to talk to anyone who might have driven down the street, especially in a vehicle equipped with bright lights, like a plow. But the State Police never talked to the plow driver, at least not until well after Karen's PR machine would start hammering this a year and a half later. Is that suspicious? A blunder?

Lead investigator Proctor would report that, upon contacting Canton's DPW, department head Michael Trotta told him Fairview hadn't been plowed before John was found. Trotta would dispute that report by the trooper. There would also be disputed claims about the GPS tracking system monitoring the plows, something that apparently drew the interest of the FBI.

In any case, the street certainly was plowed. The plow banks are visible in Officer Saraf's dashcam video… but Lucky wasn't interviewed by anyone before Paul Mackowski spoke to him almost three weeks after John's death.

And the stunning story Lucky told the private investigator added a whole new dimension to their developing theory.

According to Mackowski's report, Lucky arrived to work at the DPW yard at 2:00 A.M. and, around 2:15, took out the Frankenbeast. Around 2:30, he made a pass down Fairview with 34 on his left. Minutes later, he made a pass from the opposite direction. It was snowing lightly, with about two inches of snow on the road. At least that was what he remembered when interviewed. We'll see if it stacks up with the weather reports.

Between 3:30 and 4:00, while making another two passes, he spotted a small SUV parked "exactly where the body was found." The lights were out, and he didn't observe anyone inside the vehicle. He later told the troopers that the SUV had been parked there for a significant amount of time, "over an hour."

Mackowski walked Lucky to the parking lot at the DPW and asked if he saw any similar vehicles. Loughran immediately pointed to a Ford Edge.

Brian Albert owned a Ford Edge, but he parked it in the driveway, and Lucky said he knew Brian's car, and it wasn't that one.

However, it would later be learned that someone else drove a Ford Edge, because he had been pulled over for speeding outside the college he was then attending as a freshman: Colin Albert.

# 4. NEPHEW

Means and motive. That's where any murder investigation starts, right? Motive was the big obstacle in the emerging third-party culprit theory. Why would anyone in the house want to attack John within minutes of his arriving at the after-hours party?

Brian Albert and John O'Keefe barely knew each other, despite both working for the Boston Police and living in the same town. And there's no evidence of there ever being any animosity. They weren't rivals at work; they didn't have kids who competed against each other; no love triangles… Nothing.

True, when guys drink, especially Boston Irish, shit can happen. It wouldn't be Brian's first brawl after a night of drinking.

But they needed much more than that, because if the theory was to actually convince anyone, they would have to explain not only why John was attacked, but why he had been savagely put out to die in the cold, and why so many people had gone along with it. And perhaps the hardest thing to account for was how the troopers would be enlisted to help cover it up.

Gravelly Voice had told Yannetti that the nephew had been involved, along with Brian and an ATF agent. Who was the nephew, and could this be the key?

Colin Albert is the son of Chris, Brian's brother, the owner of D&E Pizza. Chris and his wife Julie had been drinking with the group at the Waterfall, and indeed, Chris had been the one to invite John over to the Waterfall.

Karen started intently researching Chris's social media footprints, and he eventually found a picture from a few weeks later that showed abrasions on his knuckles—as though he had recently been in a fight.

Also strange: when Brian Albert listed the people at the house in his interview with the troopers, he didn't mention Colin being there. Was he trying to protect him?

Focusing on Colin became the key for Karen and her team because it explained the motive of the witnesses AND the police who were thought to be orchestrating the cover-up. It would be hard to get people to rally to the cause if this was just a matter of Brian getting into a drunken fight. It's much easier to imagine them doing it if they were protecting a 17-year-old young man.

But it didn't explain the motive for Colin to attack John.

That was the key. I always had trouble accepting the possibility of a 17-year-old kid, no matter how athletic, attacking a six-foot-two Boston cop who worked with his uncle. And in his uncle's house, no less.

Karen, no doubt seeing the same problem, seemed to arrive at a solution, telling *Boston Magazine* reporter Gretchen Voss that it all began with an incident of teens drinking on John's lawn.

Any good fiction builds on kernels of truth. John, a stickler for neatness, required people to take off their shoes in his house, and he didn't like kids playing on his lawn. Colin was a tough football player who, like many boys that age, wanted to seem bad-ass, so he adopted the language of thugs. On the stand, he came across as polite, clean cut, and respectful, but high school boys trying to establish an identity can take on different personas. Portraying him as a ruffian wouldn't be difficult for the defense. And they were neighbors, Chris and John, the Alberts living a couple of doors down. So the elements for a clash were there to build on.

Karen told Gretchen Voss of an incident where they were awoken one night by the RING alarm system. John opened the front door to see what the ruckus was and found teenage boys drinking in the bushes on the property line. One of these boys was said to be Colin, and John exchanged curses with the boy. Voss was unable to find any neighbors to confirm what happened, but could this have been the source of a feud?

Even during the early days of the launching of the conspiracy theory, I was skeptical. I couldn't buy into Colin attacking John in Brian's house, and a feud centered on a lawn incident didn't move the needle either.

But the defense absolutely played this angle at trial, highlighting the abrasions on Colin's knuckles visible three weeks later, digging for evidence that Colin had been in fights, even showing a video of the boy with his buddies, seemingly intoxicated and threatening another group of kids. In fact, the defense went so far as to suggest that the whole attack was PLANNED, with the Alberts stashing Colin in the basement waiting to ambush John. The way they imagined it, even Jen McCabe offering Karen, outside the Waterfall, to ride with them represented an effort to separate her from John.

So the family planned to attack John because Colin was upset about being told not to drink on John's lawn? That was absurd, even by the loose standards of absurdity set by the mob.

Because of that, in the summer of 2023, I unwittingly became a part of the attempt to establish a plausible motive for Colin. Speaking almost daily with a retired DEA agent who, unknown to me, had become a confidante of Karen's, I kept telling him that there was nowhere close to a plausible motive.

Then, after weeks of prodding, this confidante of Karen's suddenly produced the answer: Karen and John had presented evidence to the police that Colin was dealing drugs on the street corner.

Stop the presses, right? That's a motive! I was told that John had Karen film Colin dealing drugs, and then John called 911 and arranged to send the video. And working as a detective at the Canton Police was Colin's uncle.

Now, there's a plot line. It might be more fit for *Breaking Bad*, but at least it presents a narrative, one that could actually be pitched to Showtime: A family of small-town cops rallies to protect a drug-dealing nephew. Starring Kevin Bacon or someone connected to him.

And in fact, the video Karen made of a local drug dealer, which is now in discovery for the trial, was sent by John to a contact on the Canton Police force: Kevin Albert.

# 5. AGENT HIGGINS

A couple of weeks before the tragedy, Agent Brian Higgins received a text from a number that wasn't a contact on his phone: "Hey, Brian, it's the Weed Whacker."

Karen would later call herself the "Queen of Nicknames." You'll recall the incident when Higgins drove by as she was blowing leaves.

They were both regulars at the Hillside Pub, a place we want to take you inside later for a pint, because the Hillside is as close to Ground Zero as you'll find in the Free Karen Read movement, the place where it all began.

The texts were clearly flirtatious from the start. Karen told Higgins she liked him because he was a "kind of loner… which I used to be."

Higgins cautiously flirted back: "You're double trouble."

She replied: "You're hot."

I'll talk a lot about motives in this book, and this gives us a chance to break in with another rule from the cottage.

**YCT Rule #12: Beware of simplified narratives.**

We perceive the world in narratives. The brain is a pattern-recognition machine, everything from what we see and hear to what we think. This also applies to the subject of the moment: motivations.

Because a narrative is a boiled-down version of reality, it's incomplete at best and sometimes false. The brain is even quite capable of crafting memories that don't accurately portray events. At the very least, things are more complicated than we know, especially when it comes to understanding what moves people to do what they do. In other words, motive.

For example, take Agent Clarice Starling, the main character in *Silence of the Lambs*. Why is she so determined to catch the killer? Career ambition, of course, and she wants to overcome the barrier of being a petite woman in a field dominated by larger males. She's an underdog.

But Hannibal Lecter identifies other reasons rooted in her youth: the death of her father, who was a sheriff shot in the line of duty, and her attempt to save a lamb from the slaughterhouse.

So right there are four motives driving her: ambition, oppression, a desire to live up to her father's memory, and a deep, inner frustration stemming from the inability to save the innocent. If Clarice Starling was a real human being, we would probably find more tiny levers that moved the mountain. Maybe someone picked on her growing up, and a badge gives her a sense of empowerment. Maybe she likes a challenge, or she just hates being told she can't do something.

What was Karen's motive in suddenly flirting with Agent Higgins? The perhaps too-easy answer is revenge. We've already discussed the incident in Aruba. Karen told *Vanity Fair* that flirting with Higgins helped her to "emotionally validate" herself.

When she told Higgins he was hot, he replied, "Are you serious or messing with me?"

"No, I'm serious," she replied.

The whole flirtatious thing began and ended quickly, lasting little more than a week. But it was Karen who began and ended it. And the texts seem to reveal why. When Karen texted Higgins about what he wanted, he finally answered: "the real deal." She replied: "It doesn't exist," and then seemed to end things. We don't know what Higgins meant by the "real deal," but it sounded a little too serious for Karen, who didn't want more than a dalliance.

So maybe it wasn't at all about revenge and not so much about validation as it was about control. Karen had lost control over things with John. A dalliance with someone else would give her that sense of being on top again, but Higgins's interest in something more serious created a danger: John was more likely to find out.

Higgins's interest in her remained even after the texts stopped.

While John did ask Karen about her walking Higgins out to his car the night of the football game, none of John's friends or family have mentioned him ever being concerned that Karen was cheating on him.

So there WAS a potential source of friction between John and Brian. However, none of John's friends spoke of it, so it's unlikely John was aware of anything, and there's no evidence Higgins felt any animosity toward John. In the surveillance video, when John enters the Waterfall, he hugs Higgins, who is sitting on a bar stool.

Higgins eventually texted Karen from inside: "Ummm, well?"

It had been ten days since their last text.

During the trial, the defense would go to great pains to highlight Brian Albert and Brian Higgins at one point play fighting at the Waterfall. They got into MMA stances. The implication by the defense was that they were getting riled up and actually planning an attack on John.

As they were leaving, with John and Karen still seated at the table, Higgins looked agitated. While there's no testimony of anyone saying he was agitated, he seemed to be looking in John's general direction. We asked Chris Albert, who was right there with Higgins, if there was any agitation, and he said absolutely not.

Chris's credibility is very high with me for the simple reason that I had many conversations with him over the months, and invariably, things he told me turned out to be true. When he didn't know something, he was always honest about that. He never once tried to push any narrative, and sometimes things that seemed weird to the public also seemed weird to him. All of that really makes him credible.

Karen has never once claimed she saw Higgins agitated or confrontational that night. She has also never claimed that she and John talked about any confrontation while they drove to 34 Fairview, and obviously they would have, since they knew Higgins was heading there too.

Higgins arrived at 34 Fairview just ahead of Brian and Nicole Albert and parked by the mailbox. He would say he left between 12:30 and 1:00 A.M. and drove straight to the Canton Police station to do "administrative work," but questions remain.

Karen and John arrived a little after 12:24, and right behind them was a pickup truck going to the same destination. No one in the truck remembered seeing Higgins's Jeep Wrangler parked right beside the driveway. Is this odd? Did he leave before 12:24? It's only a five-minute drive to the police station, but he wasn't seen there until close to 1:30.

New evidence has been entered into discovery before the second trial: surveillance from the police station after 1:00 A.M. It's said to show Higgins on the phone at 1:34. The FKR mob feverishly speculates whether he was calling the people inside the house.

## Butt Dials

Higgins moved his vehicles around at the police station because of the incoming snowstorm, then drove home, arriving about 1:40. He heated up some leftovers and had a couple more Jameson and gingers, then fell asleep on the sofa until, at some point, he moved to the bedroom. That's his testimony.

But at 2:22, he had a "butt dial" from Brian Albert which lasted one second, and he returned the call, which connected for 22 seconds.

At 6:30 in the morning, both his work and personal phones started "blowing up." The first was from Chief Berkowitz, informing him of what was going on. The chief has his own place in the third-party culprit theory, which we'll get to shortly. The next call was from Brian Albert, and this had Higgins getting dressed and hurrying out in the snow to go back to 34 Fairview, where he would huddle with the Alberts and McCabes, and talk to Canton Detective Lank.

After leaving 34 Fairview, he logged in to work at the Canton Police station, where he would spend the rest of the day. Within that building, access to certain doors is regulated by an electronic key, creating a partial record of movement.

### A Strange Shift in Defense Strategy

During the trial, a long weekend interrupted the cross-examination of Higgins by the defense. Alan Jackson began the cross-examination, but because he had to return to California for personal reasons, it was David Yannetti who picked things up on Tuesday. However, he inexplicably abandoned the line of questioning begun by Jackson, a critical line which had the potential to be explosive. Would they attempt to build on that in the retrial? Or did they abandon it for a reason?

The line of questioning centered on a critical role in the alleged cover-up played by the Canton Chief of Police, Ken Berkowitz.

### Chief Berkowitz

The chief, like a surprising number of officers involved in this story, retired shortly after the events. At the time of John's death, he was out on sick leave. He was on the defense witness list but wasn't called to testify, possibly due to ill health, and sadly, he would die of cancer in December of 2024.

Berkowitz began his law enforcement career in 1992 for the Canton Police. Throughout his career, he aggressively continued his training, graduating from programs with the FBI and the DEA and many others. As chief, he would also head the Metro-LEC Mobile Operations Unit and their SWAT team. Metro-LEC is an inter-agency organization that trains units for rapid-response situations.

From his starting position as a route cop in the quiet little town of Canton, Ken Berkowitz did about as much and reached about as high a level as was achievable. But is it possible that he envied someone like Brian Albert, who fought in the Gulf War as a Marine and who did the kind of high-adrenaline work for the Boston Police that those who wish to be "in the juice" dream of doing? Another person in the juice was Brian Higgins, who for years did mostly undercover work. These are the kind of guys Ken admired. Understandable, but did he wish he could BE like them?

I don't in any way wish to disparage Chief Berkowitz. His career was highly accomplished and something to be proud of. But there were two things he did in the days immediately following the case that are very eye-raising.

First, a few days after John's death, a local reporter published a tweet identifying Brian Albert as the homeowner at 34 Fairview. The chief contacted the reporter and requested the removal of Brian's name, calling him a "pillar of the community." That's not only inappropriate, but it's also weird, which makes it suspicious. If someone is struck by a car in front of your house, how does it harm *your* reputation for that to be made public? That John happened to be found on the edge of Brian's lawn, a victim of a hit-and-run, doesn't damage *his* reputation in any way.

The second odd thing came six days after the fatality when the chief, driving by 34 Fairview, spotted taillight pieces on the street, visible now because of melting snow. He immediately called this discovery in to Detective Lank, who notified the State Police.

It's kind of unique. Why was the chief, out on leave, driving down Fairview and studying the street for evidence?

All of this created building expectations as Alan Jackson questioned Higgins on the stand.

We have to remember that it's not enough for the defense to show that the investigators might have made crucial *mistakes* in this case and that maybe they charged the wrong defendant. No, in the case of Karen Read, unless evidence—particularly taillight evidence—was planted at the scene, her Lexus fatally struck John.

In order to plant that taillight evidence, the first step was to acquire it by prying it off Karen's SUV. Well, just where and when was there an opportunity to do that?

The defense has long tried to portray a scenario where this tampering was done inside the sally port, and then the taillight pieces were hurried over to 34 Fairview, where they were planted. So, establishing that any funny business took place in the sally port was essential in creating a plausible third-party culprit.

Let's examine some of the discoveries Alan Jackson revealed at trial.

At 3:10 P.M., inside the Canton Police station, Higgins received a call from Detective Kevin Albert. And Higgins implausibly testified that they didn't discuss the death of John O'Keefe.

The call lasted 12 minutes, and two minutes later, Brian Albert called him. The ATF agent denied sharing any details about the investigation with Brian.

There would be two more calls between Higgins and Chief Berkowitz and one more with Brian Albert. The line of questioning by the defense was to imply that they were getting their stories straight and plotting how evidence would be planted.

Alan Jackson pointed out that the electronic key system showed that Higgins had accessed the sally port door at 3:57 and 4:07 P.M. That doesn't fully establish his movements… people cut through the sally port to get to and from the parking lot… but it places him roughly in the area right around the same time Karen's SUV was being put on the tow truck at her parents' home in Dighton. Were Higgins and Chief Berkowitz waiting for the Lexus?

Jackson went on to say that there was evidence Berkowitz and Higgins were moving together through the station at different times during the day. Higgins didn't deny the possibility. However, when the defense tried to place the chief and the ATF agent in the sally port together, Higgins balked. He didn't remember anything like that.

Over the weekend, every veteran Karen Read trial watcher now sat on the edge of their seat. Would the defense prove Higgins and the chief were hanging around in the sally port when the SUV arrived?

Jackson listed a bunch of specific times after 4:00 P.M., asking Higgins at each one if he was present with the chief in the sally port. The inference was that they had Berkowitz's electronic key record, which showed him multiple times opening the door to the sally port. And if Higgins was with him, he wouldn't have to use his own electronic key, so we might not know his movements in those moments.

Whether the defense actually had such a record about Berkowitz's movements, at this time there's no way to know. As we said, the chief didn't testify.

But one other thing we do know: Karen's Lexus arrived inside the sally port at 5:36 P.M. These bays are used to bring in people who have been arrested, and there's a security protocol. Someone at the control desk opens and closes the garage door. At 5:42, the order came to the control desk to close the garage door. By protocol, that order had to come from someone *inside* the sally port.

Well, the record shows that order came from Chief Berkowitz.

# 6. THE DEVIL'S DATA

On April 12, 2023, the defense filed a motion which for the first time publicly blew the lid open on their third-party culprit theory, and they included an affidavit that detailed shocking data uncovered by their forensic investigator, Richard Green.

The data was from two phones: John O'Keefe's, recovered at the scene; and Jen McCabe's, which she had voluntarily given to the police.

The main program used to extract and analyze the data is called Cellebrite. It's used by law enforcement all over the world. The forensic data analyst for the Massachusetts State Police, Trooper Guarino, used Cellebrite, as did Richard Green. But Green, using an updated version a year later, got very, very different results.

According to the defense affidavit outlining Green's conclusions, O'Keefe's Apple health app had him walking 80 steps between 12:21:28 and 12:24:37 A.M., and also "ascending/descending three floors." And between 12:31 and 12:32, according to the health app, he took 36 steps.

In the prosecution's version of events, Karen dropped John off, and he never went more than a few steps before being struck. They found him at the edge of the property where she had parked.

However, if he took 116 steps, the prosecution's narrative doesn't work.

And if he went up and down stairs, he *was* inside the house.

Green also analyzed Jen McCabe's phone, and what he found became printed on the billboards and T-shirts driving the movement to free Karen Read.

According to the version of Cellebrite that *he* ran, Jen McCabe searched… at 2:27 A.M.: "Hos long to die in cold."

Since her friend of eight years, John O'Keefe, happened to be doing just that very thing at that very moment, or in other versions of the theory soon would be, that search, if it really happened at that time, shows that something nefarious took place that night and continued to take place afterward with a cover-up that stretched all the way from the troopers into the District Attorney's Office.

# 7. TAILLIGHT TALES

It's important enough to repeat, yet again, that unless someone planted the taillight pieces from Karen's SUV, her Lexus struck O'Keefe.

There's really no way around this.

One might speculate on whether a taillight shell from the same model of a different vehicle could have been smashed into pieces and supplemented, but this is very unlikely, because the reassembled taillight shown in court perfectly matches the missing section on Karen's Lexus. So, unless the criminologists were also in on some institution-wide conspiracy, the taillight pieces belonged to her Lexus.

Therefore, in order for Karen to be innocent, the pieces *from her car* had to have been planted. Period.

The opportunities were limited. Karen pulled into John's garage at 1 Meadows at 12:42 A.M. It remained parked there until she went out to look for John at 5:08. She arrived at the McCabes' house after 5:30, then Jen McCabe drove her and the Lexus back to John's, with Kerry Roberts following. They parked it in the driveway.

Here's an interesting part which the defense for some reason chose not to exploit: the garage door at this time was stuck open. Apparently Karen was either unable or didn't bother to put the door down. We'll come back to that in a later chapter, because it might tell us something interesting when we try to answer the question of why the door wouldn't close. It's worth noting that the defense never attempted to suggest the garage door had been tampered with in any way. Maybe that will change in the retrial.

They left the Lexus in the driveway while the three women went to search for John in Kerry's vehicle. Anxiously awaiting inside the house was 14-year-old Kayley.

The driveway was under RING video surveillance, but here it gets interesting too. At least two videos were deleted: Karen getting home around 12:36, and Karen, Kerry, and Jen leaving to go search around 5:45. There's probably also a deletion at 12:42. Karen's phone connected to John's Wi-Fi sometime around 12:36, but she's heard on voicemail pulling into the garage at 12:42, so she probably parked around 12:36/12:37, went into the house, perhaps went to the bathroom, then opened the garage door from inside and pulled the car in. That should create two videos—12:36 and 12:42—for a total of at least three missing videos.

### Means and Motive

Who had the means to delete any videos and who had the motive?

It's not known when and from where the RING videos were deleted. While the State argued in the charging document that Karen deleted them, oddly, during the trial, they barely covered it. Did they contact RING? Yes, but we don't know what was said because the defense objected to that as hearsay. Did they recover the videos that they did obtain from the app on John's phone? Probably, but it wasn't discussed. Was there a digital footprint left behind, either on John's phone data or at RING? Again, we just don't know.

Is it a sign of something more nefarious?

The defense and the Free Karen Readers have long proposed that Trooper Proctor himself deleted the videos. Well, there are two ways they could have been removed. One was from the RING app on John's phone. And the other is simply by logging into John's account on the RING website from any browser. All you would need was his email and his password. Did Karen have John's passwords? A lot of men use one password and trust their girlfriends with it. So maybe.

But Proctor certainly had full access to John's phone. He *could* have deleted the videos.

The problem for that theory is motive. We can imagine why Karen deleted the videos if she's visible on them inspecting her taillight, and that's exactly what Kerry and Jen testified happened at 5:45 A.M. when they left to search for John. It was probably the same when she got home to John's house earlier, from 34 Fairview, and briefly parked in the driveway, going into the house to open the garage from the inside.

However, what motive could Proctor have for deleting a video of Karen getting back to the house at 12:36?

Finding a motive for Proctor is a stretch, but with a little creativity, we can fit it into a conspiracy theory. However, there would have to be something ELSE Proctor wanted to delete. Some other video from that morning, and he just happened to delete these other ones too, perhaps accidentally or perhaps to point investigators in another direction.

For example, what if someone showed up at the home between the hours of 1:30 and 4:30 A.M. and... well, let your imagination run wild.

Maybe I can help spark it with this: when Jen, Kerry, and Karen arrived back at the house after 5:40, they found the garage door had been left open. And they were unable to close it, so they left it open when they went searching for John. When Michael Camerano came a short time later to pick up Kayley so she wouldn't be alone, he found the garage open and had to manually close it.

Was the garage door malfunctioning? Or was it damaged?

Did whoever might have damaged it task Proctor with deleting a video?

Look, that's grassy knoll stuff. I expected the defense team might go there, suggesting to the jury that someone might have run a covert operation to break into the garage. Maybe they will next time.

It's difficult to find a time where there was an opportunity to pry off taillight pieces from the Lexus. It sat in the driveway all morning. Around 7-ish, Camerano picked up Kayley and shoveled some snow, so he probably spent about 20 minutes there. At 8:22, a patrol car stopped by to do a wellness check. They were there five or ten minutes. Around 10:30, the O'Keefe family arrived, and Paul shoveled the driveway. Between 11:30 and noon, Karen and her dad got there, and a half hour later, they drove the car to Dighton. There it sat buried in snow until the State Police came and towed it at 4:18 P.M. It arrived at the Canton Police sally port at 5:31, was pulled in at 5:36, and the sally port door was closed at 5:42. Proctor and Bukhenik are visible on surveillance within the sally port when it closes.

So, at 5:42 P.M., the troopers are still inside the sally port. At the exact same time, a five-minute drive away, the seven-man SERT team is shoveling shoulder to shoulder at the crime scene, an area the size of two parking spaces. A news truck is out front with a crew filming. Lieutenant Tully is overseeing the scene and documenting it with photos. And the SERT team finds the corner piece of the taillight at precisely 5:45. It's photographed and documented on the spot.

So where and when could tampering with the Lexus have occurred?

By the time it reached the sally port, it was too late. Look, we could tease you. This section of the book is about establishing a third-party culprit theory. The idea is to really make a conspiracy look plausible, and we're giving it every possible chance. But the notion that someone pried pieces off the SUV in the sally port and whisked them to the crime scene to be buried is too weak to even tease you with.

The defense tried, and certainly Free Karen Read has focused mightily on the sally port in social media. Karen Read's minion, former DEA Agent Seamus O'Malley, sent me pictures of the taillight; I immediately recognized them as discovery evidence. So he was clearly in touch with Karen, who was selectively leaking material to him, or at least working with someone close to her. And here's where he told me a tall tale that had an element of truth.

He told me a Canton Police officer named Brian Wanless, who also owned an autobody shop, had been co-opted into helping the conspirators. For months, he kept insisting that Wanless was the key to unlocking the conspiracy. As with many parts of the conspiracy theory, O'Malley would never fully color in the details, giving me mysterious bits and pieces and then insisting things were "obvious." They never were, but for many people, that kind of argument is enough.

What looks like a long, deep scar jags its way through the paint above the taillight. Hard to judge its length from a photo, but it looks to be over a foot. To O'Malley, who had spent 28 years as a DEA agent, this was where Wanless's "screwdriver slipped."

I'm not making this up. That's what he believed.

The idea seems to be that the troopers enlisted Wanless and had him waiting in the sally port, like an Indy 500 pit crew, for the SUV that was being towed from Karen's parents. Then, nervous about the task, his experienced hand slipped so much that the screwdriver left a scar longer than the taillight itself. Yikes. Welcome to the world of Free Karen Read.

Even within the fevered conspiracy theory swamps of social media, that's a heckuva hard sell. But should one wish to factor it as possible, remember, as that was allegedly going on, the SERT team was already finding those pieces Wanless or Proctor were thought to be removing from the SUV. So unless that classic car in the sally port next to Karen's Lexus is a Delorean time machine, it's just not going to work.

Or... unless... the entire SERT team is in on it.

And that jagged scar? As it turns out, this probably isn't even a scar but rather, is just a light reflection.

Look, here's a rule that I won't even call a YCT one because it's so common sense that every normal person should already follow it: The more people needed to be involved in a conspiracy, the less likely it is to be true.

Lieutenant Kevin O'Hara, the head of the SERT team, testified that the main piece was found after digging three feet down, at the street level. So the scenario portrayed by Free Karen Read—one where Trooper Proctor shows up at the scene a minute before the piece is found, walks out into the search area unnoticed, and drops the taillight pieces into the snow like Andy Dufresne in *Shawshank Redemption*—isn't going to work. Because Proctor needed to *bury* the pieces three feet into the snow, he would certainly be noticed, and he couldn't have reached the scene in time to manage all that.

As for Brian Wanless: he's a Canton cop, since retired, who does, in fact, own an autobody shop, and who was actually enlisted by the State Police criminologist to help remove the taillight. But that took place days after the Lexus arrived at the sally port.

During the trial, the prosecution mistakenly played an inverted version of the surveillance video from the sally port. The defense, of course, caught this over the weekend, and made a show of it on Monday. The prosecution tried to capitalize on it, but this was clearly just an error. Many cameras and surveillance systems record video in mirror mode, and the system converts it back during playback. There are technical reasons for the glitch that occurred in trial, which we won't bore you with, but it was really just a mistake that bears no relevance, because while the police were first examining the Lexus inside the sally port, the SERT team was actually finding the pieces at the scene.

So if there was a conspiracy to plant evidence, we have another either/or:

Either…

A) All the troopers involved were part of it… meaning the seven-man SERT team, Lt. Tully, Proctor and Bukhenik, the criminologists… or

B) Someone tampered with the taillight and planted the pieces *earlier* that day.

Well, if you're really thirsting for conspiracy, I've got something for you!

The crime scene was strangely unguarded from 8:30 A.M. until about 4:55 P.M., when the SERT team began arriving.

No yellow tape. No squad car sitting there. Kids could have built a snow fort and no one would have stopped them. No snow fort appeared… but did anything else go on?

# 8. FEDS TO THE RESCUE

In August of 2022, Karen and her defense team did something unheard of: they walked into the office of then First US Attorney for Boston, Josh Levy, and pitched their conspiracy theory. Now, you have to understand just how weird and rare this is. The person on the food chain right above the First Assistant US Attorney is the US Attorney, a position filled by the president and requiring Senate approval. Prosecutors this high in the chain of command don't normally grant audiences to murder defendants. It's just another unique element of this case.

We don't know what the team pitched Levy, but whatever it was, it moved him. He assigned FBI agents to the case and, within three months, started subpoenaing the communications records of people the defense was accusing of being the real killers and their accomplices. At the very least, they sought records from Apple for seven witnesses, including Trooper Proctor.

In that August moment, Karen was so thrilled that they had enlisted the First Assistant US Attorney that she messaged her friend Natalie, even sending her a flow chart showing just how high up in the government Levy was, and saying that the First Attorney had promised to "personally" handle the case.

Things that make me go "wow"... and things that make me go "hmmm."

This is upside down. Normally, the FBI finds evidence of a crime and, when they have enough, take it to the federal prosecutors. Over a hundred prosecutors work in the Boston office of the US Attorney, so only the most important cases—terrorism, organized crime—ever reach the attention of the highest levels of the office. This one not only did, but Levy promised to handle the case himself.

And he did!

Eventually, a federal grand jury would convene, and Josh Levy, by then Acting US Attorney, would personally grill many of the witnesses. Long, brutal questioning that brought some of them to tears.

Even weirder, during this questioning, he displayed a huge printout of the *TB Daily News*, the blog of Turtleboy, whom Karen was using to successfully stir up a mob. Turtleboy showed up with a cameraman to harass one of the witnesses at her daughter's lacrosse game, and he threatened, at one point, to bring his crowd to the soccer games of the children of the State's Attorney General!

Yet the US Attorney, who is just below the AG in Washington, was using Turtle's blog to grill witnesses who were harassed with information his office leaked to a murder defendant?

Over a hundred AUSAs (Assistant US Attorneys) in that office, one of the largest in the country, hundreds of investigations and prosecutions every year, hundreds of trials… from drug traffickers to financial fraud, from terrorism to organized crime… and the US Attorney overseeing it all has time to invest hundreds of hours into preparing to question witnesses?

Would this powerful person invest that much time if there was nothing?

Karen bragged to Natalie that the Feds don't "swing and miss," and that this was one of the most powerful prosecutors in the country taking this case on personally.

So there must be something there, right?

Josh Levy is an elite attorney. After graduating from Brown University, he went on to Georgetown Law, where he managed to graduate magnum cum laude in 1992. From 1997 to 2004, he worked as an AUSA in the Boston office, before moving on to private practice at elite Ropes & Gray, a top-20-in-the-world law firm, where he eventually became a partner specializing in white-collar crime and civil litigation.

But in 2020, he decided to come back to work as a prosecutor, again in the Boston US Attorney's Office, but now as First Attorney. His boss, the brand new US Attorney placed there by President Joe Biden, was a controversial figure: Rachael Rollins. Rollins, before her nomination, had been the Suffolk County (Boston) DA.

I actually talked to Rollins and found her to be forthcoming, deliberative, and cautious with her conclusions. My expectation was someone who might be a firebrand eager to settle old scores, but she was very self-reflective and made no attempt to excuse mistakes she made.

She took no shots at Levy, who had not only replaced her, but who had cooperated in the probes into her actions. But despite her careful and balanced words, one word seemed best to sum up Josh Levy: ambition.

He had campaigned to the Biden administration to become Boston's US Attorney, even trying to convince Rollins to withdraw her nomination. He wanted that job badly, and on day one, as Rollins began her stint as US Attorney and Levy as her First Assistant, he seems to have already been scheming to take her position.

Let's be clear: words like "scheming" are mine, not Rollins's. She's much too deliberate to say something like that, not due to a lack of being forthcoming, but rather out of deep self-awareness about not wanting to have some ulterior motive. After all, Levy took her job.

But she explained that the US Attorney's Office in Boston has a close relationship with certain large law firms, especially Ropes & Gray. She estimated that 30% of the lawyers at the Boston US Attorney's Office came from Ropes. These lawyers move back and forth. Like Levy, they might start out as assistant federal attorneys, then move to Ropes, then do other stints at the US Attorney's Office, then go back to Ropes.

That's a recipe for influence peddling. If you're facing federal charges in Boston, especially white-collar crime, your first call should be to Ropes. Because their connections to the Boston office are incestuous.

So, as Levy was preparing to take the job under Rollins, he already had a pipeline into the office through the many former Ropes lawyers who worked there. Rollins came in as an outsider. Levy was the penultimate insider. Rollins should have seen the handwriting on the wall and been extra cautious. She didn't and wasn't.

Rollins would be removed from office in scandal just a couple of years later, in May of 2023, right as the Karen Read case was catching fire in the public mind. A radical activist promoted into power by George Soros, Rollins had ideas that clashed with fellow Democrat, District Attorney Michael Morrissey of Norfolk County, where Read was being prosecuted. This political feud could have been at the root of why Karen got the meeting with Levy in the first place; we don't know. There was another feud where an assistant DA from Norfolk, who happened to be married to an AUSA, sued the DA because she was unhappy with her lack of promotion. Even Morrissey speculated that was at the root of the federal investigation.

However, Rollins told me she had no awareness of any of this and wasn't involved. I believe her.

When you talk to people who potentially have something to hide—and most people do—there are ways to gauge whether they're telling the truth. A good technique is to broach a subject that you know makes them uncomfortable; but don't back them into a corner, just broach it and give them room to react. Listen carefully. You'll pick up little response patterns that you can use later, like tells in poker.

I did this with Rollins, with issues I knew would put her a little on guard. I listened carefully to how she reacted. Then I talked about things like Karen Read or Sandra Birchmore, another high-profile case. And Rollins seemed completely comfortable in saying she had no involvement with or awareness of the beginning of the Karen Read investigation.

She thought it was unusual that Karen and her team got a direct audience with Levy in August of 2022, but she wouldn't use the word "suspicious." She lamented that not everyone could have that kind of access, and the entire theme of her public service had been to try to give those with less access to power a fairer shake. She speculated that perhaps Yannetti had some personal connection to Levy outside this case, but she knew of no such connection. Karen's special access to power didn't bother Rollins; she just wished everyone had such access.

Still, even supposing that Karen had special access to the powerful US Attorney's Office through a family connection or through her lawyers, could that explain how Levy became convinced Karen was being framed by corrupt cops and prosecutors?

Another point Rachael Rollins made was this: a District Attorney's Office is reactive. A crime happens. They're obliged to investigate it and seek justice. But the US Attorney's Office is proactive. They're looking for what crimes they want to investigate.

How do they choose? Well, very often it comes to one word: headlines.

The US Attorney's Office pays very, very close attention to headlines. And at the end of the day, that also plays a huge part in that they choose to do… generating headlines.

Does this eagerness for headlines make them easier to dupe?

Would the federal government actually use its immense powers against seemingly innocent people to help a murder defendant if there was nothing to the case? Levy continued the grand jury inquisition long after they removed Rollins. He was the acting US Attorney when he himself was doing something unprecedented, grilling witnesses merely because a murder defendant had fingered them.

Weird, wild stuff.

And it got weirder. The Feds were working so closely with the defendant that, incredibly, Karen knew what days the witnesses would be testifying before the federal grand jury, using that information to help her social media bullies target those people.

*Excuse me, shouldn't that sentence end with an exclamation point?*

Certainly!

Seemingly, the Feds themselves fed the defendant information about a federal grand jury so that a mob, stirred up by her proxy, could harass the federal witnesses.

This was something Josh Levy himself had to be aware of, given his eagerness for headlines… and given the fact that witnesses reached out to his office BEGGING for help against the mob.

He ignored them.

Just as he ignored many messages from the frustrated and bullied O'Keefe family.

And in November of 2023, months before the trial, Levy would hold a conference call with Karen's attorneys, David Yannetti and Alan Jackson. In that call, he actually advised them to delay the trial!

This kind of interference in a State's murder trial is unheard of.

I learned that FBI agent LF was coordinating a little too closely with one of Karen's social media agents, Seamus O'Malley, the retired DEA agent down in Florida. It looked fishy.

All of this unusual federal activity led by a very high federal prosecutor makes it hard for us to avoid another either/or.

Either…

A) The federal investigation was corrupt… or

B) There really was a conspiracy to cover up John O'Keefe's murder by framing Karen Read.

# 9. ARCCA

In November of 2022, the federal investigation swung into high gear. Subpoenas for the communications of the alleged conspirators went out, the FBI began digging around Canton, and the US Attorney hired an independent accident reconstruction company called ARCCA to determine whether John O'Keefe had indeed been struck by a vehicle.

Two PhDs from ARCCA would testify at the first trial for the defense. Dr. Daniel Wolf said that the damage to the back of the car, mostly the broken taillight and the small dent about a forearm's length away, was "inconsistent" with being caused by an outstretched arm. He found the back of the car overall to be "remarkably intact" for a pedestrian strike. He said that we would expect to see damage to the bumper, but there was none.

Dr. Andrew Rentschler testified that the injuries to John's arm were inconsistent with it being held extended while being struck by the SUV.

In general, the two PhDs from ARCCA came across as highly competent and articulate, and while they didn't say it was impossible that John was struck by a vehicle, it was clearly their impression, based on the evidence they viewed, that it was unlikely.

If these two "independent" experts were completely on the level, then John was probably not killed by Karen.

# 10. PROCTOR EXAM

I've already introduced you to Michael Proctor, but since he became, from early on, the focus of the conspiracy theory, we need a much closer look.

There were no marks on Proctor's exemplary record before this case, and he had been a trooper for 10 years, assigned to the homicide unit for five. He had been involved with several high-profile cases. And there's no evidence of any wrongdoing in this case in regard to the actual investigation.

There were, however, some very insensitive private texts discovered by the Feds.

Also, a few of the details of the case seem to have been discussed with people outside the investigation. That's always a no-no. Some of the discussions were with old high school friends, and some were with his sister. None of them involved important details, however, and what details were discussed is comparable to probably the kind of minor stuff that always happens on private phones, because no one expects the Feds to get those communications.

I have firsthand experience with very honorable police officers who say things in private messages that would be perceived as offensive—and which are, in fact, offensive—but which really are just dark humor. Not excusing it, just putting it into proper context.

The reason the defense made Proctor the focus of the case is supposedly because friends of Karen's from the Hillside told her that lead investigator Proctor was connected to the Alberts. Searching social media, Karen found Proctor's sister Courtney's account on Facebook and searched through over 1300 photos. Eventually she found a young Colin Albert as the ring bearer at Courtney's wedding, and another photo showing Proctor's parents and Courtney with members of Chris Albert's family.

In fact, Chris and his family, including Colin, had been at pool parties at the home of Proctor's parents. Michael Proctor had also attended these.

And this is the actual connection. Trooper Proctor's sister is friends with Chris Albert's wife Julie and her sister.

Was this the connection that tied it all together?

Remember, without the planting of evidence, Karen is… well, let's just say the prosecution's case is strong. And there was a lot of evidence to plant! Taillight pieces in the yard, microscopic taillight pieces on John's clothing, cocktail glass pieces on the bumper, John's DNA on a taillight piece, one of John's hairs on the rear panel of the Lexus, his shoe, his hat, the shattered cocktail glass. And don't forget the straw. Did I mention that investigators found the straw from the cocktail glass in the gutter?

That couldn't all take place without some troopers being involved.

Pointing the finger at both Colin and Trooper Proctor is actually essential for the conspiracy theory. Because what if Colin did indeed get in the car with Allie McCabe, as all evidence suggests, and leave several minutes before John and Karen pulled up, and therefore can't be included in the third-party culprit theory? If Colin can be ruled out as a suspect, then the effort to ascribe MOTIVE to Proctor is really weak. If John was attacked by a jealous Higgins, why would Proctor be willing to actively cover up for a man he didn't know? And he didn't know Brian Albert either.

You might be willing to theorize that it was just a cop looking out for fellow cops, but John was a cop too, and more importantly, why would Proctor risk his career, his freedom, and the welfare of his family to plant evidence for guys he had never met?

But there might, however, be more incentive to protect Colin, who had been in his sister Courtney's wedding party. It's a huge reach, but it's as close as one can get in creating any kind of a plausible motive for Trooper Proctor to risk it all in planting evidence in a murder case.

# 11. KAREN

Now, let's take a shot at seeing things from Karen's point of view… assuming her innocence.

Two years invested in this thing with John, and she for damn sure wasn't letting it go down the drain. Relationship run its course? *Fuck you, John.* After all she did for him? She never wanted kids, precisely because it restricts your lifestyle, dramatically reduces your choices, not to mention your money. Having no kids meant she'd been able to buy two properties, one in Mansfield and the other in Medfield, and the rents were paying off the mortgages. She would be all set financially and would be able to always live the way she wanted. Nice clothing, nice shoes, nice cars, traveling to fun places.

*Run its course*? After all that time she'd spent with his kids?! There had been a Karen-sized hole in that little family before she arrived to fill it.

And they weren't even his kids! That was the problem. He'd stood up, done the right thing because he loved his sister so much, but he wasn't cut out for the job. He was built to be the fun uncle, not a parent. *He* didn't want to give up his lifestyle either.

What did he think she was, a babysitter with benefits?

No, he needed her and just didn't know it. This was merely something they had to get through, a normal hiccup before the next step in the relationship could be reached.

She didn't ever want to *have* kids, but she did actually *like* Patrick and Kayley. It felt a little weird to care about someone else—not really her strong point—but she did care about them. They were very well behaved, having been through so much in their lives, and they were both really smart. It would be fun to guide them as they got older, see what they might become.

She was especially close to Kayley. It was really cool to be able to mentor her, talking about clothing and boys. Kayley had just found out she'd gotten into an elite high school, and John was out celebrating with Mike and Curt at C.F. McCarthy's.

Now that she thought about it, it was kind of weird that he didn't want her drinking with him tonight. He always took her with him. Was he flirting with that bartender? She didn't think John was cheating on her, but he was naturally friendly, born to flirt, and women were always drawn to him.

Shit, she better text him: "Can I meet you?"

They'd had a nasty fight this morning over something stupid. He accused her of spoiling the kids. WTF, what did she know about being a parent?! He should just be grateful she liked the kids and took some of the weight off him.

But what bothered her—what worried her—was how unwilling he was to repair things, even saying the relationship had run its course. She'd lost all leverage, and as a financial planner, she understood leverage. All that time invested in this relationship over the last two years was about to go down the drain.

And now he wasn't replying to her text. Another bad sign.

So she called.

No answer.

*Run its course?*

Damn him. She called again.

And again.

Finally, he picked up. She could tell by his voice he'd had enough beers to be feeling good.

*Yeah, come meet us!*

Patrick was staying at a friend's house, and Kayley would be fine by herself for a few hours. She was very mature, and she would just spend the time mostly on the phone.

John had allowed Karen to park in the garage because of the impending blizzard, so as she backed out, she remembered to be careful not to back into his Traverse. In the driveway, she stopped to point the garage door remote he'd given her, but it didn't work. Dead battery. Fucking annoying. Just another sign of how lost he would be without her.

She put the Lexus in Park, went into the house, and closed the garage door manually, then hurried back into her running car. God, it was freezing!

So cold, and the car engine still wasn't putting out heat by the time she reached downtown and lucked into a good parking spot. Shivering a little as she scrambled to McCarthy's, anger warmed her, remembering how he'd behaved all day: starting an argument in the morning, ignoring her much of the day and drinking while she hung out with his kids. Still seething when she found him at the bar, she readied to launch into a tirade. But then he embraced her warmly. Her anger quickly defused. No one could really stay mad at John; that was his superpower. What mattered was that he was happy to see her now, and she was in her element, relaxing at the bar.

The place was surprisingly busy! It felt good to be out. The last year two years had been a nightmare with the pandemic lock-downs. The waitresses were still wearing masks, but otherwise everything looked normal.

John greeted her warmly, already ordering what she liked—vodka and soda. They were sitting at the bar; good, that's where she liked to be, part of the action. She'd always been comfortable at the bar, especially in places with a regular clientele, where people knew each other and guys did shots. She liked being with drinkers, and she could hold her own both with the drinking and the back-and-forth talk.

The drinks were a little weak here, not like the Hillside, where they really hook up the regulars, but it was a good atmosphere… keep 'em coming, bartender!

After several rounds, Mike skipped out to go home, the "Irish exit," no goodbye, and John got a text to meet Chris Albert at the Waterfall. Cool, the party was just starting.

She walked out with a drink… No way was she going to leave it unfinished, and who the fuck was going to say anything to her? She was dating a Boston cop.

It was only a two-minute walk to the Waterfall, but damn, it was cold. Inside, a band was playing. Middle-aged guys, not the type to draw a young crowd, but this was Canton. Young kids went out in the city on a Saturday night.

The McCabes were here, of course. Jen was an alpha female—or at least, Karen reminded herself, thought she was. Jen would be the social director here, making sure everyone within the group felt connected, no one left out, everyone engaged. Karen couldn't help feeling territorial. Jen had her claws into John and Kayley and would even stick them into her if she allowed it.

Chris Albert and Julie were here. And Brian Albert and his wife Nicole, who was sweet and quiet. She didn't know Brian well. He always seemed like he didn't want to be there, like he had better things to do or more fun people to be with. Aloof. Cop's eyes, like he missed nothing.

And Brian Higgins. Shit, this could be awkward. She'd flirted with him a couple weeks ago, something she initiated, but best to keep him at a distance. He seemed like the kind of guy who could get obsessed, especially because she was so out of his league. That's what had made the whole thing so exciting in the first place. He was a huge man, and a federal cop to boot, so no one at the Hillside or anywhere else would fuck with him, and he carried himself at all times like he knew no one would. That aroused her, but even more arousing was the idea that she could tame that lion, make him her pet. She was smarter than him, and they both knew she was out of his league, and that gave her the very thing she'd lost with John: leverage.

But she didn't want him to fuck things up with John. She felt nervous about whether she could trust that. Higgins seemed like a guy with too much heart. A fall-in-love kind of guy. She liked having that kind of power over men, but here it could fuck things up. Though it was exciting too, having them both in the same room and knowing the federal agent was desperate for her attention.

He texted her now: "Umm, well?" Yup, desperate. She didn't reply. Let him stew.

They settled into a couple hours of drinking. John got along with everyone, as always. Higgins kept his distance. She knew he was seething, but she was in control.

Near the end of the night, she felt starved. You know, the way you can get after several hours of drinking. Pizza would be great!

She tried to talk Chris into opening D&E to cook for them. She was used to guys giving in to her in these situations. So what if she was a bit of a princess? But Chris wasn't relenting, saying he was starting a low-carb diet.

So with the bar closing, they decided to go to Brian Albert's for an after-hours party. The idea didn't thrill her. Higgins would be there, so it would be even more awkward, and Jen would be even more in control in that setting. Plus, she was wasted and her stomach was starting to act up. At 43, her body was no longer conditioned for drinking till the wee hours, and it's not like they were in college. And John was pretty wasted too, so they should just go home.

In the car, John sipped a drink he'd swiped from the bar. He was a beer drinker, but sometimes he closed the night with a nightcap. They argued a little. She didn't want to go, but he insisted. They didn't even know where Brian lived.

On the way, he called Jen to get directions. It pissed her off to hear Jen's voice, the alpha, always directing events. And didn't she purposely mention someone John used to date while giving directions? John entered the address into Waze while their argument grew more bitter.

*Damn, it's freezing in this car!*

Where the fuck was Waze taking them? She would never be able to find her way home from here. Oakdale Road? She demanded they go home. John told her to chill. Finally, the heater showed signs of warmth. She blasted it.

They came to the intersection with Cedarcrest. Waze was telling them to turn right, but she stopped at the intersection and again tried to convince John to go home. Going left would bring them to Dedham Street, and from there getting to John's was easy. Dedham went straight downtown. They could be home in five minutes, having another drink, going to bed, where she would again have some leverage.

But John insisted she turn right. Why did he care about these people? Yes, Brian Albert was some kind of big deal cop in Boston, so what? His brother Chris lived a couple houses down from John until he moved a couple of weeks ago. Where Brian was pretty aloof… You know, that cop thing where they're always watching but saying little. Chris was very outgoing. He owned a pizza shop; the food was good. John had taken Patrick there today.

At the intersection, they argued for maybe a half minute, but finally, John prevailed. She spun the Lexus right onto Cedarcrest, rage building. It was dark. Hard to see the street signs or even the intersections. They were still arguing and didn't quite catch it when Waze told them to turn left onto Fairview.

Now she heard Waze re-calculating. Fuck! They'd missed the turn.

John told her to pull a U-turn. Pissed, she cut the wheel left, slammed the brakes, and threw it into Reverse. John, trying not to spill his drink, laughed a little, which pissed her off more.

"This is bullshit," she told him. "They don't even really want us there. Why would they invite us?"

They arrived back at the intersection, but a big pickup truck was coming from the opposite direction, and it also was turning onto Fairview. Fuck 'em, she had the right of way. She screeched the Lexus into a hard right turn.

Waze told them their destination was on the right. It was so dark. They crept toward the driveway. Only a few cars. Some party. Fucking lame.

"It's dead," she said. "Let's go home."

The pickup pulled up behind them. Must be someone else coming to the party. She recognized Higgins's Jeep Wrangler parked by the mailbox. Shit.

"Let me check it out," John said. "You wait here."

Cocktail glass in hand, he climbed out, loose as a goose from hours of drinking. She watched him walk to the house. What if the pickup was trying to park in the driveway? She couldn't stay here blocking it. Having never put the car in Park, just sitting there for about 10 seconds with her foot on the brake, she took her foot off it and moved up to the property line and again stopped without putting it in Park.

At that moment, she noticed something on the seat: John's phone.

She picked it up. If only she knew the password, she could see if he'd been flirting with anyone by text. She never knew him to do that, but she herself had been flirting with Higgins by text, so why not?

She squeezed the phone hard inside her fist. What was taking him so long?

The idea came to call or text him, see what was going on… but here was his phone. Fucking idiot!

She opened the window and tossed the phone out into the yard. Fuck him.

Taking her foot off the brake, she started forward… then realized she didn't know how to get home that way. Damn it!

In a rage, she threw it in Reverse and punched the gas. She must have gone 100 feet backward. Exhilarating! What a rush!

Coming to a stop, she caught her breath a moment, then more carefully turned back in the direction of Cedarcrest.

Pounding the steering wheel in anger, alcohol and rage blurring her ability to think clearly, she raced down Cedarcrest.

Anger flamed again. He was probably hooking up back there!

She pulled out her phone and sent him a call. Maybe he was outside looking for her and would see the phone in the yard.

She turned onto Dedham Street, barely slowing at the intersection. No other cars around. She sent another call. And another. And another. Maybe he would walk out and spot the phone lighting up in the yard. There were no stop signs, so she gunned it. Fuck them all.

The stoplight ahead, guided by sensors reading the traffic, turned green well before she arrived. She spun a left onto Washington Street, which was the town's main street, still sending him calls. The next set of lights also anticipated her arrival with a green light and she screeched a right onto Pleasant Street, another long stretch with absolutely no stop signs.

It took her about a minute to reach Meadows Avenue. John's house was on the corner of Meadows and Pleasant, so after turning down Meadows, she immediately turned into John's driveway and parked in front of the garage, unable to open it from the outside because the damn remote wasn't working.

From the car, she called and left her first message: *"John, I fucking hate you!"*

She went into the house, using the digital lock to enter. Spent time in the bathroom. Then she opened the garage door from inside and went out to move her car in. While she was doing this, she called John again, and once more it went to voicemail. Getting out of the Lexus, she didn't leave a message.

She checked on Kayley. Maybe she was up and had heard from John. But she was asleep.

She made herself a drink and heated up some leftovers.

At 12:59, she left another message. *"John, I'm here with your fucking kids, nobody knows where you are, you fucking pervert!"*

Minutes later, she called again but left no message.

At 1:11, she called and said, *"It's 1 A.M. in the morning, I'm with your niece and nephew, you fucking pervert, you're a fucking pervert!"*

After ending the call, she remembered that Patrick was staying with a friend.

She should get the fuck out of here. Let John take care of his own kids. He just didn't appreciate her. She wanted to see Daddy. Dad was always there for her, both Mom and Dad. Maybe she should drive to Dighton. She dialed their number.

No answer.

She felt so alone, so isolated. All those health issues she had to struggle with, and her parents were getting older. For the last two years, settling down with John had been the plan. He had the house, he would have a pension, and she had two houses, had invested wisely.

Now it was all crumbling, and it felt like there was nothing she could do. The only way to strike a deal, the only way to move a human being, was with leverage, and she had none.

Except…

She called John again. "John, I'm going home. I cannot babysit your niece, I need to go home. You're using me right now, you're fucking another girl, your niece is sleeping next to me, you're a fucking loser, fuck yourself!"

Maybe if he thought the kids were alone, that would bring him home.

She curled up into a ball on the couch and went to sleep.

**(Author's note)**

*To be honest, this was about as far as I could get with the Karen narrative. There just doesn't seem to be a way to make sense of her actions. She claims to have taken a nap on the couch, which seems likely to us based on what we know from her cell phone activity. At 4:38, she called John but left no message. She called her parents twice, at 4:40 and 4:42. No answer. Kayley heard her screaming in the hallway that something had happened to John.*

*A moment later, she burst into Kayley's room and had her call Jen McCabe. Kayley and Jen both testified that Karen tried to say she last saw John at the Waterfall, but Jen reminded her that they had driven to the after-hours party. Remember, John had called for directions while they were halfway there.*

*After the call with Jen, Karen called Kerry Roberts and screamed, "John's dead! Kerry, Kerry, Kerry!" Then she hung up.*

*A moment later, Karen called back and told Kerry that something had happened to John and maybe he was hit by a plow. So when the call ended, Kerry called 911 to see if anyone had been found. They played that call in court. Then she called the hospital.*

*There just doesn't seem to be any innocent explanation for why Karen would go to sleep thinking John was hooking up and then wake up a few hours later thinking he was dead, hit by a plow, no less.*

*Another problem with this re-creation is that Karen has never said she tossed John's phone out the window. But what else can she say? As we'll explain to you shortly, the GPS data on John's phone shows that the phone absolutely never went inside the house. We'll explain later how the health app misinterpreted his activity as being ascending and descending stairs, but in the rock/paper/scissors game of movement data, GPS trumps a health app the way rock beats scissors. That phone never went up and down stairs because it never went inside the house.*

*They found John on the lawn 80 feet up the road from the driveway, almost at the property line, with his phone underneath him. Karen has said in several national TV interviews that she dropped John off at the foot of the driveway and watched him walk into the house. If that is true, then he must have left his phone in the car... and indeed at 12:24:40, less than a half minute after they arrived, John's phone reached the end of the property. So, whether John still was or he wasn't in the Lexus at 12:24:40, his phone must have been. Therefore, either John got out of the car at the edge of the property with his phone and was subsequently struck... or Karen tossed it out into the yard because John exited the car in the driveway and forgot his phone. There simply is no other way, which means if we're going to write this from her POV with the idea that she's innocent, it has to include her throwing the phone into the yard.*

# 12. REASONABLE DOUBT?

In a few moments, I'll bring you right down to Ground Zero, in the days immediately following John's death, when the conspiracy theory first came together. I'll buy you a pint of Guinness as we cozy up to the bar with the whispers around us growing louder as day turns to night and alcohol lessens inhibitions.

The question for now is whether the elements of the third-party culprit theory actually add up to reasonable doubt.

We have to understand: stuff where you say "that's weird" exists in every case, and the more witnesses who are involved, the more the chance to find "that's weird" kind of stuff.

The crucial thing is to weigh those odd or seemingly mysterious things sensibly. For example, in the O.J. Simpson trial, when the defendant tried on the glove, it famously didn't fit. The relevance we attach to that depends on the weight of the *other* evidence. Had there actually been video of O.J. killing Nicole and Ron, the glove still wouldn't fit, but we would just conclude that it had shrunk, or his hands were swollen, or he was acting. The video evidence would outweigh the "that's weird" evidence, so the weirdness wouldn't bother us.

Very rarely is there video of a murder. There could be witnesses, but of course, witnesses can lie or be confused.

In many cases, maybe even most, we actually have to weigh primarily circumstantial evidence. In the Karen Read case, we have data, taillight pieces, the injuries, damage to the Lexus, DNA, cocktail glass pieces, clothing, and a human hair. The State's experts have the burden of explaining to us what happened. A jury has to decide if their arguments are strong enough to overcome any unexplained odd things.

But there always will be odd things. In every single case.

Most of the odd things in this case, it turns out, actually have very good explanations, and we're going to provide them. A handful of things have explanations which don't *fully* satisfy. And a few of the odd things remain somewhat mysterious. This is normal. For example, we'll never know why the glove didn't fit O.J. Simpson.

Let's repeat in the Karen Read case: either she struck John with her Lexus, or there was a massive cover-up that included the planting of all the substantial evidence. Without being able to say evidence was planted, Karen has no defense. They *have* to be able to argue that someone had the means and the motive to plant taillight pieces. Unless, of course, *everyone* was in on it: the seven-man SERT team that found the first pieces, Lt. Tully, Troopers Proctor and Bukhenik, the criminologists, the prosecutors, and so on. But… if everyone *wasn't* in on it, the only way for the defense team to argue that evidence was planted is to show it was plausible that someone could have planted the evidence *before* the SERT team arrived around 5:00 P.M.

The opportunities for doing this were incredibly unlikely but perhaps can't be completely ruled out.

But then we get to the problem of motive. Who would have the motive to plant all this evidence? It's important to recognize that the third-party culprit theory is essential for the defense to create doubt in this case, because it not only involves pointing the finger at someone else who *could* have done it, but it's crucial to explaining *why* someone—namely the troopers—planted evidence.

However, this creates a challenge for the defense: while they don't have to *prove* their alternative theory, they do have to defend it. And to the extent that the prosecution can poke holes in it by showing there was either no means or no motive, the third-party culprit theory does actually collapse.

But this book isn't meant for a jury or the prosecutors. It's meant for the public. Because Karen and her team have very actively tried to influence the jury pool by manipulating public opinion, and to do that, they've been pointing the finger at people who aren't on trial. Those people are subjected to merciless daily persecution. So, there's much more at stake than justice for Karen and for John. If these witnesses are, in fact, innocent, the destruction unleashed on their families by the mob is unjust.

In a moment, I'll go over the compelling evidence in favor of the prosecution so we can weigh it against the intriguing third-party culprit theory and the numerous seemingly odd things. But there are other reasons the conditions were ripe for this conspiracy theory to grab the public's attention.

A year before John's death, a 23-year-old woman named Sandra Birchmore was found strangled in her apartment in Canton. Authorities ruled her death a suicide. However, over the next couple of years, this came into doubt with the public and, as it turns out, for very good reasons.

Birchmore was pregnant, and the presumed father was a Stoughton cop who had been grooming Birchmore since she was at least 14, and who had been sleeping with her since she was under the age of consent. Surveillance video shows the officer, face disguised with a mask, going onto the elevator of her apartment building, then returning a short time later. It's hard not to see that video and feel suspicious and horrified.

But since the medical examiner ruled it a suicide, the investigation seemed to quickly wither on the vine.

However, it was kept alive by true crime podcasts, and it eventually became the focus of the State's Attorney General and of the FBI. Weeks after Karen's trial, US Attorney Josh Levy held a press conference and announced that the Feds had arrested Matthew Farwell that morning, charging him with murder. That day, the FBI filed documents, the product of an outstanding investigation. The case against the Stoughton cop seems very compelling. Farwell, according to the Feds, had planned the murder weeks before carrying it out. His motive was to prevent Birchmore from going to the authorities and to Farwell's wife to reveal the affair. Additionally, Farwell had long enjoyed fantasies about strangling a woman, which Birchmore played along with in role-playing games, and which was uncovered by the Feds through text messages recovered in the I-cloud.

The Karen Read conspiracy theory had grabbed the public's attention long before Farwell's arrest, but now it further feeds the idea of corrupt State Police investigations involving murderous cops. There is no evidence, as of this writing, of any corruption with the State Police investigation of Birchmore, yet the public has made up its mind, and they lump it all together, holding vague and amorphous impressions of a police force so determined to protect their own that they'll readily cover up murder cases.

In that environment, it's easy to buy into conspiracies… as long as those conspiracies aren't too specific. Because if you examine them too closely, they tend to evaporate.

Now, that being said, there's plenty of unique material in the Karen Read case to stitch together a conspiracy theory that looks impressive from the vantage of a 2000-foot flyover. John's injuries—and lack of injuries—seem hard to understand, and the State did do a horrible job explaining them in the first trial. The ARCCA guys, hired by the Feds, didn't say these injuries could *not* have been caused by a vehicle, but they did consider it improbable.

And then there's the very existence of the federal investigation itself. That kind of thing is so rare. At the very least, it does grab one's attention. Could the US Attorney have been duped? Is there a corrupt connection between US Attorney Josh Levy and Karen or her team? Or did they discover some powerful piece of evidence that predicated their involvement?

**Unprecedented Showdown**

The Feds are required, by the Brady rule, to turn over any exculpatory evidence before the trial, even though the trial is being prosecuted by the State. Indeed, a few months prior, the US Attorney's Office signed a protective order, with both the prosecution and the defense agreeing to hand over any relevant material, both inculpatory and exculpatory. The protective order ensured that this material, containing grand jury testimony, remained private.

However, a dramatic showdown erupted when Judge Beverly Cannone weighed making the federal material public. The *Boston Globe* and other news outlets petitioned the court for access to the federal materials. They argued that the public has a right to know, especially given the high-profile nature of the case and the allegations of corruption and misconduct.

Cannone seemed to be about to grant this request on the basis that the protective order didn't apply to her. SHE hadn't signed it. But she had been given access to the material from the parties as the judge.

In a pretrial hearing, the judge gave a hint about the nature of the federal report when she told the parties that she had seen absolutely no evidence to support a third-party culprit theory. She was acutely aware that the very existence of the federal investigation had been a primary factor in stirring up public belief in a conspiracy to murder John O'Keefe, and she likely wanted to dispel that.

Of note, the defense vigorously objected to the release of the federal material to the public. Instead, they made claims which were no doubt distortions. For example, Yannetti said in a pretrial hearing that the FBI had confirmed the 2:27 search for "Hos long to die in cold." But the defense never presented any evidence of that confirmation at trial. The FBI likely just ran the phone extractions through the exact same VERSION of the software that the defense's hired gun did, and not surprisingly, got the same results. Of course they would.

But that isn't at all the same as saying the FBI confirmed the actual search was made at 2:27. That's just another trick.

It's a familiar defense tactic that came up again and again in this case. They would claim there were "gaps" in videos, or "nonhuman" hairs, for example, none of which proved true.

So it was much better for the defense to be able to make imprecise *claims* about things in the federal trove, claims which danced very close to being complete distortions, but where the public can't check the documents to understand what's being said. And making the federal findings public hindered their ability to perform such tricks, so the defense absolutely didn't want any of this public.

Why couldn't the US Attorney trust Judge Cannone to decide what should be made public? Common sense tells us they just didn't want to look bad. They had invested enormous federal resources into an investigation that seemingly turned up nothing other than a rabid mob used to intimidate witnesses. The US Attorney, Josh Levy, had taken the unprecedented step of questioning the witnesses in the grand jury himself, almost unbelievably using an article by the defense team's discredited blogger as their prop in court! That shows just how much of his reputation was on the line here. He wasn't going to let some State judge embarrass him, so he invoked an ancient law that hadn't been applied since the Jim Crow South, using it as a basis to threaten to take over the trial.

That might have provoked a constitutional crisis that ran all the way to the US Supreme Court. Those are the wild stakes here.

### Integrity Is Rare

This case has shown that personal integrity is a rare quality. It's easy to think you have it, even easier to *say* you have it, but you really only know you have it when you have to make decisions of courage, decisions where you have to risk losing something. The federal investigation into the Karen Read case has played a huge role in stirring up a frenzy which led to a witch hunt atmosphere. A mob has been subjecting innocent people to attacks that have taken a tremendous toll. The US Attorney could take the heat off them, and largely end this destruction, just by holding a press conference saying that, despite rigorous and intrusive probing, they found absolutely no evidence of a conspiracy to kill John by the people inside the house.

That's exactly what DA Morrissey did. There's no law or rule against it.

Levy hides under the excuse that they don't comment on grand juries that fail to indict. That's a bullshit excuse. Staying quiet isn't a legal requirement; it's a policy, and it's based on the notion that just reporting a grand jury investigation into someone does them great harm even if it results in no charges. If it came out that a grand jury investigated you for embezzlement or fraud, the very fact that you were investigated would smear you and damage friendships and business relationships. So, it's a good policy.

But in this case, word of the grand jury, who was testifying, and what was being looked into had already been leaked out. In fact, if the State is correct, the Feds were the ones leaking it! So these people have already been smeared by that federal investigation. The only way to protect them is to clear their names by admitting nothing was found.

The real reason they don't do that (at the time of this writing) is because they don't want their own wrongdoing exposed.

The best thing that can be said about the third-party culprit theory is that, except for the oddness of John's injuries, there's nothing there. We'll explain why shortly.

However, the odd lack of injuries to a man struck by a vehicle does create powerful questions, as does the fact that the ARCCA guys, who are highly qualified, doubted John was hit by a vehicle. So let's see if we can:

A) Show you the compelling evidence presented by the prosecution;

B) Show you how pretty close to impossible it would be to manufacture that evidence;

C) Clear up most of the odd things with convincing and mundane explanations.

Before bringing you to Ground Zero where, in the immediate aftermath of John's death, the conspiracy theory congealed organically, we need to go back on the trail with the investigators as they gather the clues. But the storm that would become known as Free Karen Read wouldn't erupt until two summers later, and at the heart of that tempest emerged something new in this story: a true villain.

### Yellow Cottage Tales: Delphi

The series on Lizzie Borden marked the first time I was narrating my own videos. It would be almost another year before I would be doing live shows, and almost two years before I would be making appearances on Court TV or doing interviews on Boston news channels and for documentaries. Being in front of a camera doesn't come naturally for me, and while over time I've reached a level of comfort with it, it's certainly not my mug of pilsner.

For the Borden series, I carefully read every single document on the case and consulted experts, and it became an exercise not only in logical analysis, but in persuasion, as I tried to argue certain conclusions. However, there were no stakes because everyone involved had been deceased for many decades. There was no way to hurt anyone.

For the first time, the channel began to grow, as a certain number of people enjoyed my analysis. One of these new listeners asked me to look into another case: the Delphi, Indiana murders of Abigail (Abby) Williams and Liberty (Libby) German.

I vaguely recalled that case as the Snapchat Murders. In 2017, the junior high schoolers were brutally abducted at the end of a long railroad bridge and slaughtered a short time later in the woods. One of the girls had heroically managed to take some video of the killer moments before he ordered them "down the hill."

The idea of investigating this didn't appeal to me at all. The crime was too horrible to imagine. If someone had suggested looking into this a month before, I wouldn't even have considered it. But after working my ass off on videos with other narrators that didn't really get any traction, now that I was finally getting some positive results, I felt open to it.

And this is important to note, because this is how it is with YouTubers. You work really hard to create the content: learning how to edit video, doing research, trying to master the equipment. But then you discover that it's incredibly difficult to find an audience. Yellow Cottage Tales wasn't my first channel. I had worked thousands of hours on another channel I set up during the year before, but it didn't draw much of an audience, and this is true for thousands of content creators.

Mike Crawford runs a channel called the Young Jurks, and after 10 years, his videos were still only getting a few hundred views. But then he did an episode about Karen

Read, one where he took the conspiracy side, and the views jumped immediately to seven thousand! One can only imagine how that feels after 10 years of achieving essentially no audience growth.

So when something finally works, it's really hard to NOT continue down that road. In fact, this even applies to standard publications, documentaries, and news shows. It's a very Darwinist world. Ratings and numbers mean survival for them just as views and subscribers do for YouTubers.

We'll see more of Mike later, as he and other YouTubers faced the same choice I did.

So, I dove into the Delphi case. As it turned out, a few months later, police would arrest Richard Allen. In October, he was convicted of the murders. But at the time, I began going over all the documents, news reports, and interviews. Police were still stumped, and Allen wasn't on anyone's radar.

I learned that the only way I could get through these cases was by focusing on the intellectual challenge of figuring out the puzzle. I still remember editing those videos on Delphi, adding in the images of Abby and Libby and feeling heartbroken every time I saw their faces. They should have been in college doing college-girl things. But as long as I kept my brain zeroed in on the puzzle aspect of it, the emotional part of me was distant enough that I could get through it.

My approach was the same as with Lizzie Borden: use questions, develop possible branches on the logic tree, and eliminate the branches that were very unlikely.

With each episode on Delphi, the channel grew more and more. I discovered that this case had tremendous global interest. However, something else became clear: the dark side of the true crime community.

The channels with the most views on the Delphi case were creating content built on outrageous claims of ritual killings and conspiracy theory. The more bizarre the claim, the better the channel did. People sent me images taken from on top of the Monan High Bridge, images which they said showed the girls being slaughtered in some kind of satanic ceremony.

All I saw was pixels.

The lesson applied to the Karen Read case, and to most other unsolved cases, is obvious. It's kind of a true crime version of the squeaky wheel gets the oil: the more unusual the theory, the more attention it gets.... as long as the unusual theory can be made at least a little bit plausible. It's not that different from what makes urban legends and creepypastas appealing. There's just enough hint of possible reality that they excite something deep within us.

There were other lessons from Delphi. Using logical deduction from known facts, weeks before Allen's arrest, I put out a profile of the killer that would prove to be eerily accurate.

None of it was rocket science, either. Remember, there are no geniuses, and this old bartender is definitely no genius… except at making Long Island Ice Teas that will leave you crippled! No, it was just a matter of simple logical deduction.

The killer was in his mid-40s. Why hadn't he killed before?

And he probably hadn't, because the area is extremely rural, and there had been no similar crimes in recent decades.

I had spent a lot of time researching serial killers, people who kill for the pleasure of killing. And that urge doesn't happen overnight. Their sexual impulses, like everyone else's, develop around puberty. Most serial killers don't begin to act on their urges until their 20s, but whenever they do begin, it starts after many years of fantasies that involve stalking and violent control.

To hold off acting on that compulsion until the mid-40s isn't the normal trajectory. So in Delphi, something must have prevented the budding killer from killing.

That could just be a lack of opportunity, but it struck me that maybe something internal was holding him back. He had stopped himself from acting on his fantasies for 20 years. So the key questions are:

What?

And what changed?

To be a serial killer, you generally have to be either born with a psychopathic brain, or through oppressive circumstances in early youth, you become a sociopath, where the result is very similar. The key thing is that you're incapable of feeling emotional empathy for other human beings.

Only a small percentage of psychopaths develop fantasies about killing… Many become doctors or CEOs, where lack of empathy can be a strength. But especially for males, who already have a normal urge to dominate (think sports, adolescent fights), if they don't have a natural sense of empathy to put boundaries on their adolescent urges, they can start to develop abnormal fantasies. The normal boy dreams of winning the fight, but the idea of torture would repulse him because of empathy. However, without empathy to cause revulsion, there's only stimulation. And the need for more stimulation will build. This can lead to fantasies of killing.

However, there's something else that will put on the brakes and prevent these fantasies from getting dangerous: an internal sense that this kind of thing is wrong.

If that sense of wrongness is strong enough to nip those fantasies in the bud at an early age, then the boy will probably not grow into a monster. But for some males, a kind of endless war develops inside their head. The fantasies continue to grow, but the sense of wrongness is just powerful enough to prevent the boys from acting on them. In a male who remains unmarried, it's almost inevitable that the young man will eventually lose the battle to those urges and begin killing. But to a man who marries and has a family, those urges have a better chance of being contained.

There's no shortage of men who maintained normal family lives but who became serial killers: BTK, the Green Mile killer, and Richard "the Iceman" Kuklinski, to name a few. But in Delphi, it was apparent that this didn't happen, because there were no other murders in the area that matched. So how would someone like this resist the killing urge all the way into his 40s?

The answer: self-image.

If someone with those fantasies and urges doesn't like the image of himself as a killer, it might be enough to keep things in check.

But this guy did ultimately kill two innocent young girls with whom he had no connection. So he held off until his 40s, but then eventually gave in to his fantasies. That suggests something changed in his life. It suggests something might have triggered him.

What made the most sense to me was that the killer was a father. He had an image of himself as a good father. Probably as a good husband too. This is a very Christian part of the country, and a man who stays with his wife and raises his children is extremely valued. That's the self-image that a man is most likely to have: good father, good husband.

But someone born with a truly psychopathic brain doesn't view his wife and kids in a normal way, no matter how much they might want to. The reason is that he has a brain incapable of emotional empathy, and he has a hard time seeing anyone else as a real person. As Bryan Kohberger said in high school, he sees other people, even his family members, as nothing more than video game characters. They almost aren't real to him. This is what happens to a brain that goes through its entire development unable to emotionally put its owner in other people's shoes.

So to a psychopath, his children are, in some ways, possessions. On an intellectual level, he'll know this is wrong, but in a deeper, primal way, his kids belong to him. And once those kids start going out on their own, he'll take that as betrayal. It triggers powerful feelings of rage. I believed that in Delphi, all of this would topple the precarious balance which had stopped the killer from acting on his urges all these years.

There was one last thing that influenced my thinking. In 2019, Indiana State Police Superintendent Doug Carter had done a carefully planned press conference in which he directly addressed the killer. His words were obviously scripted. And he began with a strange reference to a movie called *The Shack*.

Why *The Shack*?

I presumed that his comments had been crafted with the help of professional profilers, perhaps the FBI Behavioral Analysis Unit. *The Shack* is about a man whose daughter is abducted by a serial killer and, during the search, he confronts memories of his own abusive father and his guilt for murdering him.

Trying to understand what message Carter was sending to the Delphi killer, it didn't seem likely to me that the profilers expected him to just surrender out of some pang of conscience. Serial killer types don't do that. But what did make sense was that Carter was appealing to him to not kill again. They believed the killer's image of himself as a good father had prevented him from killing until now, and appealing to that sense might help him get the urge back under control.

I took the theory one final step. What could have triggered the Delphi killer to kill for the first time in his mid-40s?

One possibility was the loss of a child to death or terminal illness. Maybe that provoked a kind of rage against the universe.

But the murders of Abby and Libby felt more personal. More targeted. Not because he knew the girls... I believe they were just in the wrong place at the wrong time, because they hadn't told anyone other than Libby's sister, who dropped them off, that they were going to the bridge. Rather, they were targeted because they were girls who fit a profile. This was projected rage, rage he didn't want to direct at his real target: his daughter.

That was pure speculation of mine done when Allen wasn't even a suspect.

So I did something I'm absolutely in no way, shape, or form qualified to do—and probably won't ever do again. I put out a profile. I predicted that the killer was a dad who saw himself as a good father and husband. That he had committed no crimes similar to this before. And what triggered him, I proposed, was his daughter leaving the nest, perhaps to go to college.

Three weeks later, when they arrested Richard Allen, we learned that he had been with the same woman since the age of 19, and that they had one kid, a daughter. I queried to find out what was going on with that daughter right before the murders, and the answer was quickly found by talking to someone from Delphi: two months prior, she had gotten engaged.

So I had been close.

Maybe I should have quit while I was ahead, but then I put out a video entitled "Antlers." I predicted that signs of antlers left at the scene by the killer would have been found. You'll have to watch the video if you want to know about the convoluted reasoning. Did that prediction prove accurate?

Weirdly, the defense claimed that the killer arranged sticks and branches around the bodies in order to symbolically form antlers.

So I did it again, right? I thought you guys said there are no geniuses?

Well, actually, no, I got this wrong. Allen did arrange branches around the bodies, but there's no way of knowing what was in his sick mind, and there's nothing to suggest he was creating antlers. So I should probably leave profiling to the experts.

***"Just when I think you couldn't possibly be any dumber, you go and do something like this... and totally redeem yourself!"*– Harry Dunne, *Dumb and Dumber***

But simple deduction had succeeded in leading me to a correct general profile of the killer, and that did encourage me to keep putting speculations out there.

I was starting to believe that true crimers, people with no training or experience, could, in theory, have useful insights. People like Michelle McNamara, who wrote *I'll Be Gone in the Dark*, and who helped catch the Golden State Killer.

I was certainly not naïve enough to think that kind of thing would happen on my channel. Not only was that not an ambition, it wasn't even a daydream.

Rather, what I was starting to think was that my channel could play a very small part in the conversation. And that felt worthwhile.

## True Crime Creepypasta

I think we can also sneak in a new rule while no one is looking.

### YCT Rule #20: It's just pixels.

I'll never forget that feeling when someone I love and trust, and greatly respect, sent me screenshots from a video taken from on top of the Monon High Bridge between the railroad ties.

In the woods below was a group of what seemed to be teens. The screenshots then zoomed in real close to the brush, so close that you make out the rectangular pixels. Well, the claim was that you could actually see the forms of Abby and Libby being held down and sacrificed.

But all I could see were pixels. My brain just couldn't connect the dots into patterns that other people were seeing.

Of course, now we know for certain that the girls weren't killed beneath the bridge. They were killed right where they were found, in the woods across the creek and about a half mile away from the bridge.

But why were people seeing things that weren't there?

Don't be ashamed if you're one of those people. It doesn't make you a bad person, and you aren't crazy.

But there ARE lessons for you... and us... to learn. Look, it's perfectly normal for people to be intrigued by the mysterious. This is why conspiracies fascinate us. The idea of JFK being killed by a secret faction within his own government is a million times more interesting than him just being killed by a lone nut. The notion that Andy Kaufman faked his own death is way more compelling than the fact that he died prematurely of lung cancer. Our lives tend to be routine and drab, so these entertaining thoughts provide escape.

However, you have to be careful of true crime creepypastas.

A creepypasta is a horror story that is like an urban legend. It's presented as a true tale, and there are just enough plausible elements to make it easier to suspend disbelief for a moment. The possibility of the story being true is what makes it interesting. Andy Kaufman was exactly the kind of person who WOULD fake his own death; he loved tricking the public and blurring the lines of reality. As you read a creepypasta, deep down you know it's not true, but for the sake of entertainment, you willingly buy into the premise.

I like a good creepypasta!

But for some people, they don't so much "suspend" disbelief as they just plain believe. That can be a problem. You don't want to start thinking Slenderman is real.

The same thing applies to true crime, cases that really grab the public's attention can take on aspects of a creepypasta. The mind starts looking for seemingly strange elements and then begins to stitch them together into a titillating narrative—turning pixels into images that don't exist.

# PART FOUR: INVESTIGATION CONTINUED

# 1. ON THE TRAIL

A photo would emerge during the Free Karen Read frenzy that showed John's clothing piled on the floor of the emergency room at the feet of Trooper Proctor.

"Aha!"

In other words, look how reckless he was with the evidence. Only it turns out it's very easily explained. And that's how it went throughout this case, continuing to this day: "Aha!"s followed eventually by mundane explanations... rinse and repeat, no lessons ever learned by the mob with its insatiable thirst for conspiracy.

This is all human nature, of course. We love the mysterious, the unsolved, the unexplained.

Even if you don't believe alien ships from other worlds are likely plucking people from their back yards and then returning them to their beds after a night of experimentation, who doesn't love a good story?

So let's say this headline appears one day in your local paper: "Strange Craft and Unusual Beings Seen in Nearby Woods." Aren't you at least intrigued enough to read the story?

But how about this headline: "Local UFO Story Debunked"?

We'll probably believe that headline, but skip the article and move on to the sports page.

So in a case like Karen Read's, which is only popular because of the conspiracy theory, we have to keep that in mind and understand there are always going to be a lot of YouTube channels and even regular media blowing air into the theory. Those of us more interested in the truth need to be alert to all these false "aha!" moments.

I'll list the seemingly odd things soon, along with reasonable explanations where it applies. If something odd remains unexplained, I'll absolutely and honestly point it out, and people can decide whether these remaining mysteries potentially add up to a cover-up or not. But you're going to see that the vast majority of these odd things did eventually have simple explanations, though sometimes we had to wait for the trial to get them.

Let's first finish reporting the results of the investigation into John O'Keefe's death.

## Evidence Collecting

In the ambulance, the paramedics were racing to save the victim's life. They hastily cut off his clothes. When they arrived at the hospital, after delivering the patient, the paramedics dropped off this clothing. Not a single paramedic, doctor, or ER staffer was thinking about evidence. They have no training in evidence preservation and no evidence bags. They were just trying to save a life.

So when the troopers arrived, they found John's clothing stored in the usual way in an emergency room: in a pile on the floor. Mystery solved. Now we know why the clothing is seen in the photo on the floor at the trooper's feet.

John's clothing was soaking wet and smelled of vomit. They bagged it in evidence bags, listing the data and initialing it on the seal. Every time the bag is opened, the seal is broken, and it has to be sealed and initialed again.

They also bagged one sneaker. The other remained missing, something they knew was typical of a hit-and-run.

By the end of the day, all of the evidence would be taken to the offices at the Norfolk County DA, right there in Canton.

At these offices, there is an Evidence Room where only three troopers have access: the commander of the Detectives Unit (STDU), and two "evidence officers."

Proctor and Bukhenik didn't have access to this room.

Outside the room is a "processing area." One of the evidence officers will take the bagged and marked evidence from this location into the Evidence Room for secure storage. By the end of the day on January 29, that evidence would include John's phone, the broken cocktail glass, and the taillight pieces found after 5:45 P.M.

The troopers left the soaked clothing on a table in the processing area to dry. A few days later, once it was dry, an evidence officer moved the clothing into the Evidence Room.

**Logging Evidence**

Are you ready for the next trick the defense team attempted to conjure in order to dupe us gullible members of the public? They pointed out that the Massachusetts State Police didn't log the evidence into their system until six weeks later.

Those sneaky bastards!

What were they doing with that evidence in those six weeks?

The actual answer is mundane. The primary storage area for the evidence is actually not with the State Police. It's with the prosecution. In other words, the DA's Office. In the Evidence Room.

However, some pieces of evidence in a criminal case—in fact, many pieces—need to be eventually brought to labs for testing. There are no labs at the DA's Office. The State Police run the labs, and all of the county prosecutors use them. In this case, John's clothing—bagged and sealed—

was sent six weeks later to the labs for testing. And THAT's when it was logged into the State Police evidence system.

See, once we learn how things actually work, not only is it not surprising, but it's completely logical the way it's set up. Unless we really, really need there to be a conspiracy, we say, "Oh, yeah, that makes sense."

This isn't to say there aren't real conspiracies and that maybe there isn't one here… We have a lot of odd things to examine. But it does mean that in our eagerness for titillating stories, we have to be careful not to leap to conclusions just because they're juicy.

Testing on the clothing revealed tiny pieces of taillight that were barely visible to the naked eye, basically red plastic dust. Did Proctor have a test tube of taillight plastic just for when he needed to frame people?

The State eventually swabbed John's clothing to test for canine DNA and found none. "But," the FKR world shouts, "why didn't they test the wounds?"

Because they never had any reason to believe John had been attacked by a dog, and by the time the defense put that theory out, John had long been buried.

Mundane explanations.

"But, but, but…"

Don't worry, FKR, we'll get to everything, but we want you to take a moment to recognize that reaction in yourself. There's nothing wrong with it, but you should also be starting to recognize a pattern here. Many things that you thought were super suspicious ended up having common-sense explanations. That should result in you stepping back and being more skeptical.

In every murder trial that has ever taken place since Cain and Abel, the defense team has tried to propose someone else did it. It's their job to create doubt by making the ordinary look odd. So, shouldn't we in the public:

A) Be a little more self-aware, recognizing our thirst for an interesting story?

B) Be much more patient as we wait for the common-sense explanations?

Six weeks after being stored in the county DA's Evidence Room, where evidence is normally stored for a trial, some of the evidence was transferred to State Police labs for further testing and evaluation. Forensic scientists examined the clothing under a microscope, reassembled the taillight pieces, and analyzed the glass fragments found on the bumper. This specialized work isn't done in the offices of prosecutors.

Ho-hum.

At the hospital, doctors showed the detectives John's wounds. Always a difficult part of any unattended death case, this moved the troopers even more because it involved a fellow officer, someone around the same age as them. They noted the abrasions on his arm, a scratch above his left eye, and one on the right side of his nose. The ridges around his eyes were badly swollen. Blood marked the back of his head.

They called Karen Read on the phone.

To their surprise, she had just arrived at her parents' home in Dighton. So the troopers climbed into Bukhenik's truck, which they had been using so Proctor would be free to make arrangements on his phone.

In Dighton, after the troopers told Karen they were on their way, she made an interesting google search: "DUI lawyers."

***

On the drive to Dighton through the pounding blizzard, Proctor did something that common sense tells us he would

NOT have done if he was on the way to tamper with Karen's SUV: he called the Dighton Police to alert them to the fact that they were coming. This was done as a jurisdictional courtesy, but also because they were going to need a tow truck and someone to plow the driveway.

Again, put yourself in Proctor's shoes from the POV that he's conspiring to cover up a murder. Wouldn't it make more sense to get to the Lexus *first* so they would have access to the vehicle *before* the Dighton Police got there? What if the Dighton cop had taken a photo of the damage? Or detailed notes?

Karen's SUV sat parked in the driveway under RING surveillance, which was later obtained by the prosecution. The vehicle was facing the camera.

Officer Nicholas Barros of the Dighton Police met the troopers at the home of Mr. and Mrs. Read. He noted in his report that the right taillight was "damaged" but wrote no more detail than that. He would testify that the taillight was "not completely damaged," "cracked," and "missing pieces."

Which is, actually, exactly what we would *expect* him to see.

The main part of the taillight, the part facing directly behind the vehicle, remains intact. It's only the corner that's missing pieces, and by then, the exposed interior would have been filled with snow.

Had Barros or the troopers thought to take a photo of the taillight at this time, it would have settled a lot of debates, but it's probably not reasonable to expect that they could have foreseen an accusation of planting evidence.

Trudging through several feet of drifting snow, as the winter sun set, the troopers glanced at the taillight, then went to the home's door, where Mr. Read greeted them.

An almost cartoonishly waifish man, Bill Read led a quiet and respectable life. College at UMass Dartmouth, MBA from Babson, PhD from Virginia Tech, followed by a teaching and research career in the field of accounting at Bentley College, a business school in Massachusetts. For a period of two years, ending a year before O'Keefe's death, Read served as dean of the school. So, a very well respected man, someone caught in a tragedy no parent should ever have to be put through.

Karen had called him at 1:15 A.M., but he didn't wake. Then again, at 4:40. And again at 4:42. The calls went unanswered. We all think we're light sleepers, but especially on a night like this, with the wind howling, we sleep pretty soundly.

Later, as Karen and Kerry left 34 Fairview to meet the ambulance at the hospital, Karen texted her father: "John's dead."

Now he called right back. And he quickly became worried about her state of mind, so he called the police, who got Kerry to bring her back to Fairview so they could put her in protective custody. Then Mr. Read traveled to Good Samaritan Medical Center to collect their daughter a little before noon.

When the troopers arrived at the Read house in Dighton, Bill Read led them inside to where Karen sat on the couch. They had a 40-minute conversation. Karen said she had dropped John off at 34 Fairview. They'd had a lot of drinks. She mentioned doing a three-point turn. The troopers seized her phone, putting it in airplane mode to prevent remote access.

While they were doing this, Officer Barros called a plow to clear the driveway and arranged for a tow truck.

A year and half later, on national TV, Karen would say that she remembered dropping John off "at the foot of the driveway" and seeing him open the door and cross the threshold into the house. She said she waited about ten minutes, texting and calling him, before finally driving off.

She didn't tell the troopers any of this that day, and *phone records show that she didn't text John at this time.*

The first call from her, at 12:33, likely came when she was already driving back. And she tells multiple versions about whether she intended to go into the after-hours party. In one version, she seems to be waiting to see if John is going to stay, and in the *Dateline* version, she actually seems to be waiting for John to signal to her that it's okay to come inside herself.

One year after saying this, in another national TV interview, she changed her story, no longer saying she called and texted John before leaving. So, her stories are kind of all over the map, evolving as needed.

The RING video from the Read home shows the Lexus loaded onto the tow truck and leaving at 4:18. Though it's a distant shot, the taillight is visibly missing pieces on the corner, white light flashing when the truck applies the brakes. There would be no white light if the red plastic was intact.

The tow truck lumbered its way to I-95 and brought the vehicle back to the Canton Police station, with the troopers following in Bukhenik's truck. It's normally about a 45-minute trip, but in the middle of a historic blizzard, the journey took about an hour and 10 minutes.

I'll come back to this transportation when we talk about timelines, but let's stop to discuss the decision about where to tow the alleged murder weapon.

**Why not tow the vehicle to a State Police garage? Was this decision unusual? Who made it?**

The sally port attached to the Canton Police station has only two bays. It's a small extension built onto the main building, and one thing about it sets it apart from most police garages: it's heated.

As we've talked about, a State Police homicide investigation is a team effort that includes many individuals with very specialized roles and training. At some point after the vehicle arrives, technicians will be crawling all over the vehicle, dusting for fingerprints, looking for DNA, documenting everything inside and out. Technicians will remove the taillight to reassemble it with the recovered pieces. Before this can be done, however, the car has to be free of ice and snow. Thus the advantage of a heated garage.

Standard training books also recommend storing the vehicle close to the crime scene in case it's decided to return it there in order to run certain tests. For example, in pedestrian strikes, investigators usually conduct tests to determine pedestrian visibility. They didn't do that in this case, but because it's standard procedure, it's not suspicious that they decided to bring the vehicle to a police facility near 34 Fairview.

Finally, the main reason for bringing it there: the County DA is in Canton. Their offices are a mile from the sally port. Giving the prosecutors easy access to the murder weapon only makes sense.

So, maybe I can hit you with another rule…

**YCT Rule #4: Things that at first seem odd often really aren't.**

If your reaction is "No shit, Dick Tracy," I hear you. But the Karen Read case has shown us how big a problem this is, and not just with the public, but even with many so-called experts. Media coverage has been filled with defense lawyers and retired cops—people who *should* know better—who won't wait for the mundane explanation. And even when it comes, they don't pay attention.

If you've been following this case, and you thought that the decision to tow the Lexus to the CPD sally port was very odd and suspicious… don't beat yourself up! It's okay. I did too! Without an explanation, it does seem weird, right?

But learn from the experience. Remember that there was a straightforward explanation, and we just had to wait for it.

Yes, it seemed weird to us in the public, because we don't really have an understanding of how homicide investigations run by the Massachusetts State Police work.

As we've explained, the State Police run all investigations involving unattended deaths, except in the state's biggest three cities. But these investigations are:

A) Run in partnership with the local police;

B) Run by troopers assigned to the county DA.

In the Karen Read case, the local police were "conflicted out" because Kevin Albert is a Canton Police detective. But this mostly meant no Canton cops would be present for witness interviews. That's it. They would run everything else as usual.

Many of us have this false conception where we imagine the State Police swooping in like the FBI and running their own independent investigation, doing everything themselves and using all of their own facilities.

But that's not at all how it works. Generally, these investigations are *led* by the Staties, but they're cooperative efforts.

Once you know all this, the decision to tow Karen's vehicle to the CPD sally port wasn't only not unusual, it's completely expected. It would actually have been weird if they didn't tow it there.

A) It's a heated facility, and the vehicle was covered in snow;

B) It's only a mile from the Norfolk County DA;

C) It's a facility owned by the local police, the usual partners in a homicide.

So, it's another seemingly odd thing that people can now cross off their list. Go ahead, we'll pause here a moment while you do.

(AC/DC blasts "It's a Long Way to the Top," Angus Young so lost in his guitar playing he barely knows they're being filmed.)

Oh, you're back. Okay.

Now, keep your red marker handy, because we'll be crossing a lot of odd things off the list.

## SERT Team

Lieutenant Kevin O'Hara, leader of the SERT team, arrived at the crime scene at 4:57 P.M.

Canton Police had tried to tape the scene off that morning, which proved futile during a howling blizzard. By 8:30 A.M., they abandoned not only that effort, but the crime scene itself, leaving it unattended all day. When O'Hara arrived, one member of his team was already present.

SERT is a highly trained unit designed to respond rapidly to various critical situations. They assist with missing person searches, civil disturbances, and crowd management. They also have extensive training in evidence collection.

Why would SERT be called to investigate 34 Fairview instead of the Crime Scene Services Unit?

The State Police Detective Unit (SPDU) is assigned to the DA's Office and consists of only four troopers. Another 10 to 15 troopers are also assigned to the county, and they perform specialized tasks such as data forensics, sex crimes, narcotics, and white-collar crime.

Other State Police resources aren't directly assigned to a county. This includes the SERT team and the Crime Scene Services (CSS). CSS troopers and criminologists do the majority of the evidence gathering: bagging it, documenting the location, dusting for prints, swabbing for DNA, photographing, and measuring.

The decision to call in the SERT team was based on the weather. The team is trained in rapid response and in extreme conditions. Snow was piling up at the crime scene.

Normally, the SERT team wouldn't be called in to a hit-and-run evidence recovery operation, so this was a decision that required a moment of discussion. It wouldn't have been made by Proctor or Bukhenik.

Because the team wasn't assigned specifically to the County, its members drove from across the state in a blizzard, causing delays. Seven members of the eight-man squad were able to make it, and the last arrived at 5:39. By that time, some preparatory work had taken place, but they wouldn't begin shoveling out the crime scene until they were all there.

Also on scene were a couple of other State Police officers, including the commander of SPDU, Lieutenant Brian Tully, and possibly some unidentified Canton cops, just there to observe.

While they waited for the last SERT team member, with a WBZ News truck setting up to film their work, the tow truck was arriving at the Canton Police station sally port a five-minute drive away.

**Sally Port**

Events at the sally port would become the focus of conspiracy theory and drama at the first trial. The tow truck arrived at 5:31, visible in the outside surveillance video. At 5:36, grainy and glitchy surveillance from inside shows Karen's SUV being driven in by the tow truck driver. Within the other bay is stored a classic police car.

Inside the bay were a handful of people, some not yet identified. This included, of course, Troopers Proctor and Bukhenik and the tow truck driver. Likely Chief Berkowitz was there too. They never touched the vehicle, though they did examine the broken taillight. Of course they did.

They brushed blown snow out of the open bay. And the door closed at 5:42. Both troopers were still within the sally port and, in fact, they used police caution tape to seal off the vehicle.

Who were the unidentified men?

A big deal would be made about a strange exchange of "butt dials" by Brian Albert and Agent Higgins around 2:23 A.M. on the night of the after-hours party. Albert made a call to Higgins that went unanswered, then Higgins called right back with a call that lasted 22 seconds. Both would describe these calls as butt dials.

Around 7:30 A.M., Higgins had calls with Albert and with Chief Berkowitz. Higgins then drove back to 34 Fairview.

Chief Berkowitz, out on injury leave at the time, has been described as someone who admires and wants the approval of the kind of cops that are "in the juice"... guys like Brian Albert, who spent years hunting down gangsters and other dangerous bad guys, and Agent Higgins, most of whose work was undercover. It had been the chief who gave Higgins an office at the station, and the chief would contact media after John's death to try to keep Albert's name out of it. Berkowitz would drive down Fairview Road six days after the tragedy and spot taillight pieces on the road.

Higgins was actually at 34 Fairview when they called back Detective Lank at 8:30 in the morning to give him more information about what had happened just hours before at the after-hours party. So Higgins was at the party, then also back at the scene as the Canton Police were wrapping up their part in the investigation.

He then reported to work at the Canton Police station and would spend the day there. The electronic lock system inside showed him to be in or near the sally port around 4:30, right as Karen's SUV was beginning its journey back to Canton on the tow truck.

The defense seemed to be trying to build a case that Higgins and perhaps Chief Berkowitz were the unidentified men inside the sally port when the vehicle arrived after 5:30.

But they never quite got there.

Did they develop contrary evidence over that weekend? We don't know, but they strangely abandoned that line of attack over the weekend as the cross-examination of Higgins extended from Friday into Tuesday.

From time to time, I'll remind everyone that the Karen Read case is an either/or. Either Karen struck John with her SUV, or someone planted taillight pieces that same day. We'll come back to examining possibilities with the taillight later.

But for now, let's close the curtain on the sally port with the bay door being lowered at 5:42. Both Proctor and Bukhenik are present. Surveillance is working. And a five-minute drive away, at the crime scene, the SERT team is shoveling shoulder to shoulder in an area the size of two parking spaces. Three feet down in the snow, at ground level, they find the first taillight piece.

It's 5:45.

**34 Fairview**

Because it's so important, let's linger over the shoulders of the digging team at 34 Fairview. There's a WBZ News truck filming. The area is bathed in floodlights set up by the SERT team. Lt. Tully, in command, is documenting the scene personally by taking photos. There may be some unidentified cops with him. That would be expected.

The SERT team received information that they're searching for taillight pieces and a missing shoe.

How well is the street plowed? It's not clear. Was the DPW informed to not plow the street in order to preserve the evidence? There's no evidence of that. At the time John was found, there was only a plowed path up the middle of the road. But since the crime scene remained unprotected for most of the day, the snow may have been pushed more toward the curb.

The SERT team members understand that the evidence they seek will be at or near street level. Over 22 inches of snow have fallen, but in addition to that, there's a bank made by the snowplows, perhaps by Lucky. The key evidence is found about three feet down in one of these snowbanks.

Lt. O'Hara described going through two feet of snow, then the harder plowed snow, which added another foot. Investigators found the red corner piece of the taillight at ground level near the curb. The trooper who found it with his shovel dropped it on the snow pile to be photographed. They documented its precise location. Then they went on digging.

They found several more pieces, and crucially, John's shoe. The team completed its search at 6:22.

Everyone went home.

Except John O'Keefe.

## 2. TAILLIGHT

Court TV had a scoop. Karen's team had leaked them an interesting piece of discovery evidence. RING video from John's home at 1 Meadows showed Karen backing out of the garage into the driveway at 5:08 A.M. It's snowing hard, maybe two inches on the ground. John's Chevy Traverse is parked in the back, where he left it so Karen could park in the garage during the storm.

Slowly easing her way into the driveway in jerks and starts, Karen edges toward the Traverse so she can turn in the direction where the driveway extends to Meadows Ave. She comes very close to the SUV, seemingly bumping it ever so slightly, before cutting the wheel. The video shows her pulling away, and we get our first glimpse at the right taillight.

The special reporter for Court TV tells the audience that, according to the defense team, THIS is how Karen busted her taillight, not at 34 Fairview. The reporter adds that *the defense team says* the taillight is clearly damaged here and *"missing pieces."*

Except the condition of the taillight in this video wasn't clear enough for people to agree. Those who believe Karen is innocent now say it's actually NOT missing any pieces at this time, but is merely CRACKED. However, zooming in on the SIDE of the taillight does seem to show significant pieces missing.

Enter Yellow Cottage Tales.
Unwittingly.

***

Seamus O'Malley spent almost three decades as a DEA agent. Retired and living in Florida, he grew up in Canton. Perhaps because of that connection, perhaps missing being "in the juice," he became interested in this case when it took off in social media. He looks every bit the part: the stereotypical big Irish cop from Boston.

Seamus would first become prominent in social media circles covering the case, and because of his status as a retired agent, he quickly became a respected authority on the case. He clearly believed that Karen was innocent, and that there was a massive conspiracy to frame her. To many of us without law enforcement experience, his thoughts carried weight. He began following YCT, and soon both Dave and Kevin struck up a relationship with him, talking regularly on the phone about the case.

*What we had absolutely no idea of was that he was also talking to Karen Read and her famous Los Angeles Attorney, Alan Jackson.*

*And the FBI.*

When Court TV showed the driveway video, I studied it over and over but couldn't be sure. RING video uses infrared light to film in the darkness, and algorithms within the software process the input to create what we see.

It's certain that no pieces fell into the driveway when she backed into the Traverse, because they would be clearly visible in the fluffy, fresh snow around the Traverse, and nothing had broken the surface.

However, could the taillight plastic have been pushed in so that there were dislodged pieces, but the pieces remained within the housing?

In the summer of 2023, we were still trying to lock down exactly where Karen's SUV was all day before the SERT team found the main piece at 5:45 P.M. If that piece had been planted, someone had to pry it from the Lexus first.

When?

This logic seems simple and common sense, but remember YCT Rule #1: There are no geniuses. Neither Karen nor her team understood, at the time that they released the RING video, what we were about to say privately to Seamus on the phone: If we could find any image of the taillight which showed it CRACKED, but not missing pieces, then Karen was framed! Contrarily, if the images showed it was MISSING PIECES, she was almost certainly… well, facing very long odds.

Amazingly, Karen and her team didn't understand this when they released the video to Court TV and therefore told them it shows the SUV clearly "missing pieces." Nor did they understand it when Karen, in the presence of her three lawyers, discussed inspecting the taillight and dropping a piece in John's driveway.

But days after I told Seamus on the phone that we needed a clear image of the taillight from as early on January 29 as possible, he texted me with photos which he said we couldn't share or show on the channel. Images which could only come from the discovery material.

Wow!

Was he talking directly to Karen?

This was my first clue to that. The images were closeups of the broken taillight taken from the sally port after the vehicle was in police custody.

And he introduced me to a name that he claimed would prove there was a conspiracy: Wanless.

### Wanless

I've mentioned Brian Wanless, a Canton Police officer, having since retired, who also happened to own Brilliance Autobody. According to Seamus O'Malley, Wanless had actually been forced by the troopers to help them in their conspiracy by removing pieces from the taillight so they could be delivered to the crime scene. It's not clear why the conspirators would need any special skill to pry broken pieces off a taillight... a hammer and pliers should do the trick.

Try to understand what it has been like to be in the middle of all this. Speculation about Wanless's role went on in Free Karen Read circles for 10 months, especially those led by Seamus, who became very prominent when he launched his own YouTube channel and has been interviewed in national publications. They envisioned a scenario where the poor Canton cop with autobody skills was forced to wait in the sally port, like a pit crew, for Karen's Lexus to arrive, so they could hurriedly pry pieces, race to the scene, and... what? Bury them three feet down into the snow in front of WBZ News and the SERT team?

Apparently.

Living through this case has been like playing *Whac-a-Mole*. When one weird theory or unexplained aspect is debunked, the conspiracy believers just jump right over to something else without skipping a beat, without ever pausing to ask themselves if they should step back and be more careful. And when I say *Whac-a-Mole*, I'm talking about a lot of moles.

***

### Late March of 2023

While Karen's defense team was preparing to officially inform the court that their data guy had discovered two electrifying pieces of information—Jen McCabe's alleged 2:27 search and John's supposed stair climbing—I got a message from someone who had just watched my video on Andy Puglisi. He had recently published a book on Andy's alleged killer. His name was David McGrath.

It's a good thing we first spoke by phone, because Dave would surely have been disappointed in a face-to-face meeting! You see, the video I did was hosted by Tom Pfost, a professional narrator. I had extensively researched the Andy Puglisi case, added my own analysis to the work done by Melanie Perkins McLaughlin, and created a script for Tom to narrate with his golden vocal chords. So, Dave thought those chords and that face belonged to me. No, sir.

But Dave and I found that we had a lot in common in how we analyze evidence. The Puglisi case was deeply personal to us for reasons that at first seemed different, but at the heart of it were the same: we're in the habit of putting ourselves into the characters' shoes.

The fact that Andy had been the same age as me and lived a mile away when he went missing was only a small part of it. That night, when John was dying in the cold and I was watching *Have You Seen Andy?*, began a months-long journey for me where I immersed myself into the details of the case, wrote a screenplay, and created the video for my YouTube channel. Through my years of writing fiction, I learned how to see the world through my characters' eyes, and this could be applied to real people too. I could go back in my mind to 1976, to the Stadium Projects in Lawrence, to when the Red Sox were in a pennant race and *The Bad News Bears* was playing in drive-in movie theaters, when summer heat still drove sticky kids to the public pool, even though soon they would be going back to school, and sunset was coming alarmingly early.

Dave had also obsessively walked in the shoes of the people he investigated, though he came to it from a different angle. He himself had grown up in the projects, in the part of Boston called Dorchester, and he had been a victim of abuse to predators like the one who took Andy. And when he researched the case, he learned to be in their shoes by literally walking in their footsteps. From Lawrence, Massachusetts to Great Falls, Montana and many spots in between, he traveled to where both the victims and the predators lived and operated.

It's a process that is both unpleasant yet addictive. We all have human minds, and even though the end product can be very different, we're all using the same essential ingredients for the meal. This is why, with practice and deep introspection, we can enter the lives of even monsters, because if you look hard enough, you'll find the clues within yourself.

Dave was like an encyclopedia of true crime, so if I had a general theory, he could immediately plug in some relevant case that was similar. With his help, I was able to zoom in deeper and deeper.

The highest level of consciousness that we can achieve involves being both in the moment and at the same time flying above it, looking down so you can see the forest through the trees. Shakespeare is said to be the true master of that, but we're all capable of it, and we get better at it the more we do it.

Dave and I started talking every day about how monsters think and how they might be caught. It felt promising because there actually was a way to kind of test our theories. We could make a prediction about what one of them might have done back in the '70s or '80s and then look into the documents to see if he did actually do it. And we were finding a lot of confirmation too. For example, we might speculate that a predator had learned certain things if he spent time in prison with others like him, and thus explain his evolution. Then we would do the research and find that, indeed, he had spent time with similar men in the same institution.

The reason that writers have to learn how to put themselves in the shoes of each of their characters is so we can understand what choices that character will make in every situation. This is where you want to be able to both zoom in and take the bird's-eye view at the same time.

I'm a fan of *The Sopranos*. Brilliant writing. There's an episode where the plot is set in motion because Ralph makes a joke about the fat wife of a NY underboss, Johnny Sack. To further the plot, "Paulie Walnuts" Gualtieri hears about it in prison and betrays Tony by reporting it to Johnny Sack. Blood flows.

But why did Paulie betray Tony and his own crew?

The writers really put themselves into Paulie's mind. Ambition alone wouldn't make him do this, so they looked deeper. What does Paulie love the most? His mother. So, while Paulie learns about the joke, he also learns, a moment before, that while he has been in prison, Tony hasn't been over to check on his mother. That has Paulie seething, so he calls Sack and tells him about the insulting joke, triggering a war.

We can attempt this kind of thinking when trying to understand the choices Andy's killer faced in Lawrence in 1976. For six days after his disappearance, thousands of people, including the National Guard and the Green Berets, searched the woods behind the State pool. There's a chance they could have missed seeing Andy's remains, but more than likely he would have been spotted.

Remember YCT Rule #7: Don't just ask why someone DID something, but why they DID NOT.

Put yourself in the shoes of the monster. If he killed the boy in the woods, would he hang around to bury the body? No, he would hightail it out of there, and the body would have been found. Would he risk being seen by carrying the body out to his vehicle (a converted bread truck)? No, not in a crowded city like Lawrence.

So, it's more than likely to me that the killer walked him out of the woods alive and drove off with him. And while it's possible he forced the boy into his truck, more probably he tricked him. That way, there were no cries for help.

Andy was more vulnerable to a trick than normal that day because his home had been really tense that morning. His mom had just given her latest boyfriend, a layabout pothead, his walking papers, but with nowhere to go, the dude was lingering. There's evidence Andy wasn't eager to get home because he was among the last to leave the pool.

So when the predator tried his usual trick of asking the boy to help find his dog, Andy would be more willing than usual to help. If the guy walked him through the woods and suggested they get into the truck—maybe sweetening the deal with an offer of a cash reward—Andy was more likely to say yes on that day because of those tensions at home.

By putting ourselves into the characters, we see ranges of choices at each turn, and we try to eliminate branches based on evidence and logic.

As Dave and I discussed these things, it felt like we were getting meaningful insights. I also felt a great respect for him as a family man with a wonderful wife (smarter than both of us… but that doesn't take much) and a couple of All-American kids… and because of his tremendous service to his country. But also because, like me, he was an aspiring writer. It's not easy to get a publisher to even respond to your query with a polite "no thanks," let alone get one to consider your work. So, I identified with his struggle.

We had been working together for about a month when he sent me a fateful text on April 18 about Turtleboy's article on Karen Read.

Let me explain my approach to life since I was diagnosed with stage IV lung cancer in 2018. I live three months at a time, from scans to scans, trying to cram as much as I can into those months. What am I cramming? Work.

It's not about money, and it's not about keeping busy just to take my mind of things. It's actually not easy to put into words what drives me, but I think the closest is this: the quest to make it all meaningful. I don't want to be lying there at the end thinking that it was all for nothing.

But drilling deeper, maybe it's also the stench of failure. My world had crumbled to the ground. I lost my business, my home… my whole life. From the moment that happened, I've been trying with all my might to climb back up the rubble pile. Writing, researching, studying, and working crap assignments. The cancer diagnosis didn't actually shift my efforts so much as accelerate them. Time was running short.

I had written books but didn't have a publisher. I had written screenplays, and only a couple sold. I started websites, launched YouTube channels, and joined a sports podcast. Basically, I was willing to try anything that might work.

But nothing really did… close but no cigar.

When I started a new series on the channel about the Karen Read case, I called it *Framed?* That's right, with a question mark. I scripted, narrated, and edited the productions, understanding that the public interest in conspiracies was insatiable, and here it seemed like there might be a real one, a truly wild case.

Why the question mark?

Because I understood that we knew very little at that point. All we had was the original charging document by the prosecution and the conspiracy theory put out by the defense through her conman blogger, Turtleboy. And though some of it was quite compelling, a lot of it was very nonsensical.

But because of the *Framed?* series, something new started happening. Turtleboy had a big show, thousands of people watching live. And if I showed up in chat, people immediately recognized Yellow Cottage Tales and said how much they liked my channel. That was kind of a wow experience. It felt good.

Pretty soon, I would make the next big step: live shows.

### Taillight Pieces

The taillight pieces were either red or clear. None were found by the Canton Police.

The first, the red corner piece, was found by the SERT team at 5:45. It was found three feet down in the snow at ground level. Lt. O'Hara, head of the SERT team, described having to dig through the older, harder snow a couple of feet down.

These pieces weren't found by the Canton Police because they never took a shovel to the scene. They only investigated the grass area where John was found. That location had been clear of snow when John was taken away—kept clean because of his body warmth—but snow had been building up for over an hour by the time the Canton cops were searching with a leaf blower. They only found the remnants of the cocktail glass.

To repeat: the taillight pieces, John's shoe, and other items were buried in the snowbank made by Lucky Loughran.

With the missing sneaker and the main taillight pieces, the investigators knew they had a strong case, but they also understood that more taillight pieces were buried in the yard and on the street. The high-speed impact, the 50 MPH wind, and the snowplow would have scattered the pieces to some degree. So the investigators repeatedly returned to the scene to look for more pieces as the snow melted, particularly on the "January thaw" type days that we typically get in New England every once in a while in the height of winter. Chief Berkowitz was also aware of this, explaining why he found a piece while driving down Fairview.

Each piece they found was documented, so we know when and where it was found. This created a spray pattern that Trooper Paul, the accident re-constructionist for the State Police, was able to analyze. He determined a likely impact zone that was about 15 feet from where John was found. The margin of error on the impact zone was five feet.

Because it can take time for snow to melt, and because some outlier pieces will always end up outside the spray pattern, some pieces—including one of significant size found by the fire hydrant, about 30 feet from where John was found—end up outside the impact area.

The defense's Alan Jackson tried to suggest this meant the impact zone was 30 feet from John, but that isn't going to fool the dudes in the Yellow Cottage. No sir! The impact zone was about 15 feet from where John ended up.

**Trooper Paul's Explanation of Injuries**

Trooper Joe Paul was the most important witness to testify.

Clean-shaven from the neck up, Paul looks younger than his 43 years. At five foot seven, he's not imposing. Joe Paul is that guy you want as a neighbor or to coach your kid's soccer team. A Marine veteran from the Iraq War, he's actually typical of many Marines: quiet, undersized, thin, and neat, the kind of men who do a job without making a lot of noise, seeking fanfare, or complaining. He wouldn't want to tell anyone he was a Marine, but he knows his fellow Marines will know, and that's enough. Semper Fi.

Trooper Paul is more comfortable socializing with a very small group of friends, and in that situation, he's garrulous. But in a large group, he'll wait quietly until someone needs him. A problem solver, he's happy to help.

He loves cars, long dreamed of having a hobby car to work on, so not surprisingly, when there was an opening on the CARS team for the Massachusetts State Police in 2015, he jumped on it. This is the Collision Analysis &

Reconstruction Section responsible for investigating and analyzing serious motor vehicle crashes. They use a lot of tools, such as an aerial mapping with drones, and spend much of their time in training. Because Paul had been doing this for nine years, he actually also spent a lot of time training other troopers on the CARS squad.

Joe Paul isn't from New England, so he's a bit of a fish out of water, and that metaphor also applies to him when he had to testify in one of the most-watched trials in years. He had testified in a handful of trials before, but never anything like this. He did fine under direct testimony by prosecutor Adam Lally, but cross-examination by elite defense attorney Alan Jackson will trip anyone up, and the former combat Marine seemed agonized and tripped up under the onslaught.

Part of the problem... a huge part... was the lack of preparation by the overwhelmed prosecutor, who only met once with the most important witness in the trial.

But the prosecution mistakenly didn't see his importance the same way. They unwisely believed that Karen's own words at the crime scene would prove her guilt to the jury, so they neglected the most crucial aspect of the charges: convincing them exactly how John was struck and how the wounds were made.

Unfortunately, this proved to be the weakest part of the State's case. And that's a problem.

Trooper Paul explained that John was facing across the street, with his arm out, when the Lexus swiped him, avoiding the rest of his body, except possibly the mild laceration on his right knee. His explanation left unclear whether the arm was straight out, bent, or held in some way to shield him just before impact.

The impact caused the abrasions on the arm and launched or spun him at an angle toward the lawn. He landed on the back of his head, the frozen ground causing the three-centimeter-long laceration and crushing his skull. The injuries to his head weren't fatal but caused him to lose consciousness. He was then unable to move on his own, and the cold finished him off.

Would this type of collision cause a taillight to shatter?

While no question like this was asked to any of the experts, Dr. Daniel Wolfe, from the ARCCA guys hired by the Feds, said that at over 15 MPH, significant damage to a vehicle occurs upon collision with a human body. This collision was over 24 MPH.

The ARCCA guys did say damage should be visible on John's arm, such as broken bones.

But this part of the ARCCA guys' performance wasn't very impressive. John's body wasn't X-rayed, so there was no way to know if there were fractures. We only know that there were no fractures visible to the naked eye.

Still, with the defense having an expert testify that the wounds on John's arm were from a dog attack, and with experts hired by the Feds saying the wounds were inconsistent with a vehicle collision, and with the State's own medical examiner saying these weren't classic pedestrian collision injuries… the prosecution badly needed to explain to the jury not only how his injuries happened, but why there were so few injuries.

They fell far short.

Trooper Paul wasn't asked to explain how the injuries to John's arm were caused. Neither was the medical examiner. In fact, the prosecution actually made no attempt to explain these injuries at all despite knowing for a year that the defense would focus on those injuries. That's nothing short of stunning.

And yet they expected to win?

Amazingly, inexplicably, yes.

### Human Hair

A human hair, found on a vertical panel above the rear bumper, would prove to contain John's DNA.

This hair took on significance for different reasons at different times in the months leading up to trial. In September of 2023, a lab used by the defense determined that "no human DNA" was found in the tiny sample they were given to test. The defense leaked this to their social media minions, who falsely trumpeted that it was a "nonhuman" hair. Days later, in court, Alan Jackson dramatically made the exact same claim.

Remember YCT Rule #20: It's just pixels?

Anyone with a minimal understanding of science could see through the charade. What the lab had actually concluded was that the sample didn't contain enough DNA because it was too small.

By the time of the trial, this magic trick by the defense no longer worked. The independent lab, Bode Technology, agreed to by both sides, had found a match to John in the mitochondrial DNA. The defense didn't dispute it.

Instead, they now suggested the hair had been planted. The hair had indeed survived a harrowing journey, from 34 Fairview to John's garage, then in the windy blizzard to the McCabe house and back, where it sat outside with snow piling up, then a one-hour journey to Dighton, where it again sat in the driveway, then was towed to the sally port.

But ask yourself a common sense question: if someone was going to plant the hair, why plant it on a VERTICAL panel? Why not plant it on something horizontal, such as the bumper, so it wouldn't fall?

At the end of the day, we can't say how the hair survived. Perhaps several other hairs didn't survive the trips. The hair—possibly from John's arm—had been pressed on during high-speed impact, then possibly iced over. It wasn't critical evidence, in any case, so we can feel free to dismiss it, and it won't impact our analysis.

## DNA on Taillight Piece and Cocktail Glass

None of John's DNA was found on the underside of the Lexus or on the taillight housing. However, his DNA *was* found on the cocktail glass and on a taillight piece.

## Glass Pieces on the Bumper

Five pieces of glass were found on the bumper and nine pieces were found on the ground, in addition to the broken remnant of the cocktail glass.

Glass pieces are actually very difficult to scientifically match. One technique is to look at optical properties under a polarized microscope. There's also a device called GRIM, or Glass Refractive Index Measurement system.

But at the end of the day, the primary way to match glass is to sit down with the pieces, as though attempting to do a really hard 3-D jigsaw puzzle, and come up with physical matches. Yikes. Who wants that job?

You can see why this matching is difficult and the results will probably seem incomplete. And that's what we have here.

None of the five pieces found on the bumper matched the cocktail glass remnant. However, the pieces on the ground matched the cocktail glass, and one of the pieces on the bumper matched with six of the nine pieces on the ground. In addition, two of the pieces found on the bumper likely originated from a similar cocktail glass, though no physical match could be found.

We also have to understand that the glass in a cocktail glass can really vary a lot in the way it's blown. The base, for example, will usually be very different from the walls or the lip.

So it's likely, though far from certain, that all of the pieces found on the bumper were from the same cocktail glass.

## GPS

Every cell phone has a special chip in it designed for one purpose: to pick up signals from whichever of the 24 GPS satellites orbiting the Earth are in range. In order to determine the phone's location, it must pick up a signal from at least four satellites; the more the better. The process of pinpointing location is called triangulation.

Apps like Waze, Google Maps, and Uber access this GPS data.

During forensic analysis of the phone, an extraction—a digital, bit-by-bit copy—is taken. This extraction is available to both the prosecution and defense teams, so they're working with the same copy, the same exact data.

GPS points are normally accurate to within about 15 feet. However, if some of the satellite signals are blocked, the overall signal strength is weaker and the margin of error expands.

But the key thing to understand is this: the signal strength for every second, every plot point, is always known, *so the margin of error is always known.*

This is something that many FKRers get confused about. They will say, "Well, the signal is known to be weak there."

No. That's the cell phone signal, which comes from cell towers. This is different, and more importantly, the signal strength is always known, second by second.

Karen had turned off her location data, so no GPS points were available from her phone. John's phone, however, provided crucial data.

We can unequivocally state this: John's phone never went inside the house. It just didn't.

And that isn't data that could be manipulated or manufactured. Remember, the defense has the exact same data.

There are different locations within the phone where the GPS data can be found. One place is the phone's registry, but what's stored there depends on the settings. Another place is within the databases of the apps that use GPS, such as Waze.

We'll provide a more detailed view of the timeline of John's GPS points later when we discuss the crucial correlation, but for now:

A) 12:24:18: They turned onto Fairview Road;

B) 12:24:40: They reached the far edge of the property, within 15 feet of where John was ultimately found, because this was his last GPS position, which was reached almost eight minutes before his phone stopped moving.

What we know from witnesses in the pickup truck behind the Lexus is that it briefly pulled up near the driveway, then moved up to the far edge of the property, a distance of about 80 feet. It reached this location at 12:24:40.

Did the signal strength ever weaken enough that the margin of error expanded beyond 15 feet and included the house?

Yes.

The margin of error for the whole time John's phone was at 34 Fairview held at 15 feet, with the exception of a quick period of several seconds.

The front door was 72 feet from where John's body was found. At 12:25:30, the signal weakened and the margin of error expanded to 108 feet. So at that point, the phone could have been anywhere within the circle with a radius of a 108 feet.

At 12:25:31 the margin expanded to 200 feet.

At 12:25:32 the margin shrank back to 95 feet.

At 12:25:33 it was 88 feet.

At 12:25:34 it was 72 feet.

At 12:25:35 it was 59 feet.

At 12:25:36 it dropped to 52 feet.

After that, it remained within 15 feet.

So, there's only a four-second period during which the phone, based on the margin of error, could have been inside the house.

At no point are there any plot points that indicate movement in the direction of the driveway or the house.

To believe John went inside the house with his phone, you have to suppose he flew across the yard and then back to where he was found in just four seconds. To achieve this, he would have to be moving close to 25 MPH. Usain Bolt could just about do this at his peak. But even if John O'Keefe had Olympic speed, it gives him no time to go inside, get mauled by a dog and beat up, then carried back unconscious to where he was found.

And this evidence can't just be dismissed. There's no way corrupt police could fudge it. It is what it is. John's phone never went in the house and Elvis is dead. There, we said it.

So, the stories Karen tells about seeing John walk "across the threshold" can't really be true.

Unless… he forgot his phone on the car seat and as she drove off, in a fit of anger, she tossed it out the window into the yard. If that's what happened, she has conveniently forgotten it. And now the defense has to explain how John ended up unconscious on top of his phone.

**John's Health App**

The app is INTERPRETING his movements and imperfectly trying to understand whether he's driving, walking, running, climbing stairs, etc. While it can't know for sure what he's doing… for example, he could be roller skating… one thing it does know is whether there is actual movement or not.

John's phone stopped moving at 12:32:16.

Therefore, either that was near the time he was struck by the Lexus and rendered unconscious, or that was the time the phone was tossed into the yard from the Lexus.

### Vehicle Data

All kinds of sensors within a vehicle are continuously sending information streams through its nerve system. The primary function is safety. Modern cars have sensors that detect objects on the path, sound alarms, and trigger air bags that automatically deploy if there's a crash. The information being measured includes speed, degree of pressure on the accelerator, brake application, and steering wheel position. These systems can help prevent accidents or mitigate the damage in them, but they're also used to gather information to improve vehicle performance, and yes, last but not least, they're used by forensic investigators.

One system that collects and analyzes all this information is the Event Data Recorder (EDR), also known as the "black box," located behind the steering wheel.

The storage capacity of the EDR is limited, so it can't create a record of everything. Unless something triggers it to stop and create an event, it records five seconds of data, then overwrites it continuously. But if something like a crash triggers an event—also called a Crash Data Retrieval (CDR)—then a snapshot is created from five seconds before and five seconds after the event.

So, let's say you pull out of your driveway and strike a telephone pole (don't try this at home, kids). The CDR will record five seconds before and five seconds after the moment you strike the pole.

The EDR in Karen's Lexus didn't create a CDR. It was actually the ARCCA guys who explained why: the difference in size between the vehicle and the object. It's typical in pedestrian strikes that the black box will not be triggered to create an event, so nothing is recorded.

However…

There's another system recording data in Toyota/Lexus vehicles. It's called Tech Stream. It does essentially the same thing, except it's programmed to record in a larger variety of situations. In fact, a year before John's death, the ARCCA guys posted an article on their website explaining that Tech Stream can access data relating to vehicle behavior from a larger number of collisions where traditional EDRs may not record an event.

During most trips in your car, you won't get in an accident and no event is recorded. The Tech Stream, however, can record more events. And the system running in Karen's Lexus did, in fact, record two events around the time prosecutors say Karen struck John. The first event was a three-point turn and the second, eight minutes and four seconds later, was an event where she went in reverse at a speed close to 25 MPH and for a distance calculated to be 62 feet. Trooper Paul explained that four seconds into that event… so, 8:08 after the first triggered event… the data shows signs of a pedestrian strike.

Those signs:

A) The vehicle suddenly slowed .6 MPH despite no change in angle on the accelerator.

B) The steering wheel shifted from 4.5 degrees left to 4.5 degrees right, after being fairly straight before that moment.

Now, one might reasonably ask: could either of these signs have alternative explanations? For example, maybe the car slowing was related to engine performance, and the shifting position of the steering wheel was due to the driver?

Yes, except the key thing is that these events occurred at the same second. Trooper Paul explained that this is recognized in his industry as the classic signs of a pedestrian strike.

Now, while the Tech Stream didn't create a timestamp, we can correlate these unique events with data recorded on John's phone, and that CORRELATION creates practically bulletproof evidence that the Lexus struck John O'Keefe at around 12:32. Patience, grasshopper, we'll get to it!

If the new data obtained turns out to have timestamps, we'll know where the Lexus was when John's phone stopped moving at 12:32:16.

We may know what route Karen took home.

We may know if she returned to the scene of the crime, say around 5:23 A.M.

Let's give you the straight dope as best we understand it. The reason they weren't able to get time stamps for the vehicle data was because the entertainment system needed a software update that just wasn't available before the first trial. Hopefully, we'll get new data for the second trial.

**Voicemails**

Karen's phone connected automatically to John's Wi-Fi "around" 12:36 A.M. Hopefully, in the second trial a more precise time can be provided. Was it 12:36:45? It matters, as we'll see.

At 12:37, Karen left her first voicemail with John. She had called him numerous times on the trip from Fairview, which took around five minutes. It would seem that she parked in the driveway and went into the house.

In this first message, which was likely either from the Lexus or the driveway, she said, *"John, I fucking hate you!"*

At 12:42, the next message comes, but Karen doesn't say anything. However, we hear the car's warning alarms... apparently from Karen moving the Lexus into the garage... then we hear the garage door closing and Karen's boots on the concrete.

So, it would seem she parked in the driveway, went inside, perhaps used the bathroom, then opened the garage door from inside and drove the Lexus in. This and other indications suggest she didn't have a working garage door opener.

At 12:59 comes the third message: *"John, I'm here with your fucking kids, nobody knows where you are, you fucking pervert!"*

She reaches his voicemail a fourth time, but leaves no message.

At 1:11: *"It's 1 A.M. in the morning, I'm with your niece and nephew, you fucking pervert, you're a fucking pervert!"*

At 1:18: *"John, I'm going home. I cannot babysit your niece, I need to go home. You're using me right now, you're fucking another girl, your niece is sleeping next to me, you're a fucking loser, fuck yourself!"*

A final message would come at 5:23, when Karen was on the road searching for John. It's unclear and, depending on what version one hears, it sounds like, *"John, where the fuck are you?"* or *"John, is that you?"*

One thing that is clear in any version: she's terrified.

**Karen's Words**

Karen says she curled up on John's couch to nap at around 1:30 and woke up around 4:30. This matches her phone history, which shows no calls during this time.

Notable in the early voicemails is both what's there and not there. She's angry and thinks John is cheating on her. John had never cheated on her before, and she never suspected him of it, but the relationship was on the rocks and she was drunk.

But there's no indication in the voicemails that she was aware of being in any kind of accident.

She also doesn't make any kind of attempt to leave a trail of false breadcrumbs for investigators. For example, she doesn't say, *"Hi, John, I'm going to sleep, there's leftover spaghetti in the fridge, goodnight!"*

But after her nap, everything changes. At 4:38, she calls John, doesn't leave a message. At 4:40 and 4:42 she calls her parents, but they don't pick up.

Then she calls Katie Camerano, who was working third shift as a hospital nurse. John had been drinking with her husband Mike at C.F. McCarthy's before she met them there. Katie tried to call her husband, at home asleep, but no one knew anything.

Around this time, Kayley was woken in her bedroom by screaming in the hallway. Karen, pacing up and down, was saying something happened to John. She was saying, "What if I hit him?" and "Maybe I did something," and "Maybe a snow plow hit him."

She burst into Kayley's bedroom and had the 14-year-old girl call Jen McCabe. Kayley testified at the trial, but cameras were turned off, so all we have is limited description from the media. But Kayley backed Jen's testimony that Karen initially said she last saw John at the Waterfall until Jen told her they had seen her SUV outside the house.

Jen also testified that Karen mentioned her broken taillight. It's not known if Kayley confirmed that.

Next, Karen called Kerry Roberts and woke her up, screaming, "John's dead! Kerry, Kerry, Kerry…" Then she hung up. A moment later, Karen called again, saying she thought something had happened to John, that maybe he had been hit by a plow.

Karen left at 5:08 to look for John. She called Kerry to say she was on her way to the McCabes' house. After looking for John near the Waterfall, and then possibly near Fairview, Karen reached the McCabes, who were by then trying to stir themselves, getting dressed and making coffee. Matt became alarmed that Karen's screaming outside would wake the neighborhood and their four daughters.

Kerry arrived, and though Karen was insisting they search at 34 Fairview, Kerry and Jen thought it made more sense to check John's house, believing that Karen must have missed him coming home. She was wasted and hysterical. So, Jen drove the Lexus to 1 Meadows while Kerry followed.

After a quick search of John's house, the women got in Kerry's car to go looking. On the way, Karen sat in the middle of the back seat, leaning forward, occasionally screaming, asking if maybe she had hit John.

Arriving at 34 Fairview a little after 6:00, Karen was the one who spotted the figure of John lying buried in the snow by the property edge. She jumped out of the car a second before Kerry came to a stop. While Jen called 911, Karen and Kerry attempted to warm John and provide CPR.

After the first responders arrived, several of them heard Karen repeatedly say, "I hit him, I hit him." At other times, she frequently asked if he was dead.

We need to parse this fairly and objectively… in a both-sides kind of way.

**"I hit him, I hit him."**

The prosecution clearly believed that this was their most important evidence. They led with this during their closing arguments, and they perhaps neglected to properly develop other parts of their case because of it.

Karen has admitted to saying this at the scene, but with a question mark, as in, "Did I hit him?"

There's a distinct difference between "I hit him!" and "Did I hit him?" Is what the first responders heard reliable?

The defense made a big effort to establish that firefighter Katie McLaughlin had invented or distorted this because of her high school relationship with Caitlin Albert, Brian and Nicole's daughter. Indeed, during voir dire, she did underplay her past friendship. No, she didn't perjure herself when describing Caitlin as an acquaintance. They had been in the same circle almost a decade earlier, while in high school, but there's no evidence they were close friends then, and after high school, there seems to be no connection. Undoubtedly if they ran into each other at Dunkin Donuts, there would be an exchange of warm hellos and a minute of catching up… and that's it. If that's not an acquaintance, the word has no meaning.

When McLaughlin heard Karen say, "I hit him," she immediately got the attention of one of the officers. And she recorded this in all in her subsequent interview with investigators.

While it would be very natural and unintentional for first responders to influence each other's memory of what they heard over the next few days, the most likely explanation, given that Karen admits to saying something similar, is that she did in fact say, "I hit him."

However, what does that mean?

To many people we respect, including several retired FBI agents, it means a lot. Their experience is that in situations like this, extreme stress can lead a person to let the truth slip out.

We're not saying this is wrong, but we do say this alone isn't evidence beyond a reasonable doubt. We don't know what was in her head when she said whatever it was she said. As they were taking John away and the women were warming up in the cruiser, Karen thought the blood on her hands was from her period. Her mind was fractured and confused in the most bewildering, world-shattering moment of her life.

And people can't have it both ways. You can't say that Karen was scheming to cover her tracks that morning and at the same time confessing to her crime.

I have long held that the jury wouldn't factor in these statements. When I sensed the prosecution was going to focus on her statements at the scene, I wished for a line of communication to them to prevent the mistake.

Juries take their work very seriously. They know the stakes and, in this case, Karen faced spending much of her life in prison.

Each of us might have different ways of processing the logic of the evidence, but with a jury, it's a collective effort, which involves a different process. Twelve people have to agree unanimously. That requires simplifying the discussion as much as possible, trying to find things that everyone can agree on, and proceeding from there.

Here's an example:

John was found unconscious on the lawn near the street. Check.

A contributing cause of death was hypothermia, so he had been outside for a while. Check.

Karen dropped him off. Check.

She was drunk. Check.

Her vehicle was damaged. Check.

But when a juror raises her hand and proposes that she confessed at the scene, there isn't going to be anything close to agreement. Some jurors will say she was merely confused and asking if she hit him. Others might say the memory if the first responders isn't perfectly reliable. With no agreement as to what exactly she was saying and what was in her mind, the jurors will discard this. Completely.

As the jury builds step by step toward conclusions, any weak link in the chain causes it to break. So, they collectively decide to leave it out and focus on the physical evidence, the data, and perhaps other testimony that might be more meaningful, such as what Karen said in her calls to Kerry at 5:00 A.M.

This was confirmed by the two juror interviews, which came out later on *TB Daily News*, and another on a podcast hosted by M. William Phelps. They gave very descriptive accounts of deliberations, and the statements at the scene don't seem to have factored into their process at all. So, the prosecution's decision to focus on this led to a predictable disaster.

We'll never know what was in Karen's head in those moments, and maybe she doesn't either. Fortunately, we don't need to. There's plenty of other evidence.

# 3. REASONABLE DOUBT?

The State charged Karen in the first trial with three crimes:

1) Leaving the scene of an accident;
2) OUI (Operating Under the Influence) manslaughter;
3) Second-degree murder.

Indications are that none of the jurors seemed convinced of charges one and three. Part of this is because both of those charges depend on proving she was aware that she had struck something, and the jurors seem to have doubts about that. But they may also have tabled discussions on those two charges until they could first reach a decision on whether the State had proven that she did, in fact, strike John with her vehicle. And on that, it seems that the jury was initially split 6/6, and by the end had moved to 9/3 in favor of guilt.

This book has focused on whether she actually struck John with her Lexus, whether at any point she became aware of it and failed to act before he was found, or at any point took any actions to cover it up.

A jury must convict beyond a reasonable doubt. Not beyond any doubt, but beyond a reasonable doubt.

Here are the standard jury instructions:

*Reasonable doubt is proof that leaves you firmly convinced of the defendant's guilt. It is not required that the government prove guilt beyond all possible doubt. A reasonable doubt is a doubt based upon reason and common sense and is not based purely on speculation. It may arise from a careful and impartial consideration of all the evidence, or from lack of evidence. If, after considering all the evidence, you are not convinced beyond a reasonable doubt that the defendant is guilty; it is your duty to find the defendant not guilty. Conversely, if you are convinced beyond a reasonable doubt, then you should find the defendant guilty.*

In many cases, the defense attempts to create reasonable doubt by using the third-party culprit defense, which essentially says, "You got the wrong guy."

And it does happen too often in American justice, where the police, under tremendous pressure to solve a case and get a killer off the streets, suffer a rush to judgment. They develop a suspect that seems to fit their expectations, and then they develop tunnel vision, tuning out other possible suspects and ignoring any evidence which points to anyone else.

Karen Read isn't one of those cases.

To repeat, either Karen Read did the crime, or there was an elaborate cover-up, one which included a large evidence-planting operation and which almost certainly required the participation by multiple troopers and investigators.

This isn't a case where the police got tunnel vision and missed the real killers.

Therefore, it's not enough to show that the investigation was flawed or that the investigators had a bias. There's a mountain of evidence that matches John's death to Karen's operation of her vehicle. If the defense is going to create truly reasonable doubt, they have to show that investigators actively "framed" Karen Read in order to protect someone else. That's why David Yannetti began the trial by making that very accusation.

They don't have to prove third-party culprit. But they do have to make it plausible enough to add up to reasonable doubt. Just keep in mind that the question we have to keep asking ourselves at every step of the way isn't whether the police could have *missed* something, but whether they could have *manufactured* something.

### Yellow Cottage Tales: True Crime Creepypasta

Remember the face on Mars? In 1976, the Viking 1 space probe sent back images that looked like a giant face crafted in stone. Kind of like a Martian sphinx, the face seemed to be remnants of some long extinct civilization on the planet.

A whole cottage industry grew around this over the next two decades. And you didn't have to be convinced it was actually a face to find it interesting. All you had to believe was that it was at least possible. The idea was tantalizing.

But another probe zipped around the Red Planet in 1998, sent back clearer pics, and it was now apparent that there was no face, just natural geological features that only looked that way from a perfect angle. So, NASA sucked the fun out of the fantasy.

Not that there aren't still believers; there always will be a handful for whom the idea is just too rich to let go. Which is fine; no one is harmed.

And, of course, there's not much harm in thinking that Jack the Ripper was actually Lizzie Borden on vacation, or that Abraham Lincoln really was a vampire hunter.

But our thirst for the strange, the mysterious, and the unsolved can be a problem with things that are current. How many people followed Alex Jones into believing the massacre of first-graders at Sandy Hook Elementary School was actually a false-flag operation pulled off by gun-control advocates?

Look, there ARE real cover-ups. There are instances where police plant evidence. And there are plenty of examples of people being falsely convicted. The system will always be far from perfect because the system consists of human beings.

In my bar industry days, I worked with and dealt with a lot of cops. I witnessed and sometimes was at the center of a lot of events involving them too, enough to fill a book. And if you'll rate my experience as worthy, I want to tell you that the majority of police officers I've known are of a kind of character where you would want them as a friend or a neighbor. Most of them brought a sense of decency and fairness to the job as well.

But of course, I've seen the other side more than a few times too. And because of the power of a police officer, it sticks in your memory. It's unsettling.

No one gets the benefit of the doubt, as far as I'm concerned. Cops are just as capable of corruption as the next bloke, and because of their position, have substantially more opportunity for misdeeds. No sir, no benefit of the doubt.

But perhaps another rule from the Cottage can help us sort our way through.

**Rule #14: It's not just about motive. It's about SUFFICIENT motive.**

This is an important rule to apply when weighing the conspiracy theory in the Karen Read case. Remember, unless the police planted evidence, Karen, as they might say down in Hannibal, Mississippi, is just plum guilty.

I've always focused on means instead of motive, motive being much harder to nail down, since the possibility of something unseen can never be eliminated. But the question of motive is frequently posed to those of a FKR inclination—as in "why would Proctor plant evidence?"—and they invariably reply with some variation of "cops stick together."

But while this provides a possible motive, does it provide a SUFFICIENT one?

See, you have to look at the stakes: what does the cop risk losing and what is the risk of exposure?

As to what a trooper is risking in planting evidence in a murder conspiracy, the charges would be obstruction, conspiracy, and perjury… So, loss of career, the destruction of his family, and, oh yeah, years in the clink.

And the risk of exposure would be extremely, extremely high. Did I say extremely? I meant to say EXTREMELY.

Most people in the FKR ecosystem believe that taillight pieces were plucked from the Lexus at the sally port after 5:40 P.M. That's 16 hours after John was dropped off at 34 Fairview. Sixteen hours for someone—anyone—to snap a pic of that taillight, or a clear video to capture it. Fifteen hours while the Lexus wasn't in police custody, so they had absolutely no idea what was being done with it all day.

Did I say extremely high risk?

And you don't think those troopers would have been aware of that risk?

Don't tell me they aren't smart enough… You've got to be (Larry David voice) pretty, pretty smart to pull off a caper like this: bringing in multiple official accomplices, influencing the medical examiner and the criminologists, and lying to grand juries.

Also, there was no way to plant those pieces without the seven troopers from the SERT team and Lt. Tully being in on it. And, of course, Trooper Bukhenik. Canton cops were there, as well as a news truck. Could they really be sure that EVERYONE would stay quiet about this murder conspiracy? What if someone in the house broke ranks? Or the medical examiner blew the whistle, saying John had been attacked?

So there has to be SUFFICIENT motive for the troopers to take on all this risk, gambling with the welfare of their families and with their very freedom, since they face the slammer if they planted evidence and obstructed justice.

Why? Because Proctor's sister went to high school with the sister of Chris Albert's wife?

I was struggling with questions like these as my series of narrated videos progressed. It was, in many ways, a lonely struggle. But I raised some of these points in a post on Reddit, which someone saw: Turtleboy.

It pissed him off, so he invited me onto his show with a clear plan to try to destroy me, and therefore silence my questions.

Well, THAT would be my first live show!

# PART FIVE: SOCIAL MEDIA

# 1. THE VILLAIN ARRIVES

On April 12, 2023, Karen's defense team filed a motion to get Brian Albert's phone, and in that motion they outlined, for the first time, what would become the conspiracy… or third-party culprit theory. It centered on the data found by their expert, Richard Green, which claimed that John walked 116 steps and ascended/descended three flights of stairs. Green also claimed that Jen McCabe searched for "Hos long to die in cold" at 2:27 A.M.

The defense further insisted that John's injuries were due to a mauling by the German shepherd inside the house. They theorized that John was attacked inside and carried outside later to die in the cold.

But the story didn't take hold with the public until Karen and her team reached out to a controversial blogger with a large following: Aidan Kearney, aka Turtleboy. After an intense 48 hours of him going back and forth with Karen's team, he released his blog article on April 18. Were it not for that article, none of us would be talking about this case.

Two things any person should have understood from that very first day.

A) That story was entirely fed to Turtleboy by Karen and her defense team. No part of it was the result of investigative journalism.

B) He saw this story as the big break he had been waiting for, the thing that would propel him into national attention.

We didn't need to know anything about Aidan Kearney or his blog to understand this. Look, as we wander through life, each in our own personal episodes of *Curb Your Enthusiasm*… getting into jams, forming observations, learning lessens, making mistakes… it's important to develop some common-sense street smarts. If you walk onto a used-car lot, and some fella with slick hair and a gold-toothed smile tells you that a certain car is absolutely perfect for you, you don't just go, "Really? Wow! Who do I make the checks out to?"

As we experience the world, we hopefully develop a sense of skepticism. Some street smarts.

In that first Turtleboy article, there was a lot of information that could only have come from the defense. And there was absolutely no attempt to question ANY of the defense claims.

So, either the article was written by the most inexperienced journalist in the world, or it was written by an ADVOCATE, someone who was essentially representing Karen Read.

That was just common sense, and if you couldn't see that on day one, we've got a car that's perfect for you!

That didn't mean the information in it was necessarily wrong or that Karen wasn't the victim of a frame job. No. What it meant was anyone with the slightest street smarts should have said to themselves that they're getting only *one side* of the story, a side being presented by someone on trial for murder… and presented by someone who expected to benefit personally in a substantial way.

Those things were obvious to people with common sense. Turtleboy wasn't seeking the truth, and he wasn't trying to bring truth to his audience. He had hitched his wagon to this mule, and he was going to ride it into his destiny.

While this was obvious enough from the start, it eventually became confirmed by police investigators. We have spoken many times to Natalie Berschneider Wiweke, who had been a friend of Karen's in college and who became her confidante soon after Karen's arrest, advising her and providing emotional support. When Karen first reached out to Aidan Kearney, it was through intermediaries, such as one of his capo de regimes, a longtime "Turtle Rider" known as the Pitbull. She would be falsely listed as Aidan's lawyer when he was in jail, presumably so prison officials couldn't listen in on his calls with her.

I would come to learn how the Pitbull functions as one of Turtleboy's bad lieutenants, digging for dirt on people they want to control, creating fictionalized smear, threatening anyone who disagrees with them, and trying to control news reporters, prosecutors, and police with the threat of social media destruction. It's fairly well organized and pretty self-conscious. They understand how much power the threat of social smear gives them, and indeed, it's really the only source of their power. Aidan would continue uttering his barely disguised threats of mob destruction from jail, using his capos to put his words out on the blog.

### Baghdad Bob

So, for the first few weeks, Karen used Natalie as a go-between for communications with Aidan. However, records also show that during this period Aidan had numerous calls, both with Alan Jackson and David Yannetti, Karen's lawyers.

After a few weeks, Karen began using the encryption app called Signal because the messages automatically disappear minutes after being read. So, she understood that what she was doing was suspect and shady.

After about a month, Karen realized that, since she was using an encryption app, she no longer needed Natalie. Therefore, she ended the friendship… which gives real insight into her nature… and from that time on, she just communicated directly with Aidan over the phone in daily calls and over Signal.

But for completely innocent reasons, Natalie had been screen-shotting the messages between Karen and Aidan. Because when you're acting as a go-between, it's the easiest way to remember the message you're supposed to send.

We've seen those screen shots. At the very beginning, Aidan did ask hard questions, because he was very wary of being duped. Aidan does have enough street smarts to be skeptical, and it wouldn't be the first time that someone tried to use him and his blog to get their version of their story out.

The issue with Aidan wasn't a lack of street smarts, but rather a complete lack of integrity. If at some point he learned he had been duped, there was exactly zero chance of him ever coming clean with his audience, and indeed, throughout this case, as evidence became available that contradicted the conspiracy theory, he just refused to report on it. He was essentially Baghdad Bob.

But something about this conspiracy resonated with the public. It's true that choosing Turtleboy was a clever decision by a defense team trying to contaminate the jury pool by whipping up a frenzy. And it's also true that there was no one else in New England, maybe even nationally, who could make this catch fire in the way Aidan did.

However, there were also aspects to the story itself that gave it tremendous potential to catch fire. We'll go over a lot of that in a minute in the Ground Zero chapter, but let's touch on some broad themes here.

**Profiling a Karen**

Karen stands out in the current world of high-profile cases because she doesn't fit the mold of the standard female killer. We asked ChatGPT to list recent high-profile female killers. Casey Anthony, charged (and acquitted) with killing her two-year-old daughter, demonstrated crystal clear psychopathic behavior. The responsibilities of being a mother interfered with Anthony's desire to party.

Jodi Arias is another classic psychopath charged (and acquitted) with killing her boyfriend. Her alleged motive was jealousy and rage.

Dalia Dippolito was a sex worker who attempted to have her husband killed by a hitman.

Clara Harris caught her husband having an affair and confronted him in a parking lot, running him over in a rage several times.

Pamela Smart conspired with her teenage lover and his friends to murder her husband.

Gypsy Rose Blanchard killed her abusive mother after being tortured and harmed her whole life.

Melanie McGuire murdered her husband, dismembered his body, and put the pieces in suitcases.

None of these cases found sympathy with the public, except Gypsy Rose Blanchard, whose murderous act was somewhat understandable, and there was no question of her guilt.

Karen Read is a financial analyst and associate professor with no criminal history. She wasn't the victim of abuse in any of her known relationships. She's attractive, well dressed, petite, upper middle class, educated… and White. Each of those things is a factor in making her the ideal victim/hero in a narrative.

What else makes an ideal victim? An underdog fighting against powerful forces. That's not at all the reality of it here, but that's the narrative, and we Americans have a huge soft spot for underdog stories. Making the main character an underdog is the surest way to success in any story, from Cinderella to Rocky.

What are these powerful forces Karen is said to be up against? Cops. Cops and their professional cousins, prosecutors. In other words, "the system." In the '60s, they called it "the man." The system represents this kind of nefarious force that's greedily oppressing people while protecting their own.

I was a bar owner in a large city and employed many cops and regularly encountered many more. The vast majority of cops are regular people, good people doing a job that at times can be hard. But there are, no doubt, some bad apples in law enforcement, and when you encounter them, because of the authority and power they have, it's disturbing.

However, because I've worked with the police, there's less mystery about them. To me, they're real people, not mythical figures. But to the general public, there's more mystery and more distrust.

Yet I've also known a lot of the FKRers who had family in law enforcement. So there really is something more than just a general mistrust of cops that feeds this.

Interestingly, there are almost no people of color within the Free Karen Read movement. The Blacks and Hispanics we've talked to tend to be baffled by the obsession with this case.

So why exactly does it resonate?

The best answer is that it's just the right combination of ingredients. Underdog character, a person with whom older White people can identify, someone up against supposedly powerful forces, mistrust of police. And, of course, plenty of things that seem odd—all of the conditions to create the perfect storm.

There could be one more aspect too: the moment was right. The public was vulnerable to this narrative at this time in history.

Witch hunts and similar hysterias, such as pogroms and Red Scares always come at a time of anxiety and during transitional periods where authority is being challenged. The Salem witch trials came in 1692. Fifteen years before that, a quarter of the population had been wiped out by Native Americans in King Phillip's War. During that war, Indians sprang from the woods, abducting men and women working in the fields, and burned down their homes. After that, the colonists lived in terror about what lurked in the woods.

But it was also a time when the grandchildren of the original settlers were questioning the strict values of the Puritans. Therefore, there was an underlying anxiety about their future and about authority. And right in the middle, between the elderly original settlers and the more rebellious grandchildren, was the second generation, the middle-aged children of the settlers. And THEY were the ones who fueled the witch hysteria, hurling accusations against neighbors and settling petty grudges.

Just as with the Karen Read mob.

The overwhelming majority of people stirred up in this case are in their 40s and 50s, not at all your usual protesters. Lacking the hardiness of their parents and grandparents, they're more dependent on the "system," so they're anxious about their future, about social security and healthcare. When you're dependent on someone, part of you grows resentful of them. Is that part of what's fueling a weird resentment of the system in this case?

Similar things happened in the Red Scare of the 1920s and McCarthyism of the '50s. As with Salem, these came a half generation after convulsive war, and they came at times of social anxiety and challenge to the old culture.

The Karen Read hysteria comes a couple of years after the deeply unsettling COVID-19 pandemic, a time of forced shutdowns and looming economic calamity. It came a half generation after wars in Iraq and Afghanistan were winding down. It came at a time when the internet had been upsetting the social order.

### Lighting the Match

The final necessary ingredient to creating this hysteria was the fact that the defendant and her lawyers were very willing and very adept at using social media to do it. They met extensively with the blogger, Aidan Kearney, who was able to spread their theories to a large audience. As other prominent players in social media came forward, they brought them into the fold. Grifters on YouTube, understanding that conspiracy sells, quickly jumped on the bandwagon, as did defense lawyers hoping to drum up new business, and Karen would bring several of these people as her guests into the tiny courtroom during the trial.

As the hysteria began to grow in the public, even mainstream journalists, ever eager to add viewers, jumped into the game.

But almost no one was asking hard questions or trying to look at the case objectively. Karen was willing and eager to take advantage, doing several national shows: *20/20*, *Nightline*, *Dateline*, and local shows such as *Fox 25*.

It was a risky strategy. Karen doesn't come off well on camera unless it's a very quick sound bite. She has very poor impulse control, and this was a problem in court. But the biggest problem was her ever-changing story, a story filled with claims that don't seem to match the evidence. The State was unable to get the unedited footage from these news sources in time to use it at the first trial, but the expectation is that they'll be used in the second trial.

### It's on us!

Finally, there's this: we in the public need to do a better job at learning how to analyze evidence. How to weigh probabilities. How to develop a sense of street smarts.

Not just us civilians, but even many people who should know better, such as lawyers. There is no shortage of lawyers on YouTube and on TV saying things that make absolutely no sense.

*Who the fuck are you to say that?*

I hear you. I'm not a lawyer. But the problem isn't knowledge of the law. The problem is a matter of being able to weigh possibilities logically.

In a moment, I'm going to bring you through that logic step by step. I'm going to provide the reasonable explanations for most of the odd things that fuel the conspiracy. And I'm going to give you powerful evidence for the prosecution which, if effectively presented, will be a nightmare for the defense to combat.

But first, let's finally drop into Ground Zero… and into the storm.

**Yellow Cottage Tales: You're Live!**

As Turtleboy began his show, I sat in front of my laptop like your grandfather trying to read the menu at the restaurant by scanning the QR code. I was in the backroom online, thousands already watching. Though I understood that his plan was to crush and embarrass me, the only thing I was stressing about was whether my mic and speakers were hooked up right.

My first live show.

By this time, a team was just starting to form at the channel. I had come up with the idea for a documentary that focused on the monsters that people like Dave McGrath and Melanie Perkins had chased, and also on the obsessions that such a chase can lead to. An old friend, Tom Fleming, who had experience and training in video production, joined the team, and we were planning our first shoot for August 1, doing a lot of work to prepare for it.

Others were volunteering to join the project, and how had they discovered us? Free Karen Read.

The movement struck a chord with people. Just why remains a hot topic for analysis by people much more qualified than me and whose names have acquired a lot of letters at the end. But something about this case really resonated with a segment of the population. And because of my *Framed?* series, many of these folks were drawn to my channel and were eager to help with other projects.

So after a decade in the wilderness following the loss of my bar, a time of struggling on my own to find relevance and meaning, this felt… good.

I was never the guy who sought meaning in his life by joining causes—you know, Save the Bedbugs, or whatever—nor did I become part of committees, volunteer groups or clubs. I was the opposite of a busybody. Your business is your business. But as a bar owner, a lot of people would come to me for help, whether employees or regular customers. I always did my best, and there's a feeling of satisfaction that comes with that.

In the wilderness years, there was none of that, so life felt a little empty. But now, because of Karen Read, we had a small community forming at the channel. We were planning other projects, nothing to do with FKR, but she was kind of a unifying glue because everyone was convinced of her innocence.

Except me.

But the others felt I at least leaned in the same direction, so that was good enough for them. And now, here I was waiting backstage for the Turtleboy show, the very beating heart of Free Karen Read. What would I do? How would it go?

You have to understand that I'm not that smart. There's a strength in knowing that. I won't be applying to lecture at any colleges or trying to build a better mousetrap. I can't fix a car, remember everyone's name at a dinner for five, or put up a shelf… at least not a level one.

But one thing I am solid at is logical thinking. It comes from a lifetime of practice, and because I TRUST in logic. I know everyone thinks they trust in logic, but I actually do.

When I was a kid, a kind of Catholic urban legend went around that if you walked up the stairs backward while at the same time reading the Our Father in reverse, when you got to the top, the devil himself would appear behind you and would try to push you down the stairs. There were two sides of me when it came to this myth. On the one hand, I was the neighborhood storyteller, the kid who scared the other kids. I could invent and embellish in a way that held their attention. I'm sure there were plenty of kids across the city who were better at this than me, but in the small pond of my street, I was the king at that one thing.

On the other hand, as the boy who created and embellished stories, I knew that stories were created and embellished. So when I heard about the devil at the top of the stairs, I was as skeptical as a dog in the car on the way to the vet. It knows something's up.

So I took the bet.

That's right. When I heard about the devil on the stairs, I told the kids I would try it. And while actually going up those stairs, reading backward from a prayer book, I was encouraged by this thought: if it was true, the emergency room would be full of kids who had been pushed down stairwells, because even though most kids would be too scared to try it, there would be no shortage of kids with something to prove.

The Sullivans and the Lafrances watched me from the bottom of the stairs as I ascended. It was Halloween season, of course, so my pulse did quicken and, in my imagination, I could feel the devil taking shape behind me, a little more solid with every step I took, his warm breath blowing on my neck. But I trusted in the idea that this story had just started somewhere with some kid like me looking to wow his buddies.

I'm tempted to tell you that I was wrong, that the devil and I shook hands at the top of the stairs and cut a deal. Obviously, I didn't negotiate a very good one, considering where things went in my life, but like I said, I'm no Einstein.

But I still put my trust in logic. Let's go back a moment to Delphi. By the time I was researching the case, five years after the deaths of Abby and Libby, a lot was starting to happen. The creep who had catfished Libby, Kegan Kline, was in jail awaiting trial and said to be cooperating about his involvement. A podcast called Murder Sheet had even got their hands on the police interrogation of Kegan, and also his roommate from jail reported that Kline said that day he had waited for his father in the car by the cemetery behind the trail, and his dad returned covered in blood. There were reports of a vast pedophile network in the region which the Klines were thought to be plugged into.

However, despite all this, I had concluded the killer had acted alone, and that the girls were just in the wrong place at the wrong time.

Why?

Because the investigators had Libby's phone and any other electronics she used. They had access to her accounts. They'd had five years to dig into that. And there was no indication that they had recovered any messages from the girls telling anyone they were going to the trail that day.

I read Kline's interrogation transcript, and the cops didn't mention any such communications. And they 100% would have. So, to me, that meant no communications like that were ever found. And it seemed likely that after five years they would have been.

It was hard to maintain this conclusion because no one else in the online community seemed to agree with it. I have a good friend from Ohio, DJ, who used to work in federal law enforcement, a man whose judgment I have incredible respect for. He remained convinced the Klines were involved... and why wouldn't he? Where there's smoke, there's fire, and there was enough smoke to raise five alarms. I told DJ that if the Klines weren't involved, it really was the Mother of All Coincidences... and yet that's what I believed we were looking at! Because if no one knew the girls were going to be there, then they weren't targeted ahead of time, but rather it was an opportunistic predator.

I stuck with that logic through hell and ankle-deep water. I kept an open mind that some communication might emerge. Richard Allen has since been convicted of murder and sentenced to life in prison.

But you can surely see my weakness: I will stick to what I think is logical no matter what, even when it's not in my personal interest. Pointing a finger at Kline would have been good for my channel, and if it harmed him, who cares, because this is a creepy and truly dangerous dude who gets off on violence against children. There was a thousand percent more interest in Delphi than in Karen Read. So why not play that angle? Push the Kline/conspiracy stuff and reap the views?

Because it wasn't what logic was telling me. And I trust in logical analysis.

When Turtleboy finally brought me from backstage onto his show, naturally I had technical difficulties. Of course I did! Wrong mic, wrong speakers, wrong camera. I don't recall exactly, but after several seconds, he was about to boot me from the show when finally, I appeared, like Lazarus, looking like I didn't know how I got there.

He started right in, reading from the Reddit post that had provoked him. I held up fine, however, because logic is the kind of shelter you can always retreat to in a storm. I said that if the 2:27 search of "Hos long..." took place, then there's something crooked going on, but that there were now competing experts on both sides. He pointed out that the defense expert had no incentive to lie, because his reputation was on the line, but the same logic applied to the independent expert hired by the prosecution, didn't it?

The episode was actually quite civil, so I survived it without in any way harming my standing with the FKR community or, more important to me, with my new team. So onward and upward we went.

A week or so later, I decided to attempt the first live show on my own channel, and we streamed a Karen Read hearing. Dave broadcast live outside the courthouse, amid a crowd of hundreds of FKR supporters, while I was at home in front of my laptop, so we had a crude in-studio/on-scene thing going on. But in a way that only we could do it, with me having trouble with my headset and Dave's phone making ear-piercing feedback, it was rough.

But as bad as it was, we actually had 2600 people watching it live! Try to understand how that feels. I never in my life had any ambition to be a broadcaster, but I had spent thousands of hours making videos that generally got, at best, hundreds of views. Now there were over two thousand listening to the show live.

Dave would approach ladies on a bench, and when they found out who he was with, they said, "Oh, we love the Yellow Cottage!"

After this, we set up a private room on Discord, a chat app, and our little team grew to over a dozen people. In preparation for the documentary shoot, we started doing nightly shows with Dave, who would prove much more popular, joining me. One of the new recruits who volunteered to join us for our documentary shoot was an intelligent woman, Erica, whom we soon invited to join us on the show. And the shows now became a threesome, with Erica and me always wondering what the unpredictable Dave and his ham-for-the-cam four-year-old son Connor would do next.

I hadn't launched the channel with exactly that in mind, but close to it in that I always wanted to build it into a team.

We now had that, and there were even enough donations coming in to help pay for the small projects we were attempting.

This was the high point of Yellow Cottage Tales.

# PART SIX: INTO THE STORM

# 1. A PERFECT STORM

In Sebastian Junger's novel *The Perfect Storm*, the catastrophe is described as an extraordinary event that might occur once in a lifetime. It was a rare convergence of three weather systems: a high-pressure system from the Great Lakes, a low over the Atlantic, and Hurricane Grace coming in from the Caribbean. The result was intense winds, massive waves, and a storm that lasted five days.

Looking further back, what led to the high and the low-pressure systems and the late-season hurricane?

Bear with me a moment, I'm cooking up a metaphor!

Cold air masses from the Arctic descended over the Great Lakes, pushing air down, creating high pressure. When the Arctic air masses ran into the air flowing north from the Gulf, the warm air was forced up, creating the low. And the hurricane began as a tropical disturbance coming off the coast of Africa. In *The Perfect Storm*, these all came together in a rare and powerful confluence of timing. It happens maybe once or twice a century.

What are the parallels in the Free Karen Read crusade? What air masses were moving, pressures falling, and disturbances forming?

Let's go back to our Mason-Dixon Line: when Karen met David Yannetti for the first time in person. It was through the prison bars shortly before her arraignment. She had been arrested Tuesday, February 1, and spent the night in jail. Yannetti went over the charging document with her: head wound and hypothermia, Karen showing people her broken taillight, saying, "I hit him, I hit him," and taillight pieces from her car found buried in the snow.

Then guards whisked her to court to be arraigned.

Yannetti told the court that his client had "no criminal intent" and that she loved the victim. He repeated this to the media minutes later on the courthouse steps.

But one thing he didn't say was, "My client didn't do this."

Which means Karen didn't *tell* him that she didn't do it.

In no way, shape, or form did Karen tell her defense attorney on February 2, a short time before her arraignment, that she didn't strike John with her vehicle. Had she done so, he would have said this in court. It can always be changed later, but the normal starting point is, "My client didn't do this; we look forward to our day in court!"

That didn't happen, though.

As we look for origins, it's important to understand that by the time of her arraignment on February 2, no one had yet planted in the minds of Karen or her defense attorney the notion that John might have been killed by someone else.

However, by then, rumors were already starting to gel in Canton.

## The Canton Bag

The drinking culture in the Canton area is unlike anything I've ever seen. I grew up in Lawrence and owned a bar in Worcester for many years, and the drinking culture in Canton seems to be unique. It's a culture that has an upside—alcohol strengthens the social bonds—and a downside highlighted by the tragic end of John O'Keefe.

When I went to appear on Court TV at the Blue Ribbon BBQ in Dedham, a restaurant without a liquor license, someone from Canton whom I had never met dropped me a gift by my plate of ribs: a Jack Daniels nip. She explained, somewhat sheepishly, that she had a "Canton Bag" with her.

*What is that*? I wondered. It turned out to be a duffel bag loaded with enough nips to turn any event into a Super Bowl party. She soon delivered me a second little bottle. (We'll leave the reader to figure out what happened to the first one!)

This type of thing was so common that they actually had a name for it: the Canton Bag. Subsequent research (some of it fun!) would affirm the popularity of the Canton Bag. School sports are huge in this town, and parents are very actively involved as coaches or helping to raise money for the teams. But these sports also become the center of social life as the parents reach their 30s and 40s and the kids reach high school. Wednesdays and Saturdays are big local sports days, but any time there's a game, one of the parents will host a "pre-game" before their child's sporting event. There will be drinks. Then they head off to the game. At least one person will have a Canton Bag with them. Then the partying will continue afterward, either at another parent's home or at a local watering hole. That was the occasion for everyone getting together at the Waterfall the night of the tragedy: a youth basketball game.

So, it shouldn't surprise you to learn that Ground Zero for Free Karen Read is an Irish tavern with excellent food and a very attentive staff: the Hillside Pub.

A townie bar with a local clientele, it's friendly to outsiders but also cautious and wary. The joint fills up before and after a local game, especially on Saturdays.

The cast of characters in the Karen Read case—witnesses, the defendant, and many key figures—were all known at the Hillside, where they were regulars in the social life that flows as smooth as the Guinness on tap.

Karen, not from Canton, fit right in once she started dating John. Before long, she didn't even need to have him with her to head over to the Hillside, and that's where she got the cell phone number of Agent Higgins from someone else who knew him, and she started text-flirting with him out of the blue. That's also likely where Karen first met Tom Beatty.

Tom Beatty is a hard-drinking hulk of a man who looks you in the eye and doesn't hesitate to buy the first round. At six foot two, 250 pounds, the construction worker has plenty of free time between jobs, and during those down periods, his habitat ranges from Dunkin Donuts in the morning to C.F. McCarthy's by noon and eventually to… you guessed it… the Hillside Pub. And if one of his two athletic daughters has a game, he wouldn't miss it for the world.

Beatty isn't what you would call a deep thinker, but he knew all the players involved: the O'Keefes, the Alberts, and the McCabes.

And he knew Karen Read, who flirted with him across the bar, and with whom Beatty wouldn't only stay in daily contact after John's death, but whom he would ask out on a date.

In that information alone, you can already sense perhaps the first gust of wind that would lead to the cyclone. But as I've said, what really moves a human being can be murky and complicated, something that we can glimpse but maybe never get a full picture of. Canton is a town where the high school kids from the last generation stick around and stay in the same cliques while their kids form their own factions. Tom Beatty, however, actually grew up in nearby but very different Dorchester. He's now a part of the social fabric of Canton, mostly accepted by the Old Guard, but he didn't go to high school with them. Does that matter? Well, the McCabes and the Alberts *did* go to that high school. So, for that matter, did lead investigator Michael Proctor. Maybe at times Beatty felt slightly… just slightly… like an outsider.

His wife left him to raise their daughters because, according to him, he hadn't "grown up." However, he's fiercely loyal to his girls. The oldest, Erin, was—like Colin

Albert and Allie McCabe—a senior in high school at the time of John's death. She also played high school sports, including basketball. For much of her life, she had been in a tight circle of friends that included Allie.

But then something happened, and she was no longer in that circle.

All of which is normal high school bullshit, especially when it comes to teenage girls. There's really no need to dig into the cause of her ejection from the circle. Who would want anyone digging into stuff that happened to us when we were teenagers? But it can be very hurtful at the time, whatever the cause. So, there seems to have been some friction within the high school circle, and given how tightly intertwined the social lives of the parents are with local sports, and how close they are to their kids, it would be natural for that tension to spread to the adults, a simmering fire that might draw more oxygen at places like the Hillside.

## 2. MYSTERIOUS CALL

That simmering fire might color the way unfolding events are interpreted. It might cast something like a mysterious phone call in a different light. A little thing that could have been, depending on one's view, either a nothingburger or a clue to an actual cover-up. It's the kind of thing that, in this case, fanned the winds of conspiracy theory in the earliest stages, because… such a call actually took place at 12:31 the night John died. That mysterious call happened right around the same time the State says Karen backed up her Lexus at 24.2 MPH for 62 feet.

At 12:31, Colin Albert called Erin Beatty. The call went unanswered. The purpose is unknown. The Beatty phone bill confirms the call.

And according to his health app, John's phone last moved at 12:32:16.

Was it that call that sprouted the idea in the Beattys' minds that the official police narrative on what happened to John wasn't the real story?

# 3. IN THE JUICE

The dream of any cop toiling away in anonymity is to find the key evidence in a homicide that leads to charging the killer. And the dream for anyone working as a corrections officer is to work as a cop.

In the spring of 2014, those two dreams came crashing together in Steve Scanlon. A gruff man, Scanlon had spent his life working in jobs adjacent to law enforcement: sheriff's department, corrections officer, etc. And he had climbed the ranks by the time he reached his 50s, reaching the job of deputy director of internal affairs in the Worcester sheriff's office.

But the dream of being "in the juice" never dies, and that's what eventually brought Steve Scanlon onto center stage of the Karen Read case.

But before that came a powerful hint of what was to come in March and April 2014 when Scanlon helped recover the body of a five-year-old boy left dead in a suitcase on the side of a highway.

With the boy missing, and the boyfriend of the child's mother sitting in the Worcester County jail on drug charges, Scanlon saw opportunity. Placing a snitch next to the boyfriend's jail cell, he motivated him to get the boyfriend talking, and by whatever methods, the suspect told the snitch exactly where the suitcase containing the body was.

This led Scanlon and a partner from the sheriff's department to search the highway location. During their first search, a trooper pulled them over in order to inquire what they were doing, and Scanlon lied to the trooper that they were looking for a lost hubcap. They ended the search empty-handed but the next day, after getting more detailed information from the snitch, they went out again, and this time they made the horrific find. They didn't touch the suitcase but called the superintendent, whom they had already informed of ongoing events, and the proper authorities were called to the scene.

The problem is that, as heroic as those actions were, they were also highly improper. The sheriff's department has no jurisdiction over homicide scenes, something Scanlon admitted on the stand. Once he had the information from the snitch, he needed to contact the District Attorney's Office or the State Police detective unit assigned to Worcester County.

So, on the one hand, Steve Scanlon showed a high level of motivation and resourcefulness in solving the murder of a child. We in the public should be grateful. On the other hand, he seemed perhaps too eager to play the part of a hero, which led to questionable judgment and got him into a bit of hot water.

Steve Scanlon personally knew Brian Albert. In fact, he had once been more than an acquaintance when he worked for the Suffolk County Sheriff's Department and did ride-alongs with the Boston cop, serving warrants on dangerous suspects. At one point, Brian had been in a serious accident and, while recovering for a lengthy time at home, Scanlon would go visit him. It seems reasonable to say that Albert was the kind of cop Scanlon envied.

Remember Gravelly Voice? The guy who called Yannetti's office and left a message under an assumed name? And who Yannetti called on the way home from Karen's arraignment?

That was Steve Scanlon.

# 4. DREAM CASE

In 2004, David Yannetti landed what he thought at the time would be his once-in-a-lifetime "dream case."

Running through the mind of virtually every law school student must be some version of the following fantasy: your factually innocent client has been unjustly convicted and sent to prison, and you swoop in and win their freedom.

Every pitcher in Little League dreams of throwing a no-hitter in the bigs, and very few actually get that experience. Yannetti triumphantly lived the lawyer's version of that fantasy. It's worth running it down for you, because there are so many parallels to the Karen Read case.

In 1990, Middlesex County convicted Ronald Douglas Phinney Jr. of murdering his neighbor, a 23-year-old nursing student named Marianne Alexander, a case that went all the way back to 1980. Phinney, then 46 years old and mentally disabled, was known for always carrying his camera with him. In 1990, ten years after the murder, he signed a confession that he had slipped into her room while she was sleeping, pulled down her underpants in order to take pictures of her vagina, and when she awoke, beat her to death with his camera. Sentenced to life without parole, he had served 16 years when along came David Yannetti.

Phinney had been a suspect from the beginning, but it was only when police somehow obtained a confession that the DA brought him to trial. By then, no blood evidence could be found on the camera, so his conviction was based almost entirely on the confession.

The epic battle to win Phinney's freedom took five years. First, Yannetti had to win him a new trial, which he did by convincing the judge that the *original* defense was ineffective because they failed to pursue… wait for it… a third-party culprit theory.

The original defense team neglected to point to a specific individual, known to both sides, who could plausibly have committed the murder.

A neighbor, Mark Barger, had a penchant for violence and had threatened to kill both himself and someone else. Two weeks before Marianne's murder, he had thrown his wife against a wall, giving her a concussion, and he was known to keep an ax handle in his car for self-defense. While the prosecution argued the camera was the murder weapon and the medical examiner testified in favor of that, the medical examiner also admitted that the handle could theoretically have caused the fatal injuries. The defense pointed out that the ax handle had disappeared after the crime and that Barger had done laundry the night of the murder. They brought in an expert to testify that, despite ten years having passed, blood evidence would have still been found on the camera.

The strategy Yannetti used to convince the judge to order a new trial was the same strategy he would later use to conduct that new trial… and the same one Karen Read would one day employ:

A) Open a tiny bit of daylight by showing holes in the prosecution's evidence;

B) Make a third-party culprit theory vaguely plausible.

Thanks, Captain Obvious!

True, but it's important to note some aspects of this. First, without opening some daylight in the evidence, there's no point attempting to bring up a third-party culprit. But it really doesn't actually take much to create a little daylight in most cases. Practically no investigation is perfect.

Second, to the degree that the defense succeeds in opening holes in the physical evidence, the tactic of being merely vague on the third-party culprit theory actually becomes a strength. If the theory is too specific, it challenges the jury to seek holes in it. It's much better to just prompt them to ask questions of "what if?"

Was it hard to find a neighbor within the three deckers of Lowell who had some instance of violence in their past and who had something in their car or home to use for self-defense? Give me 10 minutes and 50 bucks and I'll find you 10 guys like that on any block.

Could an ax handle theoretically be used to beat someone to death? Sure, and so could dozens of objects in any house.

Is it truly suspicious that the ax handle was "missing" ten years later?

Does the fact that Barger shoved his wife against a wall in any way indicate he had a proclivity for creeping into houses and committing sexual violence?

A third aspect of this case would come into play, and if the prosecution in Karen Read doesn't learn a lesson here, they'll be doomed to failure. Let's keep it simple: confessions might not mean much to a jury.

There, we said it.

There's a trial, which means the defendant isn't pleading guilty, so you don't have to have stayed at a Holiday Inn to understand that the defendant disputes the confession. So it might not take much to create a little bit of doubt about a confession: maybe they were confused, maybe they were tricked, maybe they were pressured.

In the Phinney case, they brought in an expert who testified that the defendant had been coerced after 12 hours of interrogation. It's not that the jury needs to buy into this coercion claim; they probably won't. But what they will do is say, "Okay, Mr. Prosecutor, what *else* you got?"

If there's any reason to doubt the confession, the jurors, knowing that this person faces many years in prison, will demand that the physical evidence be rock solid. And once they decide to move on from the confession to weigh the physical evidence, they've moved on from it. It's no longer part of their reasoning.

They've checked it off the list.

They won't factor it in.

As we've seen, this happened with Karen Read.

# 5. GROUND ZERO

This chapter is about trying to understand the forces at work that led to one of the wildest true crime conspiracy claims of our times. What was in the minds of the people at the source of that storm? What motivated their actions?

In Ronald Phinney's retrial, Yannetti also managed to do something Karen Readers will find familiar: question the integrity of the State investigators. And also, as with the Read case, a key element was a single human hair. A hair had been removed from the victim's bed sheets, but because DNA matching hadn't been developed by 1990, the hair wasn't a crucial piece of evidence. But by the time of the second trial, DNA testing was available. However, the State's crime lab had lost the hair in the intervening years. In his closing arguments, Yannetti would ask "What's going on here?" implying some kind of corruption.

It's incredibly unlikely the State had any motive in losing the hair… a hair which could just as easily have been matched to Phinney. Certainly, it's the defense team's *job* to cast doubt on the veracity of the investigators, but hopefully we in the public are wise enough to be alert for defense tricks.

Another powerful thing we took from the Phinney case: Yannetti firmly believed in the actual innocence of his client.

The attorney who prosecuted the case, George E. Murphy, explained after the retrial that he was sure Phinney had committed the crime because he had cross-examined him during a pre-trial motion, and under oath, Phinney admitted he had gone into the house, climbed into the bed, lifted Marianne's nightgown, and then killed her when she awoke. This confession wasn't under conditions of grueling interrogation, but simply on the stand. It couldn't be used in the retrial, but certainly Yannetti didn't forget about it.

A prominent defense attorney, one whom we respect immensely, actually told us something amazing. He believes most of *his* clients are indeed factually innocent. He even believes that it's more generally true, on a large scale, that the State is falsely charging people. Given the talent and intelligence of the person we were talking to, this seemed stunning, since it's very unlikely to be true.

Is this just a coping mechanism for a line of work that requires you to spend most of your professional time with the dregs of society?

Yannetti described his eyes watering up when Phinney won his freedom. His sister, Tanis, also a lawyer who worked the case, shed actual tears.

Put yourself in the shoes of a defense lawyer. Intellectually, you understand you have a job to do, and whether or not you actually *believe* your client really did the crime, your duty is to vigorously argue that the defendant is innocent. But how much easier must it be to do that job if you firmly *believe* in that innocence?

Finally, on the Phinney retrial, Yannetti would say, "This case could really be a movie or a book."

Again, isn't that also every law student's dream?

But how does a lawyer go from that kind of moment—a famous triumph—back to the grind of representing DUI clients, wife beaters, and rapists? Even after his headline-grabbing victory, most of Yannetti's clients still found their way to him through his website. In came a parade of troubled people who would certainly make it a challenge to sell himself on the idea of factual innocence. Was this what he wanted to do with the rest of his life?

Yannetti, quoting Teddy Roosevelt, saw himself as the "man in the arena." But by 2022, he'd about had it. Retirement looked appealing.

Then, curled up on her parents' couch… her boyfriend having been pronounced dead only hours before, drifts of snow surrounding her Lexus in the driveway, the State Police on their way… Karen Read googled "DUI lawyer."

### Conspiracy Theory

According to Yannetti, it was on the way home from Karen's arraignment, on Wednesday, February 2, that he first talked to Steve Scanlon. And THAT was the first moment that either he or Karen had any inkling that they might be able to say that she was factually innocent. That someone else had killed John.

Yannetti and Scanlon dispute what was said. Yannetti claims Scanlon told him on that phone call that John had been attacked inside the house by three men: Brian Albert, his nephew, and an ATF agent.

If true… and we think THAT part of Yannetti's story is… then by that Wednesday, Scanlon had picked up something.

In September of 2023, the troopers would finally get around to interviewing Scanlon. He told them that at the time of the call, he knew nothing and only offered his services as a private investigator, and that he didn't learn it involved the Alberts and their nephew until he met with Yannetti and their private investigator, Paul Mackowski, in Yannetti's office. Remember him? He's the roly-poly former retired Medford cop.

Scanlon's claim on this is bullshit, but as we'll see, Yannetti is no stranger to the cow pie either.

Sometime before Karen's arrest on Tuesday, Scanlon had reached out to Karen over Facebook. We don't know exactly what he said, and she told him to contact Yannetti.

But from the facts, we can deduce, to quote *The Sopranos*' Phil Leotardo, "a couple o' three things."

A) Scanlon didn't tell Karen anything in that first message that would give her the idea John was killed in the house, or she would have claimed she didn't do the crime when she met her lawyer on Wednesday before the arraignment.

B) However, Scanlon didn't merely offer his private investigation services in that call to Yannetti. No way. He had to have told the lawyer that he had at least some theory on how his client was factually innocent, or Yannetti wouldn't have scheduled the meeting. He already had his own P.I.

C) Scanlon either KNEW something or had HEARD something. And whatever he was hearing had evolved between the Tuesday message to Karen and the Wednesday call with Yannetti.

In national TV interviews, Yannetti likes to portray Scanlon, without naming him, as a whistleblower. He suggests Scanlon knows something and that he got spooked. Scanlon has said that he has no actual information, and that seems to be completely true. Suggesting otherwise is Yannetti slinging some cow pies.

Scanlon, who haunts the Canton and Dedham bars often until last call, obviously picked up some scuttlebutt. By Tuesday, he had picked up enough to reach out to Karen, and by Wednesday evening he had an actual theory to present to Yannetti. In fact, our source, who spoke directly to him, tells us Scanlon presented them with three theories by the time of the office meeting.

Remember when Scanlon used a prison informant to find the dead boy in the suitcase? In his overeagerness to turn grapevine chatter into actionable information, he violated policy by not giving that information to the proper investigators. Always the sidekick to real cops, he wanted to be in the juice, get the collar, and solve the case.

I don't mean this in any judgmental way. It's even very understandable. Who doesn't want to be the hero?

But someone was ready to exploit that: David Yannetti.

At the office meeting, Yannetti gave Scanlon a check for $1500, asking him to keep his eyes and ears open. No contract. It's too small to be a retainer for investigative services and, in fact, after consulting his lawyer, Scanlon never cashed the check. Fishy.

What did Yannetti want for that fee?

Scanlon continued to nose around, meeting with a man whose name seemed conjured by a Tim Burton nightmare movie: Jack Hallow. Hallow worked as a Medford cop, the same police force that Yannetti's P.I., Mackowski, had retired from. Somewhere along the line, Hallow had also worked with Brian Albert.

Was Hallow also paid by Yannetti?

It was Hallow who informed Scanlon that there was supposedly a beef between Colin Albert and John O'Keefe. But Hallow, in turn, claimed Mackowski as his source for that.

If your head is spinning like a nor'easter, good! That's the point. Because this is what a rumor mill—one where the defense team gives the wheel an extra push—looks like. It's NOT what real information and actual sourcing looks like.

And Karen's team didn't need anything too real. They weren't trying to solve the case, and not just because it wasn't their job, but because the very idea was to create innuendo, smokescreens, and vague dot connecting.

Doubt.

Yannetti has tried to turn Scanlon into Keyser Söze from the 1995 film, *The Usual Suspects*. The more mysterious the better, because as we've seen, a huge part of their strategy involves creating and feeding hysteria. Is that ethical? Of course not! But anything for the W, right?

Scanlon hasn't wanted to admit that he went to Yannetti with his theory about the Alberts for obvious reasons: he doesn't want to look like he betrayed an old friend because of rumors.

But if we're to wander around Ground Zero of what evolved into a perfect true crime storm, we have to go back to before Scanlon first reached out to Karen, before she was arrested. Because that's when the third-party culprit theory truly first took root in the pubs and the local Dunks and on the digital hallways of Facebook and Instagram.

It grew organically as an urban legend.

A creepypasta.

All the ingredients were there:

- a cop found dead on the lawn of another cop;
- where there had been an after-hours party;
- where a man with a tough-guy reputation lived;
- where the victim looked beat up.

And who could imagine a girlfriend leaving her boyfriend to die after hitting him? How many hit-and-runs involve people who know each other? And Karen and John weren't at all a picture of domestic violence. These were respectable people, not scumbags.

That's already enough ingredients to get the storm spinning and air pressure dropping. Then more details started to fuel it:

- an ATF agent was there;
- Colin was there, and he weirdly called Erin Beatty at 12:31;
- Kevin Albert, Brian's brother, is a Canton cop.

Canton is a blue-collar town where there are a lot of people conditioned to mistrust the police and to connect dots. You won't see this kind of dot connecting as quickly in a town like Newton or Brookline, where people don't feel as distant from the power centers.

Take a hospital, for example. Nurses, X-ray techs, and staff don't sit in on the board meetings where the big decisions are made, so there's an element of mystery for them about what goes on at that level. Is it corrupt at the top? Is it all about money? They don't know, so it becomes an opportunity for them to imagine how they THINK things are at the top. Whereas doctors and administrators, on the other hand, *have* attended those board meetings, so there's less mystery.

In places like Canton, Somerville, and Worcester, there are a lot of very hard-working and decent people who are far removed from the places of power in society where big decisions are made. So, when things happen that they don't understand, the tendency to connect dots into a conspiracy theory is much stronger.

My working theory, based on the timing of Scanlon's reaching out to Karen, and understanding how the town of Canton would react to the circumstances of John's death, was that the idea about John being killed inside the house formed organically. To confirm that, I reached out to sources in Canton and got the answer quickly.

I was sent screenshots of Facebook messages posted on February 1, three days after John's death, in which the theory can already be seen forming. One message claimed that Brian Albert beat up John with a baseball bat. And multiple other messages confirmed what was happening on the ground: a conspiracy theory was already forming.

And all of this became a way to settle petty, small-town grudges, poorly remembered incidents from late nights at the Hillside, and feuds with high school cliques. It's not a conscious thing where you decide to get back at someone.

It's more that those old grievances make you receptive to believing something bad about people you once had an issue with.

Just as the Hillside represents Ground Zero… though it could be C.F. McCarthy's or the local Dunks… Tom Beatty represents Patient Zero. Just enough of an outsider to have a bit of resentment, a fiercely loyal dad whose daughter had a beef with the McCabe girls, someone Karen flirted with and who had his ear to the grapevine in the pubs and coffee shops. He didn't start the whole thing—no single person did—but he perfectly represents the kind of person eager to give life to the whispers and willing to add new components. Indeed, he's the one who told Karen the Alberts owned a dog.

So, a perfect storm started with something weird… a cop found dying on the lawn of another cop looking like he had been beaten up. This created an opportunity for townspeople to settle old beefs, even if that all took place unconsciously. It found fertile ground in a population that mistrusts authority. And finally, the conspiracy theory that spread was actually intriguing, like any urban legend.

Steve Scanlon picked up enough of this to try to exploit it. It would put him back in the juice, like the real cop he had always imagined himself to be. And he reached out to Karen.

These were the stages that led to the perfect storm:

1) Elements of the tragedy led to the rise of conspiracy theories on the ground almost immediately. John died on Saturday, and by Monday, people were posting theories in social media about John being killed in the house.

2) Steve Scanlon picked up some of that scuttlebutt, probably in the pubs such as the Hillside or the Halfway Cafe in Dedham. By Tuesday morning, he had enough to contact Karen, but not enough to say he believed she was

innocent. However, by Wednesday evening, when Yannetti returned his call on the way home from the arraignment, Scanlon proposed that John was murdered in the house by Brian, his nephew, and a federal agent.

3) Yannetti's P.I., Paul Mackowski, was tasked with nosing around Canton to find information which could be useful in crafting the emerging conspiracy theory.

4) Meanwhile, Karen had friends in Canton, such as Tom Beatty, who believed in her innocence and, perhaps having old grudges in the back of their minds, were eager to help her find more pieces for the puzzle.

5) Searching through social media, they eventually found a connection between case officer Michael Proctor and the Alberts.

6) In August of 2022, Karen and her attorneys somehow got a meeting with then First US Attorney Josh Levy. We don't know what was said, but this was many months before Rich Green produced any data that said John was climbing stairs or that Jen was making 2:27 searches. Yet by November, the Feds were already issuing subpoenas for the communication records of not only Michael Proctor, but of members of the Albert and McCabe families. What could they have used to sell the powerful US Attorney?

This might be the most important question of the case. Shortly before the first trial, the Feds, complying with a Touhy request, turned over any relevant evidence they had to both sides. Apparently, all the Feds found, despite a massive expense and effort, was some insensitive texts by Proctor about the defendant.

Which makes it all the more baffling as to what Karen and her team used to sell the US Attorney on the need to launch a large federal investigation.

Did they falsely present Scanlon as a whistleblower?

Did they convince Levy that the friendship between Proctor's sister and Chris Albert's family could be a basis for him planting evidence?

The defense didn't make their theory public until April 12, 2023, when they filed a motion to get Brian Albert's phone. But the focus of their theory then was the data report crafted by Rich Green in March.

They also focused on John's injuries, alleging a dog attack and a beating. Did they succeed in presenting this to the Feds all the way back in August of 2022?

The Feds eventually hired two dog-bite experts, both of whom concluded that John wasn't attacked by a dog.

In the federal investigation into the death of Sandra Birchmore, they brought in their own medical examiner to challenge what the State's ME had concluded. But they didn't seem to have done that in the Karen Read investigation, or if they did, Karen's team didn't call on them to testify.

Hopefully, the Feds have an internal investigation into how their probe into the Read case began, because at this time it appears odd and suspicious.

7) Less than a week after making their theory of a frame job public, Karen and her team worked closely with blogger Turtleboy to not only put out their theory on his blog and his YouTube channel, but to begin stirring up a circus in Canton. His primary motive for doing this was to generate content for his channel, but it served their interest as well.

**Rolling Rally**

This culminated in the summer of 2023, a year before the trial, in a barbaric event created by Turtleboy and reportedly conceived with the help of Karen herself, called the Rolling Rally.

Dozens of cars and over a hundred participants drove in a parade to the homes of each of the main witnesses and Trooper Proctor. There, Turtleboy got out and blasted the occupants and their neighbors with a bullhorn, calling them "murderers." Children inside were ushered into bathrooms for their safety.

Had they considered the visuals better, perhaps they would have done the rally at night and used torches.

**Yellow Cottage Tales: Turning Point**

In many ways, everything peaked for me late in the summer of 2023. On a gorgeous August day, my new team filmed a documentary shoot unrelated to the Karen Read case. We were growing close to each other, forming friendships that seemed destined to last. And I received the kind of explosive scoop that even veteran journalists would wait many years to be a part of. But dark clouds were massing.

The first signs of trouble came within me. Guilt gnawed. Even though I was still entertaining the possibility that a coverup had occurred, the evidence for it remained, at best, inconclusive, and meanwhile, the witnesses were being bullied by a merciless mob. The frenzied rush to judgment seemed to draw from something primal and vicious, shadowy forces deep within the human psyche that can drive ordinarily decent people to become, well, evil. The mob wasn't just demanding justice. They were in truth reveling in the misery of people they didn't know.

What felt the worst was that I wasn't being myself. I'll come back to that.

During that summer, I met a retired DEA agent who lived in Florida but who had grown up in Canton. Seamus O'Malley looks straight out of Hollywood casting for the Boston Irish cop. Big guy, white hair, immaculately dressed… if your family has a Kennedy picture on the wall, you'll be immediately impressed by Seamus.

Because of his Canton roots, he began following the Karen Read case closely. And he thought something didn't smell right. If you followed Seamus by the time of the trial—

and by then he had his own channel—it might seem hard to imagine now, with his words getting crazier and crazier, but back in the summer of '23, he seemed very credible. And he was the only former cop talking publicly about the case… and this case BADLY needed experienced experts to come forward! Without that expertise, all we had was us amateurs trying to find our way through in the dark.

I struck up a friendship with Seamus over the case, and we talked by phone several times a week. I really enjoyed those conversations.

But I also felt that sorting through the branches of the logic tree wasn't his best strength. However, he did seem to care about the truth, he was far from being an idiot, and it seemed like these discussions were productive.

What I didn't know was that he was also talking directly to Karen.

Here's how I learned I had gotten played. Karen's team leaked the video of her backing out in John's driveway at 5:08 to go search for him. They told Court TV something that seems strange now, given what Alan Jackson told the jury. They said the Lexus was clearly "missing pieces" in the video.

Come again? Jackson showed the same video to the jury and told them the taillight was clearly intact. What had changed along the way?

After the Court TV segment aired, I told Seamus on the phone that what we needed was a clear image of the taillight from as early as possible. If it was missing pieces, there was no conspiracy. If it was just cracked, however, then there certainly was.

I know the cracked-versus-missing argument seems obvious now, but Seamus hadn't seen it. Yet even more shocking: neither had Karen nor her team. Because a couple of days after I had said this to Seamus, he amazingly got back to me with images of the taillight from the sally port, asking that I not share them or show them on the channel.

Did he have access to discovery material?!

Guess where he got it? Karen. Or certainly someone directly connected to her.

Though he couldn't grasp it, those images were really quite useless because they were taken while the Lexus was in custody. Still, it told me he was in contact with Karen. And these conversations with Seamus began a process which led Karen and her team to figure out something they shockingly couldn't on their own: they had to show that the taillight was merely cracked and not missing pieces.

Here's another story that shows how they didn't understand this cracked-versus-missing-pieces thing until this time. In July, *Boston Magazine* reporter Gretchen Voss, whose article on the case in September of 2023 remains the seminal piece, interviewed Karen in the presence of attorneys David Yannetti, Alan Jackson, and Elizabeth Little. That audio recording also became discovery material, and though we didn't hear it in the first trial, it remains an option for the prosecution.

In the audio, Karen amazingly describes how badly her taillight was broken, with pieces missing and internal components exposed. In fact, at one point she describes plucking a piece of taillight plastic off the housing and dropping it in the driveway!

Why would she tell such a tale? Because she was trying to discredit the State Police, who had searched the driveway and found nothing. This was also why prosecutor Adam Lally spent time in the trial showing video of the driveway being shoveled and then snow blown. Any discarded piece very likely ended up in the yard somewhere, so nothing suspicious at all.

But it shows that, in July, neither Karen nor her attorneys understood the need to say the taillight was only cracked and not missing pieces. They just hadn't really thought it through, as nuts as that sounds.

Then Seamus came back to me with what seemed like the scoop of a lifetime, even if I had been a real journalist, which I assuredly am not.

One of the things I kept hitting on in my discussions with Seamus was that the motive just seemed insufficient all around. Colin had a feud with John because of an incident on his lawn? Come on, John's a Boston cop and Colin had two uncles who were cops. That never made sense. And even if the kid was in the house, shitfaced, and started a fight with John, Brian Albert would have quickly put a stop to it. I didn't have to know Brian personally to know that. He's not going to let his nephew in high school start shit with a guy he works with.

And we're expected to believe that the chief of police, Berkowitz, was going to help cover up a murder like this just because cops stick together? No way, I'm sorry, that's loony tunes. There was just insufficient motive everywhere you looked. And that's what I kept telling Seamus.

So, one day he came back with the answers that tied it all together. Oh boy, did it do that. The story any journalist would kill for, but…

Before I let you know what I learned, it's important to add a related element. At the end of July, I got a quick call from Turtleboy. Alan Jackson wanted to talk to me. Yeah, that guy, lawyer to the stars, and of course to Karen. Turtleboy gave me his number.

Did Jackson think I had some information that could help his client?

Or did he just want to make sure I stayed under the control of Team Karen? Because I had been asking more and more skeptical questions, and since I was the only one, maybe they wanted to nip it in the bud. I know Aidan did. His cult had been slowly growing for years, but this case was giving a turtle wet dreams. You know, like all turtles must have.

I texted Jackson, telling him who I was, explaining that I had no inside information, and in case his goal was to influence me, I said right up front that I would always cover this "neutrally" from both sides.

He replied that he understood and that he just wanted to "touch base."

He never did call me. But was he in communication with Seamus? Seamus has said so privately, but I don't know if this had happened by that time. However, Seamus certainly was in touch with Karen and had even been fed discovery material (the sally port pics).

But another very curious thing happened around this time. Jackson and Karen went on *ABC News*, and Jackson claimed that on the night John died, he had walked into a "hostile situation."

This wasn't something they had ever said before, and it would presage what the defense would say at trial, that John was being "set up" when they invited him to the house. In other words, an ambush.

Let's return to the scoop Seamus gave me within days of this *ABC News* report. He said two things that, for me, tied it all together and solved the problem of insufficient motive. First, he claimed that a still-active source of his at the DEA had informed him that there was an ongoing investigation into drug dealing at the Canton Police station!

Second, he claimed that Karen had filmed Colin dealing drugs in the neighborhood, and that John had called 911 to report it, eventually sending them the video.

Neither of these things is true, though there is a kernel of truth in each. But I didn't learn this until weeks later, and when I did, I created a video called *The Anatomy of a Smear*, an effort to clear the record on Colin, who was in no way, shape, or form dealing drugs.

I grilled Seamus on his sources. He said he was talking to someone inside the Canton Police station who listened to the call come in. I should have sat on the story until I had more sources, but because of his law enforcement experience and his contacts, I trusted Seamus more than I should have.

But I was still cautious. I scripted a report and sent it to Seamus for approval. He gave it. The next day, after minor tweaks, I sent it to him one more time. Again, he approved. The show was scheduled for 8:00 P.M. I would stick to the script. Colin's name wouldn't be mentioned. I would use the word "nephew."

However, about an hour before the show, Seamus called with cold feet. He said his DEA agent source was afraid of being outed. I thought about canceling the story… and it's yet another mark on my soul that I didn't… but I went through with it, making some adjustments, and sending that final draft for Seamus's approval, which he again gave.

The truth turned out to be similar, but very different. Twelve years before John's death, a Canton Police officer was known to be addicted to drugs. No need to put his name here. Was there a DEA investigation into that? Who knows, but it was handled in-house and the officer retired. That seems to be the full extent of the drug dealing story at the Canton Police Department.

What about Karen and John reporting a drug dealer? Yup. That happened. Only it wasn't Colin, it was a troubled 27-year-old man. Karen did film him, but John never called the station. What he did do was send the video to someone on the force he was friends with: Detective Kevin Albert.

That video is part of the discovery material. If there was something useful to Karen on it, she was free to use it in the last trial. She didn't.

But that's the thing about the story Sean told me: who else could have known about that video in discovery? Not many people. But Karen did.

See, we had seen the tactic before. Karen had taken a real event—teens drinking on John's lawn—and inserted Colin into it as part of an attempt to create a motive for an attack. She had fed this story to Gretchen Voss. This here seemed like the very same thing: take something real, and falsely insert Colin into it in order to create a feud between John and Colin, only in this case, it would have created a feud with the whole Albert family.

The story fed to me sounded like a knockoff of a Dennis Lehane mystery novel. The connected Canton family wanted to protect their drug-dealing nephew, so they brought in John for a sit-down in order to put the fear of God into him, and the corrupt chief of police wanted to keep drug dealing in his department from being exposed.

I fell for it… briefly. Dennis Lehane would never write such an absurd plot, and I like to hope I wouldn't either. Eagerness for a "breaking news" story, however, clouded my judgment. What you want to do in a situation—something I'm now learning from the world's most effective teacher, experience—is take your time. By taking your time, you not only get to verify aspects of the story, but you can carefully think through the logic and see if it makes sense.

In my defense, had I known at the time that Karen and Seamus were talking, I would have been much, much more skeptical. I believed Seamus really had a source in the Canton Police Department who heard the call, and truly had a source in the DEA. I mean, not only did he seem forthright to me back then, but he's a retired DEA agent.

None of this really lessens the horror of what I had done. Without using the young man's name, I still had falsely smeared someone with the accusation of being a drug dealer. There's no way to get a do-over on that except to tell the truth about how it went down. And that truth includes this: Karen began communicating at this time with my partner, Dave McGrath. She used the encryption app, Signal, so the messages self-deleted after a certain amount of time. But Dave screenshotted them. In those messages, she tried to get Dave and my channel to put out the fact that the FBI had tried to serve a subpoena to Colin at his college campus, Bridgewater State College.

It was a big get because at the time, there was no official confirmation of an FBI investigation into the Karen Read investigation. The Feds had been leaking word of it to Karen all along, strangely working as partners with her team, but none of that was actual hard proof that could be shown to a skeptical public. So this subpoena was the first confirmation.

Karen had a "deal" with Turtleboy. He would get everything first, so he could run with the scoop, in exchange for positive coverage. But Turtle was away at an amusement park with his kids, and Karen, ever impulsive and always managing the social media campaign, didn't want to wait a few hours. So she reached out to multiple people, including McGrath.

Not wanting Turtle to find out she had broken their deal, Karen told Dave to tell Turtle that he had found out about the FBI subpoena through a FOIA, or Freedom of Information Act request. In other words, she told him to lie.

Stunned, Dave reported immediately to me about the messages from Karen, but neither of us did anything with the information and, as it turned out, there wasn't time, because though Karen told McGrath she had given him an exclusive, that also was a lie. She fed it to other social media minions, and it was all over social media before Turtle even got home from Canobie Lake Park.

But there was more. In this brief period where she attempted to turn Dave into another one of her minions, she told him that she had filmed Colin engaging in "criminal" activity. She didn't say drug dealing, but I think we can see what she was doing, given that Seamus had just fed me this very story.

For those of us covering this case, whether untrained YouTubers or experienced journalists, it's a path littered with moral hazards. There's pressure to get the "breaking news." There's a temptation to appeal to the large mob that has been generated. And everyone in the media or on YouTube understands that conspiracy theories are juicy and always get the most views, by far.

I've seen mistakes made by mainstream reporters and programs. *Fox 25 Boston*'s Ted Daniels wore a pink tie to court just before the trial, an attempt to win the favor of the FKR mob, which had adopted pink. Local channels such as NECN and Boston NBC have regularly pandered to the conspiracy theorists. Even *Boston Magazine* and the once prestigious *New Yorker* put out articles which falsely portrayed Turtleboy as a "truth seeker" with "rough edges." But truth has never been what he's after, and he has been charged with 19 counts of witness intimidation. He has even threatened to bring a mob to the soccer games of the Attorney General's kids.

So even the big-boy news outlets can't resist the lure of big numbers that comes with covering this from the conspiracy side. Conscience isn't something you acquire in journalism school… it's something you either choose to use or not.

I was struggling with all of these things that August. And remember, I had been wandering in the desert for more than 10 years, trying to recapture ANY sense of purpose and direction.

Erica, who had joined the team and who I quickly saw as a valued friend, stopped by the house one day. I noted what she had on her car: a Turtleboy sticker.

By then, it was clear to any decent person what this guy was all about. He had recently orchestrated a Rolling Rally, where he took hundreds of people to show up at the home of most of the witnesses and police investigators in the case, shouting slander through a bullhorn at each stop, terrorizing the women and children inside. That has nothing to do with truth or justice. That's just trying to generate content for his channel at the expense of other human beings.

Erica now recognized this. She had been a longtime fan of Turtle, but what she had been a fan of was the IDEA of it, the idea of someone who reports corruption that mainstream outlets won't touch. Heck, I'm a huge fan of that idea myself!

There's a bit of a process when it comes to understanding what he really is and what dark force he's tapped into. For people who were longtime fans, that process is longer. A certain amount of patience is warranted.

I went to a birthday cookout for Erica. Met her whole family, really wonderful people. They weren't too sure about this FKR stuff, but they accepted their daughter's passion. That morning, Erika had driven over an hour to purchase a FKR birthday cake, which she showed me with pride. I didn't let on how I felt about it.

You see, I had quietly flipped. More or less perched on the fence, trying my best to cover the case neutrally, I had come to the conclusion that the conspiracy hypothesis made no sense.

Dave sensed it. Privately, he asked me, and I told him I was 51% in favor of… a conclusion the mob wouldn't approve of. He was stunned.

And the FKR crowd sensed it. They could tell from the questions I was asking on the channel… and they do NOT like ANY questions, no sir, they do not. Any question was a threat. This is actually one of the many cult-like aspects to this crowd.

I was a member of the big Karen Read Facebook page, but I never posted. Then one day someone created a post directed right at me. Essentially, it said there's something wrong with Kevin from Yellow Cottage. They loved Dave and Erica, but something didn't seem right with me. And they suggested Dave and Erica leave me and go out on their own.

The post got hundreds of replies from the mob, almost all of which affirmed that sentiment, many in much harsher terms. Some said I showed signs of brain damage, mental retardation, and, weirdly, cowardice. Of the hundreds of comments, only two had expressed support, saying that I was just trying to look at things intelligently from both sides. Those two people were immediately, in turn, attacked into silence.

Little did they know this was actually exactly what I needed.

# PART SEVEN: IT HAS HAPPENED BEFORE

# 1. THE PROBLEM LIES WITH US

On July 29, 1985, 36-year-old Penny Beerntsen, a small business owner and fitness instructor, went for a run along the shoreline of Lake Michigan under a crisp blue sky. She planned on meeting her husband around 4:00 P.M. at a pre-arranged spot. Her idyllic afternoon was about to be torpedoed.

Right as she stopped to check her watch by a stretch of woods, Penny was violently pulled down from behind and dragged into the woods. Massive hands silenced her screams. It entered her mind to worry that her young daughter would later be haunted by news photos of her corpse.

After being brutally raped and beaten, Beerntsen lay bloody and unconscious, hidden between massive dunes, for two hours until two citizens on a walk stumbled across her and called for help. Miraculously, she survived. At the nearby medical center, the County sheriff showed her photos. One depicted a man out on bail for threatening a cop's wife with a rifle. That man was Steven Avery.

Avery would be made famous by Netflix in the documentary called *The Making of a Murderer*. Because of that series, to this day many thousands still campaign for his release from prison.

From the hospital, Beerntsen immediately pointed to the photo of Avery. That was the guy.

Only it wasn't.

Avery was indeed convicted. Beerntsen would even select him from a lineup. Avery's defense team put forth 16 witnesses who swore he couldn't have been in the park that day. A paint store owner presented a receipt to prove Avery had been in his store with his wife and kids to buy supplies.

But the State criminologist testified that hairs on Avery's shirt were consistent with Beerntsen, and he was sentenced to 32 years. He had served 18 years when along came the Wisconsin Innocence Project to fight for a new trial. Skin cells from under the victim's fingernails were tested, and investigators learned that the DNA belonged to another assailant. Avery not only won a new trial but was exonerated, as the DNA was matched to Gregory Allen, a man who looked a lot like Avery.

And they lived happily ever after, right?

A couple of years after Avery was released, with a major lawsuit against the County pending, a 25-year-old freelance photographer, Teresa Halbach, was summoned by him to his salvage yard in order to photograph some old vehicles the family wanted listed for sale. There she was murdered.

The premise of the Netflix series was that Avery had been "set up" by a corrupt County that was afraid of being bankrupted by his lawsuit. Eager to believe in this kind of unlikely and sophisticated corruption, many in the public were completely sold.

But it would later emerge that Avery had exhibited signs of odd behavior… behavior commonly associated with a budding serial killer… from an early age. For example, he had doused a cat with gasoline and tossed it into a fire. Details like this either went unreported or downplayed in the Netflix series.

Avery was convicted of Halbach's murder with very compelling evidence. Investigators found the photographer's camera and cell phone in a burn pit on the property. They found Avery's DNA on the disconnected battery of her car. The victim had been shot by a weapon stored in his bedroom.

And Avery's nephew, Brendan Dassey, confessed to having helped his uncle abduct, kill, and dispose of Halbach. The court sentenced Avery to life in prison.

However, exploiting any detail in the investigation that they could present as unusual or suspicious, Avery's lawyers used the documentary to spark a public outrage. An innocent man, they said, had been falsely convicted a second time. The documentary made allegations of police and prosecutorial misconduct, evidence tampering, and witness coercion. It was incredibly effective.

I'm not accusing Karen Read's team of employing the same tactics. But we in the public need to be very aware of just how effective this kind of PR campaign can be, especially when combined with social media or streaming services. Richard Allen has been convicted and sentenced in Delphi, and already we're seeing attempts, even on Court TV, to suggest that the wrong guy might be in prison. A similar game plan can be expected in the Moscow, Idaho case, where Bryan Kohberger stands charged of killing four college kids.

Look, the solution isn't to blame the lawyers or Netflix or Court TV. The problem lies with us. If I had to put the theme of this book on a postage stamp, that would be it.

*The problem lies with us.*

**Yellow Cottage Tales: Meltdown**

A sure path to unhappiness in life is not being yourself. Well, let's qualify that a bit. We all have parts of ourselves that we should try to quiet down or at least keep in check. Like when I go for coffee at Dunks, and the schmuck in front of me gets five different kinds of drinks, each more complicated to make than a hot fudge sundae, I want to tell that schmuck that diabetes is a real thing. But I don't. And it's good that I keep that asshole voice inside of me quiet.

But in general, if you're not being yourself, misery will dog you.

And I was no longer acting like myself. I had added Dave and then Erin to my live shows, and I started playing the role of host. A host tries to avoid expressing their own opinions. They're more of a facilitator who tries to coax opinions out of others. This had the effect of making me acquiescent. Sorry, that's a twenty-dollar word from a guy with mostly nickels and dimes in his pocket.

We had a woman on our team named Brit, a plus-sized professional model who suffered from a lot of health issues. She was always reporting one malady or another, and we felt genuinely bad, offering her as much sympathy and support as we could. In her way, unintentionally, she also gave me the push that I needed to stop being what I wasn't: a game-show host.

Brit was and presumably still is a big-time Turtle Rider. (This is what the cultish fans of Turtleboy call themselves.) In our group chat, I played the part of congenial facilitator, something I'm about as well suited for as a mafia gangster is for poetry jams. In private, with Erica and Dave, I was raising harder and harder questions about the alleged conspiracy, but not so much in the group chat.

Then one day, out of the clear blue, Brit said that she would "wipe the floor" with me in an argument. This was an unusual statement on several levels, including the fact that I had never been anything but supportive to her amid her daily complaining, but even more unusual since we weren't in any way discussing arguments.

It's not that I was offended. It was more like I was looking in a mirror and the person I saw wasn't me.

It was exactly what the doctor ordered! If there was one thing I had been doing all my life with some proficiency, it was making arguments. I had done it growing up in Lawrence, with the nuns in the eighth grade, with teachers in high school, over beers and bongs in college, and from both sides of the bar. One neighborhood tough guy from the bucket-of-blood, back when I was only 21, once laughed that whenever I threw him out for getting rowdy, he never realized it until he was halfway home. Words were my fists… though to be fair, that was more or less by necessity given the skill of my fists.

But at Yellow Cottage Tales, I had turned myself into something different. Something that wasn't me.

Self-analysis is like blindly putting your hand into a Haunted House hole to find a clue to the mystery. You never know what you'll pull out. When I look back to that summer, I see someone who watched people being bullied but didn't stick up for them because he saw opportunity. I see someone who was too slow to speak his mind because it seemed like literally every other person he knew or in social media believed fervently that Karen was framed. I see someone who liked his new team and didn't want to lose it.

One more thing loomed heavy on my mind. I'd had discussions with both Erica and Dave about the need to criticize some of this mob behavior. I warned them against participating in the Rolling Rally where Turtleboy took a large mob to the witnesses' homes. They agreed, but they warned me against pissing off the mob with questions. They had followed Aidan Kearney for years, and even though they admired him, they also now understood even better than me what he really was. Challenge him and he'll use his large mob to dig for dirt on you, and if they can't find any, they'll just make it up. They warned me: don't piss him off unless you're willing to pay the price.

The weight of all that was becoming heavier as the summer wore on. I needed an excuse to throw it off. The Facebook post attacking me and the comment by Brit in our chat gave me the push I needed. It's not that there was a moment of conscious decision. But the pressure had built to a point where it was going to snap at the first chance. And that chance came quick, when Aidan brought his hostile mob to chat in the next live show—producing the infamous "meltdown" episode.

# PART EIGHT: ROAD TO VERDICT

# 1. WEIGHING MEANS MULTIPLYING

Now that we've set the table with all the issues, let's clear away most of the "odd things" so we can move on to the State's most convincing evidence. First, though, let's recap some YCT rules.

There are no geniuses. Any criminal theory that requires the presence of a genius should be viewed very skeptically.

Odd things CAN add up to reasonable doubt… but also UNREASONABLE doubt. There will always be odd things in every case, so whether those odd things are meaningful has to be determined.

Don't just ask why someone did something; ask why they DIDN'T do something.

It's not just about motive. It's about SUFFICIENT motive.

When you come to a fork in the road, take it. Look for places where the logic tree branches and be careful not to miss some just because one path seems somewhat unlikely. That unlikely path might still be the most likely.

It's just pixels. Turning pixels into patterns is why we see conspiracies where they don't exist.

Let's add two more rules.

**YCT Rule #16: In high-profile cases, count on false witnesses emerging.**

It happens in every big case. This is why police withhold details from the public.

The spotlight will draw many people who say they saw something important—and they might very well believe they did—but whose account is false. These witnesses aren't usually lying. But the limelight makes people want to believe they witnessed something important, and many convince themselves they have.

Take the Lizzie Borden case again, where all kinds of false witnesses came forward. But the danger is that when some of those witnesses happen to have a story that fits a narrative taking hold with the police or the public, their testimony gets seized upon… even though it might be false. For this reason, we recommend being very cautious when it comes to witness statements unless what they say is really backed up by harder evidence or other accounts.

And now, let's drop another one:

**YCT Rule #5: Improbabilities multiply.**

I wrestled over whether to unleash this rule. Could I explain it simply? At the end of the day, it's just too important to my way of thinking to leave out.

We all use logic trees when thinking about these cases. For example, if the DNA found on a murder weapon doesn't match, then the suspect is seemingly in the clear. We can look for another suspect.

But even in that scenario, it's not always clear-cut. Maybe the lab made a mistake. Maybe the killer wore gloves. So, we look for other possibilities. Often, we're dealing not with *possibilities* and *impossibilities*, but rather with *probabilities* and *improbabilities*.

The glove didn't fit O.J. Simpson, right? Does that mean it's impossible that he was the killer? Then why did he flee in the Bronco? We keep digging.

We learn that his blood was found at the crime scene, and that the victims' blood was found in his Bronco and in his home, and that he had a deep cut on his hand that morning which was still bleeding. Now, what seemed improbable because the glove didn't fit seems very probable because of the extensive blood evidence and the suspicious wound.

But what if the cops were framing him?

That's how we all think our way through these cases: a little debate in our own mind, sorting through not only possibilities but also probabilities. Can logic apply to probabilities in the same way it does to possibilities?

Yes.

## The Key is Stacking

In our attempt to eliminate branches on the logic tree, we might not be able to say that a particular branch is *impossible*... that it can be eliminated with 100% certainty... but rather that it's *improbable*. In order to really eliminate a branch… or cross off a suspect… we have to be able to say that it's *very, very improbable*. The more "very"s we can create, the better.

This is where the multiplication factor comes in. Let's say the Boston Red Sox and the Boston Bruins both have a 1 in 100 chance of winning the title this year. Well, what are the odds of *both* teams winning it in the same year?

To calculate, we multiple the probabilities. In this case, 1/100 multiplied by 1/100, which equals 1/10,000. So, there's a 1 in 10,000 chance that both the Red Sox and the Bruins will win it this year.

The point isn't to literally calculate odds for elements of a case. No, we just need to understand the logic. If it's unlikely that the Red Sox will win it all, and unlikely that the Bruins will win it all, then it's actually very, very unlikely that they'll both win it all this year.

This is called stacking. Just by stacking two somewhat unlikely occurrences together, we can create something very, very unlikely. And we can use this when it comes to figuring out crimes.

Don't change the channel! Give me a half a minute more, because you WILL use this method when thinking about crimes, I promise.

The key thing is to find things that can be stacked together. Things that must all be true. If we can find things to stack together, we can eliminate branches on the tree—or suspects—just by lining up elements which must all be true if the theory is to be valid.

Let's play a game of Yellow Cottage *Clue*.

A female college professor is found dead in her apartment. Police suspect one of her students, a boy who had obtained a failing grade from her and lost his scholarship.

Let's see if he holds up as a suspect.

The student didn't have an alibi, but he lived with his parents a four-hour drive away, and he didn't own a car. Could he have come back?

His parents insist he never left the house. Of course, his parents could be lying.

Or he could have left without them knowing and returned more than eight hours later.

So, maybe we can assess this suspect as only *somewhat* unlikely, but very much worth keeping on the list.

One way to eliminate him is to find some things that all must be true for him to be the killer.

Say we learn that the killer entered the home by climbing through the window, and a size 10 shoe print is found beneath it. But our suspect wears a size 13. This means that unless the disgruntled student had an accomplice, he wasn't the killer. Well, what are the odds he used an accomplice?

It's not impossible. The student could have talked a buddy into making the trip. Maybe he told him they were going to rob the woman. We want to be careful about dismissing ideas in a case. The student *could* have had an accomplice.

But it's somewhat unlikely that a disgruntled student is going to convince a friend to make a long trip to get revenge for a bad grade. So now we have two unlikely things that seem to *both* need to be true for this suspect to be the killer: one, he somehow made the long trip; and two, he convinced an accomplice to go with him. Because both of those elements need to be true, and each of them is somewhat unlikely, this student is actually very unlikely to be the killer.

Let's put it in mathematical terms just to demonstrate. Say there's a 25% chance he managed to drive to the victim's place that night, and a 25% chance he had an accomplice. Or 1 in 4 for each. But because they're both necessary for this student to be the killer, we multiple, which means there's only a 1 in 16 (or about 6%) chance that he's the killer.

Now, to convincingly eliminate the student, we need to find one more element to stack, something else that needs to be true for this suspect to pan out so we can stack three elements.

Our detectives learn that during this period, when the student would need to have been traveling, the data shows that someone used his login to play *Fortnite* from his bedroom. By itself, this doesn't eliminate him as a suspect, because a clever killer could have gotten a buddy to sit in his room and play *Fortnite* while he was on the road. It's not unreasonable that he might be smart enough to think of this. He's driving back to his college to commit murder and needs an alibi. He could anticipate this. It's smart.

Would this violate YCT Rule #1 that *there are no geniuses*?

No. It's not genius to consider creating an alibi when you're planning a murder.

But it's a little unlikely, right? Let's say there's a 25% chance this student thought to create an alibi by having someone sit in his room for a while and play Fortnite. So, now we have three somewhat unlikely things that all need to be true, so we can stack them up:

- the student suspect had to somehow make an eight-hour round trip;
- he brought an accomplice with him;
- he made someone sit in his room and play *Fortnite*.

If each one of these by itself has about a 25% chance of being true, since they all need to be true for the student to be the killer, there's only about a 1.5% chance that he's our man. The point is this: as we eliminate suspects or theories, we must look to stack together unlikely elements that all need to be true for the theory to work.

In the Karen Read case, there are a lot of unlikely things which all have to be true for there to have been a conspiracy to kill John and cover it up.

Here we go.

### Why not Call 911?

If John was mauled by a dog and beaten almost to death inside the house, what should we imagine that the attackers would do? John's wounds weren't fatal. The only substantial wound was a blow to the back of the head that crushed bones and left him unconscious, but breathing. If they call an ambulance and John's life is saved, what will happen to the attackers?

Well, it will be his word against everyone in the house, who will all just say he came in drunk and started a fight. It seems unlikely anyone will get in trouble.

Contrarily, if John turns up dead, what are the odds that the medical examiner will *not* see that he was mauled by a dog and in a fight? Brian Albert and Brian Higgins are very experienced cops. Sarah Levinson is a nurse. They'll know that if John was attacked in such a violent way, there will be no way to hide it.

The common sense, self-preservation thing to do is to call 911.

But they're drunk, maybe not thinking so clearly. And someone struck John on the back of the head with an object. Perhaps careers will be ruined. Therefore, they make the inexplicable decision that John needs to die so he can never tell his story.

This leaves them with two problems. One, John is still alive; and two, what to do with the body.

Remember, the reason for disposing of him is so he won't tell the tale. Yet they decide to put him out... alive... on their own lawn?

When we run this notion by people who aren't familiar with the case, they're dumbfounded. They don't understand how people actually believe it happened this way. They're stunned that a defense team put that theory in writing and submitted it to the court.

Victoria from Dublin wondered why they would put him out like this with his phone. What if he woke up and called for help? If they were going to put him out to die, wouldn't they first finish him off the way Tony Soprano finished off Christopher Moltisanti by blocking his nose and mouth while he was trapped after a car crash? Wouldn't they make sure John never woke up, if that was the goal?

Ask yourself: what are the chances that something like this—putting the victim out, alive, onto their own lawn—can be true? Whatever probability odds you want to assign... 1 in 10 odds, 1 in 100, 1 in 1000, whatever... we then must stack this with other probabilities and multiply.

For the conspiracy theory to prove true, it also requires the planting of evidence on a significant scale: taillight pieces, cocktail glass pieces, glass pieces on the bumper of the Lexus, practically microscopic taillight pieces on John's clothing, DNA on a section of taillight, John's hair on the rear panel... even the black straw that went with the drink.

Much of that key evidence would have to be planted by the investigators… and planted 17 whole hours after the event.

The troopers involved would have been consciously taking on a tremendous—almost reckless—risk. If any photo was taken during the day, or clear video emerged, which showed the taillight intact… well, as they used to say in the movies, "the gig is up." Those troopers would be ruined, going to prison. For what reason? Because Michael Proctor's sister was friends with Chris Albert's wife's sister? Remember YCT Rule #14, it's about SUFFICIENT motive.

Let's be really, really generous to the defense theory and say the odds of the people in the house deciding to put John out on their own lawn, alive, to let the cold finish him off is 1 in 10.

Okay, so what are the odds that all that evidence was planted, much of it by police, at enormous personal risk and in a way that they were very likely to be caught? Again, for the sake of argument, we'll be irrationally generous and call it 1 in 10.

Those odds multiply, so now the defense theory is at a 1 in 100 chance of being true.

But let's just put it in terms of words. It's rather unlikely that the people in the house would put John out alive to die on their own lawn. And it's rather unlikely that multiple police officers would risk their freedom to plant evidence in a murder case involving people they either didn't know or barely did. But both of these things had to happen for the conspiracy theory to hold up. Since they both are rather unlikely, the theory is now very, very unlikely.

Now, if we can just find a couple more necessary elements to stack with this, then the theory becomes so *highly improbable* that it's safe to call it *impossible.*

It can't be exaggerated how useful this stacking technique is when it comes to eliminating possible theories in a crime.

Let's stack another element.

Nine people were in the house, and they all testified that John never came in. None of these people had a criminal history. Would they all stay silent? Would Julie Nagel and Sarah Levinson stay silent as the men in the house plotted to murder a wounded man? Their silence would make them accomplices. Would they stay silent even after they learned the FBI was investigating this? Or would one of them save themselves by cutting a deal? If they had been terrified by the killers into participating in a murder conspiracy, and they knew the Feds were about to bust it open and arrest everyone involved, wouldn't some of these witnesses be RACING to the US Attorney's Office to save their own skin?

Again, for the sake of argument, we'll say there's a 1 in 10 chance that everyone in the house remains silent, even people forced to participate, even with the Feds hot on the trail. A 1 in 10 chance is an utterly absurd number, but let's run with it.

There's a 1 in 10 chance that the killers placed John alive on their own lawn so the cold will finish him off.

A 1 in 10 chance that all of the evidence is planted, much of it by people with motive that is at best insufficient and more realistically nonexistent.

A 1 in 10 chance that everyone in the house remains silent.

10 x 10 x 10 = 1000.

So, there's now a 1 in 1000 chance that this conspiracy theory proves true. And that's being as generous as we can be to it.

And there are more things we can stack to make the probability even longer. Here are some:

**Why didn't Proctor and Bukhenik secure the vehicle?**

As explained earlier, when the troopers left the McCabe home, they didn't secure the Lexus, which was sitting a mile away. They went to the hospital.

Chapter One of the *State Police Manual for Planting Evidence to Frame an Innocent Victim* makes clear that obtaining the evidence needed for planting is Job Number One.

Let's put it this way: if the troopers were tasked with framing Karen, it would have certainly happened in the McCabe home. What are the odds they wouldn't make their next stop the Lexus?

### The Feds apparently didn't uncover a conspiracy

The federal investigation was taken on personally by the very powerful First Assistant US Attorney, Josh Levy, who eventually would continue the investigation as US Attorney. The FBI was tasked to investigate, a federal grand jury was seated, and eventually the reputation of the office and of Josh Levy became linked to this investigation. If it didn't uncover a conspiracy, there was going to be a lot of egg on their faces, because very significant resources had been invested into it, and if it didn't discover a cover-up, there are hard questions about whether the federal investigation was properly predicated in the first place.

The Feds were absolutely going to leave no stone unturned.

And it doesn't seem like they did. By November of 2022, just months after Karen and her lawyers were able to simply walk into Josh Levy's office, the Feds began subpoenaing the phone records of at least seven witnesses named by the defense team as part of the conspiracy. And they further got warrants for the content of many of those witnesses' communications. Fair to say that if something was to be found… if there was a conspiracy… the Feds were very likely to find evidence of it.

Yet they seemingly did not.

The Supreme Court case of Brady vs. Maryland established that the government must turn over upon request all material exculpatory evidence to a defendant. If that evidence is held by a part of the government separate from the prosecution, such as the Feds in this case, it must still be turned over. It's first put through the Touhy Process to make sure federal regulations are complied with.

The Norfolk County District Attorney, as required by their duty to acquire any exculpatory evidence, made this request by letter several times to the US Attorney. Strangely, they were ignored, forcing the DA to write to the Department of Justice.

Just a couple of months before the trial, the Feds submitted all material exculpatory evidence they had compiled during their lengthy investigation to both parties. No one had been indicted by the federal grand jury. No police officer had been suspended. The only wrongdoing that would eventually emerge as the result of the federal investigation were some inappropriate messages sent by Trooper Proctor over his personal phone.

A baffled Judge Cannone, overseeing the State's murder trial, implored Karen's team to give her some basis on which to allow a third-party culprit defense. Having read the federal materials, she obviously had seen none.

During the trial, no FBI agent testified. The only evidence submitted that resulted from the federal investigation was Proctor's insensitive texts. Karen did call on the ARCCA guys, independent accident reconstructionists hired by the US Attorney, and they did attempt to help Karen by saying that it was unlikely John's injuries were caused by a vehicle.

But what we're going to say now can't just be dismissed: the Feds DID NOT find ANY evidence of a cover-up by the time of the trial.

Because if they had, the defendant's Brady rights would have required the Feds to turn over any exculpatory evidence, and evidence of a cover-up certainly would be exculpatory. So even if the investigation was technically ongoing, the Feds would be required to turn over any evidence of a cover-up.

This means the only way they found evidence of a cover-up is if it was found after the trial. But this is super-duper unlikely. There are no indications that a grand jury continued. Trooper Proctor was the last to testify, and that was in early February. Whatever communications or data the Feds might have obtained would have been received many months before.

It's safe to say the Feds found no evidence of a cover-up. In fact, by February of 2025, the new US Attorney, Leah B. Foley, brought in with the new administration, confirmed that the federal investigation ended without anyone being charged.

This leaves us with this final question to add to our stack: what are the chances that there was a substantial cover-up involving at least a dozen witnesses and investigators, yet the FBI found no evidence of it?

As all of these unlikely occurrences stack together, the math against the conspiracy starts to look daunting.

The "very"s stack up.

The conspiracy theory becomes very, very, very, very, very unlikely.

# 2. CLEARING THE TABLE

At the end of the day, it's the State that has to prove its case, not the defense. And the State does have a compelling case, though it was very poorly presented in the first trial, and there are still some absolutely crucial aspects that have to be proven to a jury, aspects that strangely were not addressed much in the first trial, especially in regard to John's injuries.

A huge problem for the Commonwealth of Massachusetts was that while it did actually present very compelling evidence, the most important evidence wasn't pulled together for them in a coherent way. I'm going to do that.

But first, let's clear the table of the biggest things that make people believe something unusual happened in this case.

**2:27**

The search for "Hos long to die in cold," allegedly at 2:27 A.M., was the basis for the defense's alternative theory, presented to the court a year before the trial and to the public a week later through Turtleboy. It was on billboards and T-shirts. Defense attorney Alan Jackson forced Jen McCabe to recite it on the stand. Even though the logic of the case itself, beyond the data interpretation, renders 2:27 utterly absurd, it has become an article of faith to the faithful. They recite it online like monks doing Hail Marys as Vikings climb the monastery walls.

I'm not going to bore you with a technical explanation beyond this: Jen searched for her daughter's basketball league at 2:27, then went to sleep, leaving the browser open. At 6:23, when Karen wanted to know how long someone could survive in extreme cold, Jen used the same open browser to type that search. There were a couple of different spelling variations she tried at that time. It was freezing out, a high stress moment, and she was typing onto a phone.

The most plausible explanation has always been that the three typed-in searches were done at the same time. Karen's side has said from the beginning that the searches at 6:23 were done by Jen in order to somehow cover up the search she made at 2:27. It's easier to believe the moon is made of cheese. The idea is that Jen McCabe, this evil criminal mastermind of the ages, convinced Karen to believe she struck John, and then suddenly remembered her earlier search, and weirdly thought that typing it again would cover it up? Alrighty, then.

One of the most important things we all have to do when looking at cases is to recognize how ignorant we are of most of the complicated things that go on around us in the everyday world. Do we really know what goes on inside our phone? Or everything that a letter goes through before arriving at our mailbox?

An example I use is this: I've been voting for 40 years. I go to the polling station, give them my name, and get a ballot. After filling it out, I drop it in some ancient wooden box. Somehow my vote is tabulated. Is it connected to Wi-Fi? Does someone read a counter at the end of the day? Are there tiny Keebler elves working inside that box? I have utterly no idea.

We're surrounded by processes we don't understand. We don't know how sausage is made. And that's how it is with homicide investigations. Who does what and in what order… we don't know. We have ideas from watching *Dexter*, but we don't really know. Fingerprints, DNA matching, blood spray patterns, putting phones in airplane mode, documenting the location of spent shells, evidence storage, autopsies… and forensic data. We don't know.

When I first heard that 2:27 was found in Jen's phone, I thought data was data. Didn't you?

But then I learned at the next hearing that the State had an independent forensic data expert, Jessica Hyde, who explained that there was no search for "Hos long…" at 2:27. Whoa! Stop the presses, hold the headline. Is data open to interpretation?

It seems obvious to me now, of course, that it is. We're surrounded by streams of data on our phones, laptops, RING systems, printers, routers, alarm clocks, Rokus and, of course, our cars. These streams are guided by ever more complex algorithms written by multitudes of coders for purposes that are varied, but which have nothing to do with forensic data.

Forensic data companies like Cellebrite and Magnet Axiom Cyber create software to read the data captured on these devices. It's imperfect. The software can never keep up with the evolving programs they're trying to read, so it does its best.

To truly analyze that captured data, you need a human being. An expert. Someone who looks at the reports the software produces and applies a higher level of understanding.

It's the same thing with medical tests. I go for scans every three months and I read the results. The radiologist will flag certain things seen in the scans for the doctor to look at, and the doctor, applying many years of expertise, will interpret the radiologist's report and apply understanding.

For example, the radiologist might note a nodule in my lung. Reading the radiologist's report, I might say, "Damn, that's not good. I better finish writing this book!" But then I visit the doctor, and he says, "Just scar tissue, nothing to worry about."

Think of programs like Cellebrite as the radiologist flagging things for the doctor. These forensic data programs flag something and the expert will look at all of the other surrounding evidence and data and determine whether what was flagged is relevant or not.

We in the public have to remember that it's not the job of the defense team to solve the case. They aren't after the truth. They're on the hunt for anything that might be useful in creating doubt.

And any expert willing to accept a payday from the defense understands this.

I'm not talking about lying. This involves finding things the defense can present as odd to a jury. It involves choosing interpretations of the evidence at every turn, which helps the defense.

When I first heard the name Jessica Hyde, I looked her up and found she's extremely elite in her field at George Mason University. She has done extensive work, for decades, with the government and the military.

I couldn't find anything on Rich Green, the defense expert. And I hoped to find that he was a superstar! I thought it would make a great video to present a battle of two titans, like from *Gladiator*, Jessica the Merciless vs. General Green the Machine.

When I called the number on Green's website, it went to a generic answering service that didn't even list the company name. Huh.

Since that time, I've learned that Green has numerous LLCs listed in Ohio, Michigan, and Florida, most of them being forensic data companies. So he starts a lot of these businesses.

There were a lot of tax liens.

And a couple of arrests. The most recent was in 2016, and it involved him being asked to leave a bar in Florida called MacNasty's. Outside the door, untouched by anyone, he fell. He then called 911 and filed a false report about being pushed. Surveillance video showed otherwise.

Look, people make mistakes in life. This isn't about smearing, and I hate the way that goes on in social media. But this information seems relevant. In a hearing before the second trial, the defense argued for Green's qualifications by citing that he has testified in trials 26 times.

When I was a young man, I served my first jury duty. It involved a civil case. And I'll never forget the cross-examination of a medical doctor. The guy was about 50 years old. For some reason, he hadn't practiced medicine in a few years. But in that time, he earned a living another way: by testifying. He had testified in more than a couple dozen cases.

Again, I'm not saying defense experts lie while prosecution experts don't. I'm saying we have to have some street smarts about what goes on in the real world.

No other expert has come forward to publicly back up Rich Green on ANY of his contentions.

This is a very high-profile case, and Alan Jackson is one of the highest-profile attorneys in the country. If they could find a forensic data expert without Green's checkered past, don't you think they would have?

The prosecution also brought in the senior forensic data expert from Cellebrite itself! That's the company that created the software both Green and the State used. It's used by law enforcement all over the world.

Ian Whiffen's superior knowledge was quickly apparent on the stand. His team had reached out to Green some time months before the trial, but he didn't take the call. Whiffen offered the same explanation in court as Jessica Hyde. The search, according to him, was done at 6:23, and Cellebrite's software has now been tweaked so it no longer produces this erroneous artifact.

But let's say that, like me, you consider this data stuff mumbo jumbo. What if I told you we don't need it to disprove 2:27?

After John was taken by ambulance from the scene, Karen left with Kerry to drive to the hospital. On the way, she texted her dad: "John's dead." Now awake, Mr. Read called right back. And because she was saying she didn't want to live, he called the Canton Police, who called Sergeant Goode at the crime scene, who called Kerry and asked her to bring Karen back. There, another ambulance awaited her. She was Section 12'd, put into custody for her own safety, and brought to the hospital. Though she was still suffering outbursts of hysteria, she didn't resist.

In the ambulance, she asked the paramedic the same question she had asked Jen McCabe, prompting McCabe to make that search at 2:27: how long can someone survive in the cold?

That testimony came out at trial. That should end all belief in 2:27, but faith is very powerful.

Let's finish on the subject of 2:27 with this: does it even pass the basic smell test? The McCabes left 34 Fairview around 1:30. They gave Sarah Levinson and Julie Nagel a ride home. If they drove off knowing that the plan… plan!... was to put John out to die later, that car would have been unimaginably tense. There would have been fierce arguments. Levinson, a nurse, would have been shouting that they're not going to get away with it. If John had been mauled by a German shepherd and beat up, she would know there would be no way to hide that from the ER staff and the paramedics. No way. The McCabes and Julie Nagel would know it too. If they don't go to the police, with John still alive, they're all accomplices to murder. They wouldn't need to consult a DUI lawyer to know the prison sentences for that will be long. They would understand how unlikely they were to get away with it.

So the McCabes go home to their four little girls. Jen is wearing an Apple health watch, and it shows her heartbeat to be completely normal through all of this. They tuck the kids in, then get ready for bed. Jen plays "It's Raining Men" on her phone. She messages the coach of her daughter's eighth-grade basketball team. She looks up the league.

Oh, and yeah, she searches for how long it will take for her friend, John O'Keefe, to die when her relatives put him out in the yard. The niece that John is raising is best friends with Jen's daughter.

Jen has no arrest record, used to teach fifth grade. But maybe she really is Keyser Söze, leading a double life as an evil villain. Maybe Putin's invasion of Ukraine was originally her idea, and she cooked up COVID in her kitchen lab.

But even if one considers the possibility that she's utterly heartless, doesn't she have some sense of self interest? If she doesn't, what about Matt?

What exactly is the plan? When John is found on the lawn mauled by a dog and beaten up, what are they going to tell the police? Do they already know that they're going to frame Karen? Do they know she's going to back into John's Traverse? Do they know she's going to call Kerry and say, "John's dead, hit by a plow"? Do they know she's going to keep repeating "I hit him" at the scene?

Of course not. But what they absolutely would know is that they're almost sure to get caught and that both she and Matt will be going to prison for decades. The house will be lost, the kids raised by someone else. They stand on the precipice of ruin.

Yet Jen is casually looking up basketball leagues and making a search four seconds later about how long it will take for her friend to die?

When people are presented with all that, and they still believe in 2:27, it leaves me speechless. Maybe we do live in a virtual reality and the people who believe these things are NPCs, non-player characters created by the program as part of the game in order to provide obstacles for the real players to deal with. I have no other explanation, but I'm confounded by the prospect that real human beings believe this.

### Why No One Came out of the House

This one piece of evidence that gave me serious pause in the early days of the hysteria: with all that commotion on the lawn, they really slept through it?

Then I remembered that in small towns like Canton, the first responders don't use their sirens at night. It's like that in my town too. Officer Saraf not only didn't have his sirens on, but he didn't put on the flashing blues until he arrived.

Still, Karen was screaming and fire trucks have loud engines, right?

It was the beginning of a blizzard, winds steady at 30 MPH, gusting over 50. Sergeant Goode testified that at the scene, when talking to someone nearby, you had to shout to be heard over the wind.

At 6:15, it was still pitch dark. The shades were drawn. The wind was absorbing most sound. Karen's parents didn't wake up from her three calls, either. People sleep deeply in these conditions.

Most of us overestimate how lightly we sleep because we remember those times a noise woke us up, but we don't remember the time something really loud didn't wake us up… because we didn't wake up.

Jen made three calls into the house from the scene. Despite the defense's tricks, evidence showed that the calls went unanswered. Remember all those voicemails Karen left on John's phone? Those calls show on her records as "answered," but on John's records as "not answered."

Two of Jen's calls into the house show as answered… but only on Jen's data… because they went to voicemail.

See what I mean about mundane explanations?

As I got older, my sleep patterns changed a little. I get up around 4:00 and go to the bathroom. When I go back to sleep the second time, I find that I fall into an unusually deep sleep, with the most vivid dreams. I'm gone. And I suspect this is the time that it would be hardest to wake me, around 6:00 A.M. Especially in the depth of winter, with sunrise an hour away.

Unable to wake her sister and her brother-in-law, Jen rang the doorbell. Then she went inside. She testified that she went upstairs and into the bedroom to wake them up. Detective Lank would be in the house when the Alberts came down, and he testified they looked like they had just woken up. I know, I know, everyone's in on it, so maybe you don't believe Lank.

But if the Alberts were really inside hiding and waiting for John to be discovered, wouldn't Jen also have stayed home? Ignoring phone calls? Why would she return to the scene? Why would she call the people inside from the scene if she knew they were hiding behind the curtains?

Oh, I forgot, because she's Lex Luther.

### Ascending/descending Stairs

The raw GPS shows that John never went inside the house. GPS location data is incredibly accurate. It's designed by the military to fly missiles through a mullah's window from a thousand miles away. The Apple health app is designed to help you exercise.

The health app has John walking 116 steps and traveling stairs between 12:22 and a little after 12:24. But we know, from both Waze and the raw GPS, that Karen missed the turn onto Fairview at 12:23:46, and after a three-point 180, they took the turn onto Fairview at 12:24:18.

So in the entire time the health app says John was stair climbing and walking, they were actually still in the Lexus.

Out of desperation, the defense tried to suggest that there were multiple clocks within a phone and the apps were accessing one that was up to three minutes off. They offered Ryan Nagel's 12:23 text to his sister inside the house saying "here" as proof.

All nonsense. Nagel testified that he made that text from Cedarcrest Road when they were "two minutes" away.

The Lexus is observed going by Temple Beth David after 12:20. That's a four-minute drive from Fairview.

Atomic clocks have been designed to be the most accurate time pieces invented and they were largely made for GPS. Location accuracy is intricately linked to time accuracy.

We also have the time from when John called Jen McCabe for the address. They were a four-minute drive from the 34 Fairview.

John simply never went into the house, never ascended or descended stairs—at least not with his phone.

How did the health app come up with this erroneous conclusion?

Go to ChatGPT or something similar and ask it how the app makes these determinations. It turns out it's a sophisticated device with several sensors. But what it lacks is a drone to follow you overhead and report to the app what activity you are doing. Are you walking? Roller skating? Riding a bike? Climbing a ladder to the roof? Skiing?

It has to guess what you're doing based on a variety of sensor inputs. It uses gyroscopes and barometric altimeters. It reads the rhythm of your movements.

When we walk upstairs, what are the clues the app might use? Obviously, change in elevation, speed. But it also leans on movements that are typical of stair climbing.

However, other things can mimic those movements, such as if you talk with hand gestures while holding the phone.

According to the raw GPS and the Waze data, John was on Oakdale Street when the health app thought he was on stairs. It had him doing this type of activity for the two-minute drive from Oakdale to 34 Fairview. Google Earth shows that the change in elevation for that drive is 30 meters. Or three flights of stairs.

In addition, it was 18 degrees outside, and the car engine was cold when Karen and John got into the Lexus after hours of drinking. It would take about seven or eight minutes to warm up and be able to blast heat. That would put them right around on Oakdale St. Say the car suddenly warmed from 25 to 75 degrees. That would change the barometric pressure within the car to the equivalence of 30 feet. Or three flights of stairs.

When they got to the corner of Oakdale and Cedarcrest, there could have been an argument. If they wanted to go home, they would need to turn left. If they wanted to continue to the party, turn right. If they argued for 20 or so seconds, that would slow down their average speed during this part of the trip quite a bit.

At the end of the day, we don't know and can't know what combination of sensory streams tricked the exercise app. But we do have the raw GPS data and the Waze data. And we have the time that John called Jen for the address. There's no real argument here, but once again, it's hard to argue with belief.

### Dog Bites

It's not unreasonable to see a photo online or in the newspaper of the shallow, parallel wounds on John's arm and wonder if these are from a dog attack.

It is, however, very unreasonable for a doctor to look at those wounds and make that determination with "medical certainty," based on just a newspaper photo.

The wounds are very shallow. The attack clearly didn't contribute to the cause of death. Any number of things could create shallow, parallel wounds. Any credible doctor, scientist, or dog-bite expert would need to know a whole lot more before making that determination.

Dr. Marie Russell of Los Angeles didn't. She saw a newspaper article in an online version of the *Boston Globe*, right as the trial was getting underway, and she reached out to the Los Angeles District Attorney's Office. Karen's defense attorney had spent many years in Los Angeles as a prosecutor before becoming a lawyer to the stars.

The defense happily sent Dr. Russell files of information for her to analyze. She looked at some of it, ignoring other parts. But it was all really just confirming what she seems to have already decided after seeing the *Globe* article: these were dog bites.

There is absolutely no question Dr. Russell is qualified to give expert opinion. She had been retired as an emergency room doctor for almost 20 years. She began her college education at M.I.T. in the '70s, but when her mother died, she was forced to drop out. She eventually became a cop… the town's first female cop… in Malden, Massachusetts, and continued to complete her education, going on to medical school. She worked in the coroner's office doing autopsies for several years, and as a prison doctor, before ending up as an emergency room physician in a Los Angeles hospital. There, seeing gangsters and ex-cons coming in daily with gunshot wounds and prison tattoos, she began, on her own, to document and collect photos of the wounds. She published work on this and became in demand on the lecture circuit. She's an incredibly accomplished woman.

As part of her side project documenting wounds, she also published research on dog bites. These involved victims of bites by police dogs, which are unique wounds, since those dogs are trained to bite and hold.

We first saw images of John's wounds back at the beginning when Turtleboy published them. So, we saw the images at the same time we were told they were dog bites. That power of suggestion has a great impact on our memory. The brain is a pattern-recognition machine, and if we don't know what we're looking at, suggestion has an indelible influence.

When I saw Turtle's story, I googled "dog bites." Going through hundreds of images, I found nothing that looked like John's wounds. I tried looking for dog bites on a cadaver. Nothing helpful.

This doesn't mean they weren't dog bites, because the search showed that almost no two dog bites look alike.

But then how did Dr. Russell make this determination seemingly based solely on a newspaper article?

No other dog-bite experts have come forward to affirm her conclusion. This, despite that fact that the theory and those images have been prominent in the media for almost two years.

On John's arm, there are no corresponding wounds from the lower jaw of the dog. Dr. Russell couldn't distinguish which wounds on the arm were caused by teeth and which by nails. There are three separate sets of parallel lines, but the spacing between them is different. She couldn't effectively explain that.

After the first trial, Dr. Russell was forced back on the stand months later, for what is called a Daubert Hearing, to determine if she was qualified. It's rare for a judge to disqualify an expert for a defendant, and Dr. Russell will testify in the second trial.

But in between the first trial and the Daubert Hearing, her testimony evolved. She showed more methodology. She pointed to fibers on John's shirt being on the outside, suggesting that whatever made the rip in the shirt and the skin then pulled out fibers as it withdrew, like a dog's teeth or nails.

However, during the first trial, Russell seemed to deliberately skip over a vital piece of evidence: canine DNA.

After the defense put out their theory that John had been attacked by the German shepherd inside the house, the defense and the prosecution agreed on an independent lab to test swabs taken from John's clothing by a state criminologist. She had double swabbed the rips in the right sleeve of John's shirt. The tests came back negative. No canine DNA.

It's hard to imagine how a dog could sink several bites into someone's arm and not leave canine DNA on the shirt.

Dr. Russell is a very intelligent woman and not intimidated on the stand. Her qualifications are somewhat unique: autopsies, documenting wounds, emergency room, and dog bites.

But this just shows how complicated it is when it comes to expert witnesses. In 2001, the *L.A. Times* did an article on Dr. Russell. She was at the top of her game and very much in demand. She was a senior doctor at one of the busiest ERs in the country, teaching courses at County-USC and Cal State L.A and in demand on the lecture circuit.

But a decade later, she would retire under somewhat unusual circumstances. It seems she started missing shifts. A lot of them. The hospital let her go and she sued, claiming she suffered from hypersomnia, a condition characterized by excessive sleepiness during the day.

So Dr. Russell had really been in the juice… and then suddenly, she wasn't. And it seems to have been that way for about 10 years.

Until she saw that story in the *Globe*.

The *L.A. Times* article mentioned she had one other passion: true crime.

**The Feds**

Under normal circumstances, the mere existence of a deep federal investigation into a murder investigation would be more than enough to create reasonable doubt, and much more than that. And had the Feds not agreed to take up Karen's cause, she wouldn't have convinced Turtleboy to take it up. I've read the original messages between Aidan and Karen, which were screenshotted by Karen's friend Natalie because Karen insisted on using a go-between. And Aidan was skeptical. He may not care for truth from an ethical point of view, but he didn't want to be duped. Not good for his brand.

He actually asked some of the tough questions we have here. In fact, the conspiracy theory didn't seem to make any sense to him at the time.

But then Karen told him that the Feds were coming and that the arrests of the real killers were imminent, weeks away. That hooked him.

When I first began covering this case, my channel was small, I had never done live shows, and I barely knew what a source was, let alone had any. But I did have a friend in Boston law enforcement who reported to me that the FBI was "taking over" the investigation. The FBI?

Rumors were rife that agents were all over Canton. Arrests any day. Is that a black helicopter over the Canton Police station? They're coming!

Even Turtle wasn't saying anything on his show about the Feds then, which exasperated Karen, who wanted it out there. Did he have some reason to be skeptical?

Karen was pushing him HARD too. She was angry he wasn't talking about the Feds.

From what we now know, it was all the way back in August of 2022, eight months after John's death, that Karen and her team walked into Josh Levy's office. They had a story to pitch.

This was one month after Karen had brought Alan Jackson onto the team.

And one month after this visit, the defense would start keying on Proctor.

What the Feds did after that is a story that needs to be told, but the only way we'll ever learn it is if the Feds themselves do an investigation.

Remember the last scene from *Raiders of the Lost Ark*? Indiana Jones has brought them the powerful Ark of the Covenant. He asks the government agents who first hired him what they're going to do with it. They reply, "We have top men working on it right now." Who? "Top. Men." Then we see the Ark put in a crate and placed within an endless government warehouse filled with crates, where it will be just as lost as before.

I suspect this is what will happen to material showing the launching of this large federal investigation. The Feds know how to bury anything that makes them look bad.

According to the Norfolk County District Attorney, it was the US Attorney's Office that leaked to Karen the days and times when witnesses would be appearing before the federal grand jury. Those witnesses would be very weirdly questioned by three prosecutors, including the US Attorney himself, Josh Levy. And they would use a blown-up copy of Turtleboy's blog, *TB Daily News*, something each of those attorneys would have understood would terrify the witnesses, sending them the message that the whole thing was rigged against them.

Under the threats from the mob stirred up by Turtleboy, the witnesses went many times to the US Attorney's Office for protection. He ignored them.

The O'Keefe family has gone many times.

Ignored.

It's impossible to deny that something really odd is going on with this federal investigation. Just six months before the trial, Josh Levy would hold a teleconference call with Karen's team. And he would advise them to delay the trial. He would also advise them not to discuss the call with the media. Of course.

As the trial approached, Judge Cannone was at a loss. She had an upcoming murder trial. The defense was talking openly in court about the federal investigation, saying that exculpatory evidence gathered by the Feds was on the way… yet the US Attorney's Office utterly and arrogantly ignored her. She invited them to send someone to explain what was going on… Nothing. No one showed.

From the prosecutor and the defense team, the judge learned that the evidence to be turned over was in the Touhy process.

Remember, any exculpatory evidence held by the Feds must be turned over as Brady material. They don't have a choice. ANYTHING that could be exculpatory to the defendant.

That included all the minutes from the federal grand jury, because all of those witnesses had also testified before the State grand jury, and any discrepancy in their statements could be exploited by the defense. Discrepancy is normal and expected, but because it was potentially exculpatory, it had to be turned over.

Presumably, Trooper Proctor was the last witness to go before the federal grand jury. This was on February 8, 2024. Was there anything else for them to investigate?

Judge Cannone finally provoked a response from the Feds when she granted a hearing to the *Boston Globe* in April. They motioned for her to make public the federal materials. Frustrated with the federal interference in her murder case and their complete unresponsiveness, she seemed more than inclined to release the material, including the grand jury minutes. She had already reviewed the more than three thousand pages and said there was nothing in it that pointed to a third-party culprit.

Now, finally, the US Attorney's Office responded, sending a letter threatening to essentially take over the trial if she released the material.

Why doesn't the US Attorney's Office want any of this public? Why won't they take the heat off innocent witnesses being hounded by a mob by revealing evidence which exonerates them? There's no law against that, and ethics requires it.

Because, as I've said, integrity is rare. You don't actually even know whether you have it until you reach a time of choice, and you choose to do what's right even though it harms your personal interest. You don't learn integrity in Ivy League schools or at elite law firms. The guy fixing your car or the fifth-grade teacher working with your kids is just as likely to have integrity as the Princeton lawyer working for the US Attorney's Office in between stints at Ropes & Gray.

What originally predicated this investigation? How did Karen and her team convince then First Assistant US Attorney Josh Levy to release the Kraken… the FBI and a team of ASUS?

We don't know. It was months before Rich Green found any incriminating data. It was before they had any independent experts saying John wasn't struck by a vehicle, that he was mauled by a dog.

So what did they have?

Did they sell Levy on the idea of Steve Scanlon as a whistleblower?

Maybe they convinced him that Scanlon had gone back into the shadows out of fear, and that only the existence of an FBI investigation could give him the courage to come out.

We don't know. We know the first orders went out to the phone companies to preserve the phone data of at least seven witnesses as early as November of 2022.

We know eventually they also got warrants for the content of some of that communication.

Some of the content they got went back five years!

We don't know what else they got. Did they grab geofence data? Almost certainly. Did they check into the GPS data of the town's plows? Assuredly, since they did visit the DPW and Lucky Loughran.

They likely know what devices were in the house that night and what time those devices left. If John's phone was in the house, they would know it, and that certainly would have been revealed by this exculpatory evidence.

There's a mistaken idea out there that many have, including many lawyers and former federal agents. The belief is that a federal investigation proceeds on its own sweet time, and that nothing is revealed until they decide to wrap it up.

No.

As I've said, a defendant has the right to Brady material. If the US Attorney's Office intentionally withheld any Brady material, they'll need to slap the cuffs on themselves.

So let's close the matter of the Feds by listing what is known and indisputable.

A) The Feds did an extensive investigation involving the FBI, subpoenas and warrants on communications, and a federal grand jury that brought in the witnesses the defense claimed were the real killers. None of the witnesses pled the Fifth. None of them were indicted. None were told they were targets, and if they were under suspicion, they were required to be told that so they could lawyer up and consider their Fifth Amendment rights.

B) Absolutely no exculpatory evidence emerged from any of this by the time of the first trial. The defense lawyers haven't reported any new federal evidence as we approach the second trial.

As *My Cousin Vinny*'s Vinny LaGuardia Gambini might say, "I got no more use for these guys."

**ARCCA**

In August of 2024, I was outside the courthouse in Dedham for a hearing on scheduling the second trial. By this time, supporters of John O'Keefe and the prosecution had emerged wearing blue shirts. About 75 of them stood on one side of the courthouse stairs. On the other side, kept separated by a narrow patch of No Man's Land maintained by the State Police, massed the pink-shirted army that supports Karen. They also massed across the street on the stairs of the district court. Occasionally, a truck went by blasting a horn in support of Karen. News helicopters buzzed overhead and camera crews worked the edges of the crowd.

I was standing with the blue shirts, but I wanted to talk to the pinks. I had done a series of Court TV shoots in Dedham in April as the first trial opened. After the Monday appearance, Vinnie Politan's show manager asked us if we could try to fill the joint for the next night's show. I said, "Sure, I can post about it in social media, but it will be an all-pink audience." That didn't bother them, so I posted, and the Pink Army showed.

But in truth I got along well with them. And they liked talking to me, at least back then. Sadly, the nature of these movements is to grow more bitter over time. Much of that crowd accuses me of faking cancer and whatever else they can make up. But in that week, I met them a couple of times, and we got along. I liked them. This was just a cause they believed in.

Vinnie was friendly to any fans who showed up. He was more than willing to take selfies. The pink shirts wanted to talk about their beliefs with anyone who would listen.

I went and sat down with Nick Rocco and one of Karen's bodyguards. Nick would become a nightly rival on Court TV. This was my first time meeting him. I offered them some wings and ribs. The bodyguard looked at me like a Hatfield would look at a McCoy. But Nick shook my hand, we got along, and he expressed sincere sympathy and disgust at the just-emerging smear of faking cancer.

By the time of August came along, that type of friendliness between Pink Shirts and those of a different shade was hardly possible. But I wanted to try. I spotted someone just on the other side of No Man's Land whom I had been friendly with. So I crossed over and held out my hand. She didn't want to take it. Didn't even want to look at me. I said, "Come on, we got along fine in April." She took my hand with the greatest reluctance.

But then she moved off to make way for the angry pink crowd forming around me. Two prominent FKR YouTubers, Brian of LTL and MazzaMedia, went live and started bombing me with questions. I had met Brian and his wife in Dedham too. He seemed like a nice guy and, in fact, I had been told by my friend Dave McGrath that he's a very nice guy. Brian had parlayed his Karen Read advocacy into a healthy channel that even allowed him to rent a studio.

He was now asking me if I believed the world was round.

The angry crowd mushroomed around us. The State Troopers in No Man's Land grew nervous. I was getting bombed with questions and insults to the point where it was hard to answer questions asked by Brian or Mazza. But if my life in the bar industry had prepared me for anything, it was being alone in the middle of a hostile crowd.

See, the problem can be boiled down to one word: temptation. Brian was a hard-working guy toiling through life, dreaming of doing something more interesting than retail. And all because of one case, he now had the chance. I know a lot of YouTubers who would kill to have a studio to work out of. I work out of an attic room.

Remember Mike Crawford? I talked about him earlier. He runs a channel called Young Jurks. It had been around 10 years and seemed to have achieved no durable growth. Then along came Karen Read, and boom! Now he's booking lawyers and cops who wish to exploit the size of his audience.

Around Christmas of 2023, Turtleboy was on the run. He had been charged with witness intimidation and other crimes and had violated his bond, so they put out a BOLO. Be on the lookout. While on the run, he tried to contact the FBI, hoping against hope that the Feds really were coming to the rescue. They weren't.

When the Staties caught him, he was sent to jail. While there, Mike Crawford, who had been doing some soul searching for a couple of weeks, did a highly anticipated show. That morning, I got a Facebook friend request from him. Something was up. I had never watched his channel, but I knew he was an avid Karen supporter.

I tuned in to his show that night. Why was it so anticipated? Because word on the street was that he had "flipped" against Karen. With Turtle in jail, Mike was perhaps next in line.

The show began with a large audience, most of them FKR and Turtle Riders who were ready for blood if Mike showed any signs of flipping. What Crawford actually said was immensely reasonable, rational, and calm. He said, in effect, that from now on he was going to cover this case objectively from both sides.

At that, the mob in chat became about as violent as a chat mob can! If this had been in front of a live audience, Mike's life would have been in danger.

He even mentioned me. He said he was sorry for all the insults he had sent my way and that from now on he wanted a respectful relationship. He said maybe we would even do a show together.

The one thing he said that he did object to about me was that I talked about a "mindless mob." He said that didn't exist.

Then he looked down at his chat… and saw them. The mindless mob. The look on his face was precious. He saw vicious insults. And all he had promised to do was be fair and objective. Turning red, he whispered, "You guys are crazy."

But he also got scared. He tried to appease them by talking about related issues they were into, like a police audit in Canton.

The next day, word came out from jail: "No more wavering."

Turtleboy had people running his blog and channel for him, people like the Pitbull, whom he had falsely listed as an attorney. In jail, he heard about Mike's promise to be objective. And THAT wasn't something he was going to tolerate. The Code Red was put out.

So, Mike Crawford stepped back into line, 100% pro-FKR, asking no more objective questions. He took down one of the most-watched videos in the history of his channel. Why? He didn't want anyone to remember that he had promised to cover the case fairly.

Can you imagine that? THAT is the video he had to remove? Doesn't that tell us everything we need to know?

Many people covering this case, from YouTube and Court TV to Netflix and HBO to *Dateline* and *Fox News*, all face that same dilemma. Do they want to cover this case objectively? Or do they want to exploit the public's thirst for conspiracy theory? The thirst for an apparent underdog victim against allegedly powerful forces.

Mike allowed the Turtle crowd to scare him into covering this case in a way that appealed to the mob. We've seen opportunists like the *Boston Herald*'s Howie Carr try to ride those numbers. And we in the public have to understand that this is how things work now. When we regular people want the truth, we have to recognize this is going on and learn to be more skeptical.

So there I was in the middle of the Pink Army outside the courthouse. I looked at the cameras of LTL and MazzaMedia, questions and insults raining down, Brian asking me if the world was round.

What had them stirred up? What had convinced them that the experts confirmed John was killed in the house?

ARCCA. The PhDs from that company seemed to bear the imprimatur of science on whether John could have been struck by a vehicle. So many people were shouting at me I couldn't even answer.

Until finally I said this: "Those two guys from ARCCA are not only qualified, but they're the MOST qualified experts in the trial."

Every voice grew silent. Stunned. Jaws dropped. Every eye on me. The Pink Mob couldn't believe I was saying that.

I explained that these guys weren't only PhDs, unlike the troopers, but they were extremely articulate on the stand, and that accident reconstruction is what they do for a living.

The unblinking mob stared at me in disbelief.

"The issue is not their ability," I told them. "It's their credibility."

At the end of the day, the ARCCA had behaved like all of the defense experts, not looking at vital evidence and arguing to a conclusion that helped their client. Now, Karen didn't hire ARCCA; the Feds did. However, for some reason yet to be revealed, the US Attorney wanted to help Karen. If nothing else, by this point, helping her get off might help the Feds avoid embarrassment.

There were a couple of ways the ARCCA guys really showed their hand. One was the fact that they didn't ask the US Attorney for the Toyota Tech Stream vehicle data. And these guys are experts in Tech Stream. ARCCA's website displayed an article from the year before about Tech Stream, how data can be recovered that can't be found in ordinary black box data.

Trooper Paul, the CARS guy working for the State, hadn't trained on Tech Stream. He had to try to get up to speed, and by the time of the trial there was more he needed to learn. He could have used the help of the ARCCA guys, Dr. Daniel Wolfe and Dr. Andrew Rentschler.

Look, for accident reconstruction guys to do a reconstruction without the vehicle data is like a medical examiner doing an autopsy without a body. No one is saying the ARCCA guys needed EVERY piece of evidence, but they knew the vehicle was a Lexus, yet they made no attempt to even inquire about the Tech Stream data? They constructed a cocktail glass cannon on the theory that John had thrown the glass at the car, but they didn't want to know the speed of the vehicle?

These guys not requesting that data was ballgame for me, but there's more.

The other thing that stood out about Wolfe and Rentschler's testimony is that they only considered a very narrow range of possibilities. They were only able to use the limited evidence the US Attorney's Office gave them, which was what Karen had given the Feds. So they started with the idea that John had whipped the glass at the taillight. By the time of the trial, they were weighing whether John's injuries could have occurred if he had been swiped while holding his arm straight out, but no one thinks John was doing that, and it's kind of absurd to think he was standing in that position when struck.

The State didn't present a very effective theory in the first trial, but it seems to be that John sensed the SUV coming at the last moment and reacted by putting his bent arm into a defensive position. So the Lexus swiped the elbow and sent him flying back. Because his arm was bent, the internal structure of the taillight housing, now exposed with the covering smashed off, created the parallel wounds. John's arm snapped forward, his hand creating the dent in the rear panel a forearm's length away from the taillight.

The ARCCA guys didn't have to know this would be the State's eventual argument. They're accident reconstruction guys. They're supposed to consider all the main possibilities. That they didn't is… weird.

Or not. Because at the end of the day, they were no different from Dr. Russell ignoring the lack of canine DNA or Rich Green ignoring the call from Cellebrite. ARCCA's main business is actually not performing reconstructions. It's testifying. They need to please their client. The instructions from the US Attorney, though not explicit, would have been clear to them. They understood the Feds didn't believe the State's charges against Karen and had launched an expensive investigation into it. They understood what their client wanted.

The new prosecutor, Hank Brennan, won't make it so easy on them. He has already demanded they report what evidence they were sent AFTER the trial. Presumably, they were sent the Tech Stream data. Now, when they get on the stand and Brennan asks them if they got that data, they'll have to say yes. When he asks if they looked at it, if they say no, their credibility will be shattered. If they say yes, Brennan will grill them on whether Trooper Paul is correct that the data shows the telltale signs of a pedestrian strike. The ARCCA guys, who are very intelligent, will see this coming. So will the defense.

Will Josh Levy?

### Why Didn't Anyone See John?

If the State's theory about how John died is correct, Brian Higgins was the first to drive by him unconscious on the lawn. He didn't see him.

Brian is one of those guys who wears his heart on his sleeve. His eyes watered when he expressed regret at not seeing John. There are ways you can gauge if someone is telling the truth, and one way is when, instead of going to a possible explanation, someone reacts from the heart. When Gretchen Voss asked Karen what it was like to not be able to go to John's wake, she showed no emotion, instead talking about how busy she was that day. When Higgins was asked why he didn't see the unconsciousness man on the lawn, instead of explaining why, like he had some practiced answer, he answered with his eyes immediately watering up. He mentioned how he had a medical bag in his Jeep. He was a trained first responder. He went back to the moment he drove by his friend and lamented that he hadn't seen him so he could have saved him.

A half hour after Higgins left, the McCabes drove by. Julie Nagel and Sarah Levinson were on board. Julie remembers seeing a dark blob on the lawn, but the others saw nothing.

Caitlin Albert's boyfriend Tristan drove from Southie to pick her up at her parents' house. They didn't see anything.

The area where John was found has no streetlight, so it's dark, but headlights would light the yard up pretty well. Why didn't anyone see John?

The key to making this understandable: Lucky Loughran.

Lucky testified that he plowed four times between 2:30 and 4:00. The plow has bright lights, and the seat is high up so the driver can see the road.

But he didn't see John.

Does that mean John wasn't there?

Well, Lucky also plowed twice around 5:30. The plow banks are visible in the police dashcam video. If he went down Fairview at 5:30, he came back up the other way around 5:45. John was found by Karen, Jen, and Kerry at 6:08. And he wasn't just on the lawn but completely buried in snow.

This leaves us with two choices. Either John was placed on the lawn just minutes before he was found... or Lucky plowed the street twice around 5:30 and didn't see John either time.

If John was put out on that lawn just minutes before 6:00, how did he get hypothermia? So it's not very likely he was put out at that time, is it?

But if Lucky, sitting high on the seat in the heavily lit truck, didn't see John during his two passes around 5:30, doesn't that emphasize that whatever position John was in, he wasn't easy to see from the road?

Look, if you get in your car and drive to the supermarket, you're going to pass thousands of objects in the neighbors' yards: bushes, basketball hoops, lawn gnomes, trees, bird baths, fences, boulders, and so on. Your peripheral vision picks all of it up, but your conscious mind is aware of almost none of it. Not unless something flags it to its attention, usually something moving.

So, if you're driving by and there's a lawn gnome in the yard near the house, you probably won't register it. But if that gnome starts running toward the street, your conscious mind is flagged and your foot is ready to slam on the brakes.

And this is all during the day. If you make a trip to the store at night, your peripheral vision will be picking up shadows. If nothing moves, your mind won't register any of it.

John wasn't moving. He was well onto the lawn. He was in the vicinity of the dividing line, where there are bushes, trees, a fire hydrant, a flagpole, an old telecommunications box, and boulders. He was dusted by a layer of snow by 1:30. He blended in. When Higgins drove off, he was adjusting his plow. When the others left, they weren't alone in their vehicles, so they were looking at and talking to each other.

I'm not saying you should dismiss the fact that no one saw John on the lawn. It IS relevant.

But we have to stack it up on one side, while on the other side we stack up the evidence supporting the prosecution's theory.

And we have to look logically at Lucky's testimony. If John wasn't out there when he did his final sweep of Fairview, probably around 5:45, how did he have hypothermia just 15 or 20 minutes later? How was his body temp 81 degrees? How was he covered in snow?

At one time, in order to explain that, Turtleboy put out the idea that the killers put John in the back yard to get hypothermia, then carried him to the front lawn just before he was found.

When you find that a theory is forcing you into more and more absurdities, it's a sign that the theory you're pursuing is just plain not working.

### Why Didn't any Police Investigate the House?

I addressed this earlier when talking about Detective Lank of the CPD. He *could* have asked Brian Albert for permission to search the house. But he walked into an unlocked house in time to see the Alberts coming down the stairs looking like they had just woken up. The McCabes and Alberts all told him John never made it inside the house. Now, people can fairly ask if Lank was a little reluctant to ask Brian this because he was a Boston cop and because his brother was a Canton detective on the force.

But a cop is watching and observing, and his instincts were that these people had just woken up and weren't lying. So far, his instincts seem to have been correct, since John's phone certainly never came into the house.

We know the Canton cops weren't in look-the-other-way mode because they used a leaf blower and collected blood in cups. The evidence is that they were highly motivated. They just had no reason to believe John had gone inside the house.

What about Troopers Proctor and Bukhenik?

Let's ask ourselves this: if they were tasked with framing Karen, wouldn't they have been even more likely to go to 34 Fairview that day? Didn't they need to size up the evidence-planting job? See where John was found? See if the crime scene was being monitored?

Remember YCT Rule #7: Ask why someone DIDN'T do something.

We've already seen that the troopers were in no hurry to get to the Lexus, and because of that, it escaped to Dighton, an hour away. The same question applies here: if they're going to plant evidence, shouldn't there be some urgency in getting to the crime scene?

As it happens, the troopers proceeded methodically and slowly. They went to the CPD to talk to first responders, then to the McCabes to talk to the key witnesses, especially Jen McCabe, and then they went to the hospital to review the remains and speak to Karen, though it turned out she had left. From there, they went to Dighton to interview Karen and get the car.

Did they know when they left the McCabes it was going to be a hit-and-run? They likely had an idea. But we must remember, they aren't forming a theory because a civilian witness gives them one. They're looking at evidence themselves and drawing their own conclusions. It wasn't until they learned at the hospital about the missing shoe that the direction really took a solid turn into a hit-and-run investigation.

Because a missing shoe is such a telltale sign of a pedestrian strike.

**Colin**

Karen has a history of inserting Colin into narratives that don't seem to have involved him. Gretchen Voss could find no evidence that Colin was one of the teens drinking on the lawn. The drug dealer Karen filmed on the street corner, a story related to us by Seamus, wasn't Colin, but rather, a 27-year-old man. John never called 911 on this. He texted the video to his friend, Canton Police Detective Kevin Albert. That's the reason it's in discovery.

While Colin did have abrasions on his knuckles three weeks after John's death, another picture emerged, only 10 days after the tragedy, that showed his knuckles clean.

Higgins testified to briefly seeing a "tall, dark man" inside the house. This excites the FKR crowd. Was it John? But this was almost certainly Colin. Higgins had never met Colin, so he didn't know what he looked like. If it was John, he would have testified it was John, whom he was friends with. Colin was leaving as the Albert family was just arriving, and Higgins arrived just ahead of and walked in with them. The McCabes would arrive minutes later, but they didn't see Colin, nor did they see their daughter Allie's car. Allie and Colin had already left.

Allie had texted Colin that she was out front at 12:10. Colin said his goodbyes as he left, and then they were gone. Allie's phone had the Life 360 app on it so her parents could track the high-school senior. Because Jen McCabe's phone was volunteered to the police, the extraction from it is in evidence, and the Life 360 data is part of that. This came up in court. While it wasn't very clear from what was presented, it seems that the app shows her leaving with Colin several minutes before Karen and John arrived out front. It also seems to show what time she got home, but again, it's not 100% clear based on the trial presentation. There was certainly no evidence that showed her sitting at 34 Fairview after 12:24, or the defense would have hammered that.

Defense lawyer David Yannetti tried to terrify the young woman on the stand with innocent data that was made to seem suspicious. As the app on Allie's phone kept searching for a Wi-Fi signal when she went home, it would connect to the nearest cell tower, on the high school. Yannetti presented this as the girl making various dubious trips in a short amount of time.

The defense tried to suggest that an attack on John was planned, and that the attackers had stashed Colin in the basement with Chloe. Try putting a crazy idea like that in a screenplay and see how long it takes you to get laughed out of Hollywood.

## Why didn't the Canton cops find taillight pieces that morning?

This was a huge issue for many people in this case, one that made them believe evidence was planted. The Canton Police searched the scene around 8:00 in broad daylight, though in the middle of a blizzard, yet they found no red taillight pieces. Meanwhile, the State Police found those pieces over an hour after the sun had set.

Like almost every odd thing in this case, once you have the explanation, it's no longer mysterious.

When John was removed from the lawn around 6:15 A.M., the grass was exposed where he had been lying unconscious. Only a few inches of snow had fallen, and John's diminishing body heat kept snow from accumulating in that spot.

And that spot on the lawn was the only area the Canton Police searched.

The taillight pieces were found buried under three feet of snow, and it's where they were found that explains why the Canton cops didn't find them. They didn't look there.

The impact of the Lexus with John's elbow left taillight debris scattered, but most of the main pieces fell onto the road. Lucky Loughran plowed the road around 5:30 (and possibly at other times before that). That plowing swept the pieces in the direction of the gutter and left them buried within the plowed bank. That bank is clearly visible in the dashcam video.

Lieutenant O'Hara of the SERT team testified that the first piece, the red corner, was found at 5:45 P.M., three feet down. Canton had 22 inches of snow, but that snow accumulated on top of the plow bank made by Lucky, which looks to be about 16 inches. O'Hara described going through the soft snow on top before reaching the harder, plowed snow beneath. The taillight piece was found at ground level.

The Canton Police didn't search there and never would have. They never took a shovel to the scene and never would have taken a shovel to a scene they knew the specialized State Police team would ultimately be investigating. As diligent as the Canton cops were… and even clever, since filming the uniquely preserved leaf-blower evidence… they aren't homicide detectives. They didn't have evidence bags and were forced to use party cups, which they put in a supermarket paper bag.

The only reason the Canton cops were even searching the scene was because the accumulating snow rendered some evidence perishable. They only looked on the lawn, where they found the remnants of the cocktail glass and the blood drops.

In fact, at that time, they didn't even know this was a hit-and-run case. They didn't know the victim had a missing shoe. Therefore, they weren't looking for the shoe, also found at street level in the gutter under the plow bank.

The defense wants us to believe Trooper Proctor drove by and tossed the main taillight piece onto the snow after racing from the sally port. Keep in mind that the sally port bay door didn't close until 5:41, and Proctor was still present. The crime scene is a five-minute drive away, and that corner taillight piece was found at 5:45. At the scene was a WBZ News truck, seven members of the SERT team, and Lt. Tully, their commander, who was documenting the scene with photos. The area the SERT dug out was very small, the size of two parking spaces. And they described digging, back to back, through three feet of snow. So, unless they're all in on it…

There is, however, a serious criticism of the Canton Police: they didn't seal off the crime scene. They made a futile effort to put up yellow crime-scene tape, but that wasn't possible in a blizzard. By 8:30, they had left the scene completely unattended. It remained that way until at least 4:30 P.M.

Is that suspicious? Or just bad judgment?

I'm going to go with the latter. They should have at least left a squad car there flashing its blues.

One thing that we'll find in any and every police investigation is mistakes. The troopers should have taken custody of the Lexus before it escaped to Dighton with Karen and her dad. The Canton cops shouldn't have used a supermarket bag. The troopers should have interviewed Lucky before anyone else did. The Canton cops should have secured the scene as best they could.

Mistakes can be a sign of foul play. They can also be signs of an investigation shoddy enough to create reasonable doubt. But they can also be just ordinary human beings doing their best in unique circumstances and not doing everything perfectly. The blizzard threw everything off that day.

**Proctor**

The Feds looked at Trooper Michael Proctor's calls and messages going back five years! They wanted to get this guy. The Commonwealth of Massachusetts did something similar, going back over the whole period he was a detective. They, too, wanted to get this guy.

The State wanted to get him because of the insensitive nature of his texts. What motivated the Feds remains a mystery.

But despite spending many months looking for ammo to justify terminating his employment, they found nothing beyond the insensitive texts and some limited communication about the case with people not part of the investigation. All of that is serious enough to warrant some disciplinary action.

But absolutely no evidence was found of any wrongdoing.

In fact, Proctor's five-year tenure as a detective was so squeaky clean that this in itself almost seems suspicious.

Or maybe he was just a good cop.

No one would excuse the messages. At one point, he hoped the defendant would kill herself. These messages will hound Trooper Proctor for the rest of his career.

But no evidence emerged to indicate even a possibility that he planted evidence.

No evidence emerged that he tampered with anything.

He was never declared a target by the Feds.

He didn't know Brian Albert, though he did know the family and had a connection with Chris through his sister Courtney.

For Proctor to plant evidence, it would have to be done many hours after the crime, and every hour increased the risk. If anyone snapped a photo of the taillight during the day, he was caught.

He would know this. The risk would be tremendous, and we're talking about framing someone for murder, so the prison sentence would be lengthy.

**YCT Rule #14: It's not just about motive. It's about SUFFICIENT motive.**

Did Proctor have sufficient motive to frame someone for murder, an action highly likely to be exposed since it occurred so long after the incident, and something that would send him to prison for many years?

### What About the Butt Dials?

Let's start with this: what exactly are "butt dials"? People under 40 might have a different understanding of the word.

Back in the '90s and early 2000s, unless you had a flip phone, cell phones in your pocket could more easily dial a caller from your most recent calls. It was very common. And it seemed to happen more frequently when people put their phone in their back pocket. So, your butt, like it had a mind of its own, was sending calls when you sat down.

True story: I knew a guy who butt dialed his wife from the back seat of his car. He wasn't alone. Whatever his enraged wife heard, she went looking, knew where to find him, and you can probably guess how that story ended.

Higgins and Albert, now in their 50s, picked up that phrase in the era just before smartphones. At 58, I speak the same lingo. To me, any unintentional call is a butt dial. I do it maybe five times a week. Even though my head is often up my ass, it's never my butt making the call. Yet I still call it a butt dial. Before this case, I didn't think anything of it. Neither did Brian Higgins or Brian Albert.

When they describe calls as butt dials, they don't mean they put their phones in their pocket and sat on them. They mean an accidental call.

At 2:23, Brian Albert sent a call to Brian Higgins. It showed as answered for one second, but as we've seen, that could just mean it went to voicemail. Moments later, Higgins called back, a call that connected for 22 seconds. Was there a conversation?

According to both, no. Neither of them even remembers any type of call.

Higgins got home before 2:00, made himself something to eat, made another Jameson and ginger, and fell asleep seated on the couch. He was asleep when the phone rang. He doesn't seem aware that he called Brian back and may have done so unintentionally. He'd had several drinks, and it's now foggy.

Higgins suffers from sleep apnea and uses a breathing machine while in bed. The machine stores the data of his sleep history, and it indicates that he was asleep by 2:37.

Would that be likely if he had just committed murder?

When we weigh the evidence in a case, we must always consider the strongest evidence. What evidence seems close to certain?

It's understandable and acceptable to take something like the butt dials and use it as a basis for asking more questions. But it's not at all reasonable to take every unexplained thing and turn that into doubt.

What we want to do is look at the totality of evidence and decide if things like butt dials are meaningful.

### Why did DEA agent Brian Higgins go to work at 1:30 A.M.?

Higgins testified that he left the party between 12:30 and 1:00, and that he arrived at the Canton Police station before 1:30. Very unusual to report to work at 1:30 A.M. after a night of drinking, right?

However, his reason for going to the station presents a reasonable explanation. He had been granted an office there by Chief Berkowitz. He was allowed to keep multiple federal vehicles there. Remember, Higgins does undercover work. A massive snowfall was expected, meaning the lot would need to be plowed. As anyone who has owned a business in New England with a large parking lot will tell you, if you don't want your car plowed in, you move it to a location in the parking lot that is acceptable to the plow drivers. Higgins had to move two vehicles.

When he left for the cop's funeral in New York City, Higgins left the keys to the vehicles on the desk in case it snowed. But that meant someone else had to grab the keys and move the vehicles for him. But he had returned and didn't want to burden anyone with the task, so he went to move them himself.

### End of the Day

At the end of the day, the State has to not just disprove the defense theory. They have to prove their own. In the first trial, the jury failed to reach a verdict. On the charge of manslaughter, they were split, with nine jurors eventually voting guilty and three unconvinced. That suggests the State didn't make the case beyond a reasonable doubt.

Was this a matter of the evidence being insufficient or just an indication of a poor presentation? Let's see if we can present the evidence submitted by the State in a more effective way.

# 3. PHYSICAL EVIDENCE

David Yannetti opened the defense by telling the jury his client was "framed." He had to.

Throughout the book, I've reminded us from time to time that this case is an either/or. Either the Lexus struck John or Karen was framed.

While it's the jury's job to determine the facts, it was the defense that adopted a PR campaign to push their theory, so it's not unfair that we citizens do some evidence weighing ourselves. There's tremendous value in learning more about many aspects of the process and in learning how to use critical-thinking skills. And there's a vital role for us in helping to make sure the system is fair. People have been framed before. It's not just the system that protects our rights, but public awareness.

I've debunked many of the odd things, and others will be addressed in an appendix.

Maybe we can imagine our evidence weighing like this: you're sitting at the kitchen table with two supermarket baskets. In one, you pile all the Odd Things. In the other, you pile the Prosecution's Evidence. Pull out of the basket the odd things where we have found a satisfactory explanation. What's left are unexplained and not fully explained odd things. In virtually every case with this many witnesses, that basket is always going to have a substantial number of items.

So now you stand up, a basket in each hand. Which weighs more?

The heavier the Prosecution Basket is, the less meaningful are the items in the Odd Things Basket.

An effective defense strategy can be to make you forget what's in the Prosecution Basket just with the sheer number of supposedly odd things they point to. As long as they have you saying, "But what about....?" you tend to forget what's in the Prosecution Basket.

In the Karen Read case, the Prosecution Basket had a lot of stuff in it, some more compelling than others. The prosecution's case went nine weeks; that's an enormous amount of information for a jury to absorb. But the biggest problem was this: the most crucial evidence wasn't put together for the jurors before the prosecution rested. It wasn't put together until closing arguments. And that's too late.

**The Evidence**

John's shoe was found ten feet from his body in the gutter against the curb, as were the black drinking straw and several taillight pieces, including the corner piece. Reassembled by the State's criminologist, the pieces perfectly matched what was missing from the Lexus.

The debris field existed in a pattern consistent with a strike about 15 feet from where John ended up.

They found the cocktail glass base with John, several feet onto the lawn.

DNA swabbed off a taillight piece and the cocktail glass matched to John, as did a hair found stuck on the rear panel.

They removed pieces of cocktail glass from the bumper.

Very tiny pieces of taillight, a sixteenth of an inch, were found on John's clothing.

The physical evidence found at the crime scene and on John's clothing and matched to the Lexus leaves no room for a theory involving a different vehicle. This means the only way the Lexus didn't strike John is if there was a very substantial planting of evidence.

What would the minimum number of people be who would have to be involved in this planting operation?

After Turtle's first article in April of 2023, I spent a month exploring this case. Ignorant about forensic data, I believed the 2:27 search for "Hos long…" was an accepted fact. And for me, there would be no innocent explanation for that search. Then I learned that the search was not at all a fact, but disputed by the parties' experts, so I pushed deeper and deeper into the logic of the case. I did this by asking fundamental questions: How did John's phone end up in the yard by 12:32? How come there were practically no signs that John had been in a fight? Why was Karen acting so bizarrely that morning at a time when she couldn't have suspected she was being framed and supposedly didn't even know John was in trouble?

I focused on timelines, trying to determine when someone could have had access to the Lexus and when they could have planted the pieces of taillight. No one got a benefit of the doubt… the police, the prosecutors, the witnesses, or the defendant. Focus on facts, not things that are open to interpretation. We have no recordings of Karen's statements at the crime scene, so there's no way to know what exactly she said and what was in her head when she said it.

But the timeline isn't open to interpretation. I needed to find out where the Lexus was all day. What time could some hypothetical conspirator have accessed it?

It was in John's garage until 5:08 A.M. It was then parked there, under RING surveillance, until a little after noon. Then it was on the road about an hour before being parked in Karen's parents' driveway, where it was quickly buried in snow and where it was again under video surveillance.

The tow truck picked it up around 4:18 P.M. The tow truck drive from Dighton to Canton, at rush hour during a blizzard, would take over an hour. The first taillight piece was dug out at street level by the SERT team at 5:45. The crime scene is a five-minute drive from the sally port where the Lexus was towed to.

Some conclusions were possible, even back then.

A) There was no way taillight pieces were rushed from the sally port to be buried in the snow within the tiny search area where the SERT team was working unless everyone there was in on it—Proctor, Bukhenik, the SERT team, and Lt. Tully. Unless Lt. O'Hara, commander of the team, was lying, the piece was found three feet down, meaning it had to have been buried there by hand if planted after the Lexus was towed. With a WBZ News truck filming and all those men working an area the size of two parking spaces, it wasn't remotely possible to plant that piece unless they were all part of the conspiracy.

B) Because the Lexus was either being driven or was parked in front of surveillance cameras all day, it didn't seem at all likely anyone could have tampered with the vehicle after it left the garage at 5:08 A.M.

C) The fact that the troopers made no attempt to secure the Lexus after they left the McCabes' tells us that there was no plan by that time to involve them in planting evidence from the vehicle. Had the troopers been in on the scheme at that time, there would have been urgency to get to the SUV.

This all made it highly unlikely that the pieces found by the SERT team at 5:45 P.M. had been planted after the towing of the Lexus. And if they weren't planted, it's hard to avoid concluding… well, I'll you finish the thought.

### Karen's Statements at the Scene

Multiple first responders, including paramedics, heard Karen say, "I hit him, I hit him," at the scene. This wasn't a "confession," and in my view, these statements are important, but only in the context of the other evidence. It's impossible to know what was in her head when she made those statements. Could she have been confused?

It's not unreasonable to wonder if the first responders' memories might have been innocently influenced by what they heard others talk about later. That is in no way a suggestion of anyone lying… and no one had any incentive to. But human memory is very malleable and suggestible. Books have been written on that very topic alone. False memories can seem just as real to someone as things that actually happened.

But placed in the context of what other witnesses heard her say, the statements fit neatly into a pattern. According to Kerry Roberts and Jen McCabe, Karen was asking that very question as they searched for John: could I have hit him? And once they found John, it seems to have morphed into "I hit him."

But this could also be seen as exculpatory when it comes to the issue of intent. If Karen was in cover-up mode by the time they found John, would she have been making statements like that?

However, there's one witness she can't get past.

### The Crucial Testimony of Kerry Roberts

Kerry Roberts is practically a member of the O'Keefe family. She barely knew the Alberts or the McCabes, having met Jen once. She picked up John's parents in Braintree during the blizzard and brought them to the hospital for that terrible time. She would have no reason to help cover up the alleged murder of John O'Keefe. When she testified in trial, the defense chose not to even question her and, indeed, that would have been a mistake. Her testimony was emotional, credible, and compelling.

At 5:00 A.M., one hour before the women would find John in the yard covered in snow, Kerry received a call from Karen that woke her and her husband up.

"John's dead!"

Then the call from Karen ended.

As Kerry wiped sleep from her eyes, heart racing, the phone rang again.

"Something has happened to him, he didn't come home, maybe he was hit by a plow."

Or words to that effect. When the call ended, Kerry called 911 and spoke at length to the dispatch officer, Sergeant Goode. The call was played in court. Had anyone injured been picked up? No.

She then called Good Samaritan Medical Center. Had anyone been brought in? No.

For anyone who doubts Kerry's testimony about John being hurt, consider that the calls to the police and to the hospital back up what Kerry testified Karen said on the phone.

So unassailable was her testimony that the defense chose not to cross-examine her.

## 4. GPS

Spoiler Alert: the GPS on John's phone proves he… or at least his phone… never went inside the house.

This is as much a fact as where the Lexus was parked at 8:22 A.M. or that they went drinking at the Waterfall.

In saying that, am I contradicting my previous contention that data must be interpreted?

Some data isn't open to much interpretation. Karen's first call to John that morning was at 12:33. Her first voice message came at 12:37. That type of data isn't in dispute. It is what it is.

The GPS is close to that. I've gone over it in detail earlier. The defense wants us to question whether the clock that the GPS data linked to was accurate. For example, GPS shows they turned onto Fairview at 12:24:18, and they want us to question whether that time was accurate. They argued it could have been off by as many as three minutes.

That seems like a desperate argument made just because all that stair ascending/descending stuff took place at the time that GPS shows they were driving, but for the sake of argument, let's accept their theory that the clock was off. That still doesn't change the fundamental fact that GPS shows he never went in the house.

And get this… Shhh… The defense doesn't dispute it.

Though the legions of FKR didn't notice it, the defense didn't try to argue the fact that the GPS shows the phone never went in the house. They argued that the clock was off, but whatever time we want to ascribe to those GPS points, they still never go in the house. Whether John didn't climb stairs at 12:24 or he didn't climb them at 12:22… he didn't climb them.

Every second of GPS data comes with a known signal strength and, from that, we get the margin of error. The signal strength is always known, so the margin of error is always known. Remember the data I reported earlier. There was only a four-second window when the signal weakened enough to allow the margin of error to include the house.

At no time is there a signal showing John in the driveway.

Or on the lawn.

Or moving in the direction of the house.

Four seconds isn't enough time for John to run from the street into the house and end up back where he was found. It's definitely not enough time for him to go inside, get mauled by a dog, and beaten up.

The defense's hope is that with all this argument about data, the jury's eyes will glaze over and they'll tune it out.

That wouldn't work on me. And it wouldn't work on most of you.

The phone never went inside the house.

# 5. KEY CORRELATION

By far, the most compelling and crucial evidence is the correlation between the Tech Stream vehicle data, the location data on John's phone, and the movement data on that phone.

Amazingly, while this data was presented to the jury by the prosecution, it wasn't done in a way that the all-important correlation was made clear. The reason is that it was presented by two different troopers, and neither of them had access to the other's work. The prosecutor, Adam Lally, did try to pull this together during his closing arguments, but it was really too late by then. This needed to be fully established in the jurors' minds by the time the prosecution rested its case. And it needed to be explained by one competent expert.

Trooper Paul had the vehicle data but not the phone data.

Trooper Guarino had the phone data but not the vehicle data.

It's correlating these two that makes the prosecution's case pretty much bulletproof.

Ready? We're almost there!

Karen and John didn't quite know how to find the house, so John called Jen McCabe from a little over a mile away to get the address. He punched it into Waze from Dedham St. Waze directed them to Maplecroft Rd., then Oakdale. They took a right on Cedarcrest. Fairview is the third left.

But they missed that turn. And we know the exact time: 12:23:46.

After missing the turn, Karen performed a three-point turn on Cedarcrest in order to could get back to the intersection. But that three-point turn was unusual, because the Toyota Tech Stream data recorded an event.

Let's briefly go back to how vehicle data works. Every car has a black box, also known as an Event Data Recorder (EDR). If the car gets in an accident, this "triggers" the creation of a Crash Data Record (CDR).

A CDR records five seconds before and five seconds after the triggering of the event.

The black box (EDR) in Karen's Lexus never recorded a CDR, so it never detected a crash. But the ARCCA guys explained why: pedestrian strikes typically don't produce a CDR because of the size differential.

Sorry guys, apparently size does matter.

However, Toyota/Lexus vehicles come with an additional event recorder called Tech Stream, and Tech Stream records a wider range of events.

Within the Tech Stream data of Karen's Lexus, only two events in the history of the vehicle were triggered to create a report. Both occurred that night, with the second event coming eight minutes and four seconds after the first.

Again, as of the first trial, these events in the Tech Stream data didn't come with timestamps. It's possible the recent new chip off might produce these timestamps, but even if not, we know the times of the events because they can also be found in the GPS and Waze data found on John's phone.

The first event triggered in the Tech Stream was a three-point turn. Trooper Paul explained that the algorithms of the Tech Stream created an event because the accelerator had been punched at more than 30% while in reverse. In the few years Karen had owned the vehicle, which she bought new, she had never done something similar because there were no other triggered events besides these two from that night.

We know from John's Waze that they missed the left turn onto Fairview and therefore had to do a three-point turn on Cedarcrest. And that turn is also visible in the raw GPS data.

After turning around, they arrived back at the intersection from the opposite direction. The truck carrying Ryan Nagel arrived from the other side at the same time. Karen had the right of way and turned right onto Fairview at exactly 12:24:18.

What time exactly was the three-point turn on Cedarcrest? The State should have this within the GPS, though Trooper Guarino didn't reveal it in the first trial, probably because he hadn't been given the vehicle data and didn't understand the crucial importance of the correlation. But we know they missed the left turn at 12:23:46 and took the right at 12:24:18. So, if the three-point turn was exactly in the middle, that would be about 12:24:02. It's safe to say the turn was at that time, plus or minus five seconds.

The next triggered event comes 8:04 after the three-point turn. What triggered it? Again, it was the unusual accelerator depression while in reverse. This time she punched it 70%, reckless and dangerous while in reverse.

So an event was triggered in that moment, creating a snapshot from five seconds before and five seconds after. That snapshot shows the car in drive for a few seconds, then it suddenly brakes and slams in reverse.

Eight minutes and eight seconds into that event comes what Trooper Paul describes as the telltale signs of a pedestrian strike. While the foot remains on the accelerator at the same rate, four seconds after the event was triggered, the vehicle slows from 24.2 to 23.6 MPH. At the same moment, the steering wheel jolts from 4.5 degrees to -4.5 degrees.

This means the Lexus struck an object large enough to create these slight but noticeable changes. Could it have been the curb? A trash barrel?

One might argue this was possible until we include the last piece of data. This one hammers the nail.

John's phone last moved at 12:32:16.

The phone, found underneath him that morning when the first responders arrived, didn't move at all between 12:32:16 and that time.

So eight minutes and eight seconds after the three-point turn, the Lexus struck a pedestrian-sized object. That's at 12:32:10, plus or minus a few seconds. And John's phone last moved at 12:32:16.

That correlation was never made for the jury. At least not in the first trial.

But that correlation is as bulletproof as if the event were caught on video surveillance.

### A Lingering Problem?

This leaves what at first looks like a problem. Trooper Guarino testified that Karen's phone connected to John's Wi-Fi "around 12:36." Assuming the striking of John happened seconds before 12:32:16, could she have made the journey in that time?

If we enter the trip from 34 Fairview to 1 Meadows into Google, it says six minutes.

However, I had someone from Canton test this route late at night. We don't know what route Karen took home, but I believe she did another turn on Fairview and went back the way they had come, down Cedarcrest. From there to Dedham Street there are three stop signs, including the one at the corner of Dedham. In that quiet neighborhood at midnight, she would have no reason to slow much at those stop signs.

She would then take Dedham for a long stretch to reach Washington Street, which is Canton's main street. There are no stop signs on Dedham, and it would be easy to reach speeds of over 50 MPH.

There's a signal light at Dedham and Washington, but sensors detect the vehicle coming so that when it reaches the intersection, if there's no traffic on Washington, it's green when she gets there.

After turning down Washington, the next intersection again has a signal light that is sensor activated, and she's taking a right on red anyway onto Pleasant Street. Another long stretch of road with no stop signs, easy to reach a high speed without worry.

Pleasant connects to Meadows, and John's house is the first on the right. Actually, we can see in the RING video that Pleasant Street is just a few feet beyond John's fence, so it's possible Karen's phone connected to John's Wi-Fi from Pleasant. But in any case, she would turn onto Meadows and then right into the driveway.

What about the weather? The storm hadn't really started by this point.

The phone connected to the Wi-Fi "around 12:36." Seconds matter here, so if only we knew exactly, was it 12:36:05 or 12:36:45?

We may never know. The route I just gave you isn't the fastest one. Other routes, even using the conservative speeds calculated by Google, take only five minutes. But even the longer route, which I believe she took, was completed in four minutes and eight seconds by our driver. I told her to drive safely, just go a little fast. She only needed to average 35 MPH to reach John's home in 4:25. So this wasn't the Cannonball Run. Driving home on empty streets, she just had to drive like most people in Massachusetts do, using the speed laws more or less as helpful suggestions.

Though we can't be certain what route Karen took and how fast she drove, the times match up pretty perfectly, as long as "around 12:36" means something between 12:36:30 and 12:37.

# 6. FINAL HURDLE

Surprisingly, despite knowing for a year that the defense was claiming that the shallow abrasions on John's right arm were the result of a dog attack, the prosecution didn't offer a detailed explanation of their own for those wounds. They made little attempt to describe the lack of bruising on the arm. They didn't present a theory as to why no bones were visibly broken despite the arm being struck by a 6000-lb. SUV.

What they told us was that John's arm broke the taillight, and the Lexus swiped him in a way that launched him at an angle toward the lawn, and the head injury was caused by the frozen ground. It wasn't at all satisfying.

What is needed—badly—is an independent accident reconstructionist to give the jury a convincing explanation for what probably happened. Countering Dr. Russell's conclusions on the cause of the arm injuries by simply saying that "the taillight caused it" isn't going to work. The jury needs to know specifically how that taillight left those parallel tracks on John's arm.

The County now has opened up the purse to hire an accident reconstructionist and a dog-bite expert. We don't know at this time what they'll say.

We do have a clue from Special Prosecutor Brennan, who mentioned in a Daubert hearing of Dr. Russell that John's arm was bent in a defensive position.

Therefore, we can conjecture that the State will attempt an explanation similar to the following:

Sensing the speeding Lexus about to strike him, John put up his bent arm in a defensive posture. The elbow took off the corner of the taillight, exposing the internal housing. Plastic ridges within that housing caused the wounds on his right arm.

As the Lexus pushed through at high speed, John's forearm snapped toward the rear of the Lexus, and his hand—which was holding the cocktail glass—caused the dent on the front panel. That dent is exactly a forearm's length away from the taillight for a six-foot-two man.

The taillight also pushed John's elbow into his torso, so that for a moment, the Lexus was impacting John center mass, though his torso was protected by his elbow, and his arm was in turn cushioned by his torso. This had the effect of launching John with significant momentum, even though it was just a sideswipe.

The cocktail glass was found near John's body, and that's strong evidence that tremendous force was imparted on the body, because that same force was transferred onto any object John held, so that the object ended up where he did.

The State's explanation is going to be something along those lines. It doesn't need to be perfectly convincing because there's a lot of other evidence, but it needs to be much more convincing than what we got the first time.

When I first started looking into this case, multiple friends who worked in law enforcement and who had experienced responding to car crashes and hit-and-runs all told me something similar: that really unpredictable things happen to the human body in these high-speed encounters with heavy machines, and that it takes a trained, experienced specialist to understand what occurred. I was really shocked and disappointed, therefore, that we didn't get that explanation in the first trial.

But the defense strategy deserves criticism as well. Yes, they did an incredible job portraying the mundane and ordinary as odd and suspicious in a way that stirred up the masses. It generated hundreds of thousands of dollars used for Karen's defense fund.

But it did much more than that. One morning late in the trial, the start was delayed for over an hour. What was going on? We learned that a jury member had been dismissed, and the judge was now questioning the jurors seated next to her. The dismissed juror seemed to be fighting to stay on the jury, a very emotional and unexpected disruption.

I have the story from multiple close sources. In fact, I have the story in much, much more depth than I will share here, because I wish to protect the anonymity of the juror, even though her conduct was egregiously wrong and threatened to undermine a fair trial.

The educated and intelligent woman was an avowed Turtle Rider. During the year preceding the trial, Turtleboy had covered practically nothing else. And far from covering the trial like a journalist, he covered it like P.T. Barnum would have had he lived in the age of YouTube—ruthlessly accusing the witnesses of being murderers in order to generate content and revenue for his channel.

During the ten-week-long trial, the juror, on more than one occasion, went out drinking in bars, got inebriated, and began telling everyone in the bar that she was a Turtle Rider and that she was going to acquit Karen.

The night before she was dismissed, it happened again, only this time the incident included her driving into Boston, where the bars are open an hour later, and being pursued by the Boston Police. Some version of that story must have made its way to Judge Cannone.

Yikes. This juror didn't suddenly become a Turtle Rider during the trial, so she had to have lied on the questionnaire in order to get on that jury. She obviously had made up her mind long before being impaneled. It also means that every morning when the judge had the jurors raise their right hand to swear they hadn't followed the case in the media, she was likely lying under oath.

Her dismissal left the jury at 14. After closing arguments, two jurors were selected by lottery to become alternates. The next day, one of those chosen as an alternate showed up to court dressed in pink, tears in her eyes. She obviously was a Karen Read supporter too.

So certainly one, and likely two, jurors came into this with their minds heavily influenced by the PR campaign run by Karen and her lawyers.

However, the defense strategy, as applied in court, might also have prevented Karen from having any chance of getting 12 acquittal votes, despite a weak presentation by the prosecution. The third-party culprit theory they had carefully crafted was one thing on YouTube or Twitter, but something very different in court. One witness after another took the stand and came across as an ordinary, decent human being. This wasn't a mob trial where the witnesses were in the Witness Protection Program and had lived criminal lives. These were first responders—some cops, some firefighters—people who came across as the kind of decent human beings you would want working in a small town. They came across so well that it had the effect of making the Boston suburb seem like a great place to live. Were they all part of some criminal scheme to frame an innocent woman? The witnesses from the house also came across as decent, ordinary people: a former fifth-grade teacher, a hospital nurse. And Kerry Roberts is a longtime friend of the O'Keefe family.

But the defense tried to make them all seem suspicious. Tried to portray them as willing participants in framing an innocent person for murder.

Most of the jury likely looked at these first responders and witnesses as being ordinary, decent people very much like them. They may have resented the grandstanding by the defense.

So, perhaps it depends on the goals of Karen's team. If acquittal was the desired outcome, their strategy strikes me as a doomed one because it seems very unlikely to convince 12 jurors.

However, if the goal is a hung jury, it's extremely effective, because there is a very good chance of getting one or two jurors through who have already made up their mind.

## Yellow Cottage Meltdown

I've talked a lot in this book about mistakes. Mistakes by the prosecutors, the defense team, the Canton Police, the State Police. Perhaps I haven't talked enough about my own mistakes.

I'm not talking about *getting* something wrong. I'm talking about *doing* something wrong. Intentionally.

Rumors were swirling about incidents involving some of Karen's old boyfriends. Even if true, that kind of testimony is inadmissible and, to be clear, there's no substantial evidence confirming any of these rumors. I had discussed these reports with my co-hosts, Dave and Erica, and all three of us had agreed that even if we had solid evidence verifying these rumors, we should keep it to ourselves.

But I had been manipulated into falsely reporting that Colin was a drug dealer, so I felt maybe the line had already been crossed.

Now, that was a double line, because not only was Colin being smeared, but smeared with complete fiction. And not just Colin, but virtually all the witnesses.

So, the ethical guidelines became a little bit loosened for me. That was a mistake.

What happened was that I found a back door. I cheated. I saw a way to allow the topic to be broached without actually reporting any specific rumor.

Seamus O'Malley, our retired DEA friend, told me he had run the records and found no court documents related to Karen and these alleged incidents. I asked him if he was willing to come on the show and report exactly that. Not sensing any ulterior motive, he obliged.

Say what you want about Turtleboy, he's no fool. He understood. And he set out to stop it.

The show began innocently enough. Seamus said his piece, then Erica and Dave joined the panel. We said nothing about this talk of incidents, and Seamus merely reported that any rumors about Karen and her old boyfriends weren't true. End of story.

But Turtleboy was there in the channel's chat with hundreds of followers, and really, at that time, most of our followers were also fans of Turtle and Karen.

Turtle tried to goad me in the chat. Erica warned me in private not to take the bait. Now, that would have worked a couple of weeks before, but I was unconsciously looking for a reason. So when it came, I readily gave into it.

The triggering words for me were when he accused me of "both sides-ism." Can you imagine a "journalist" thinking that covering something from both sides is a problem?

In any case, that was all the trigger I needed, and I let loose a barrage that upset my team, my family, and the neighbors. It was loud.

I accused him of working with the defense. He denied it, calling me a liar. We now know beyond any doubt that this was true. The State documented dozens of calls between Aidan and Karen's lawyers and hundreds with Karen herself. Those communications began as the story broke. At first, they used a go-between, Natalie, for text messages, and eventually switched to an encryption app, knowing the legal shadiness of what they were doing.

Aidan's connection to the defense team was known to me because he had tried to set up a call between Alan Jackson and me, but really, anyone following his coverage of the case who DIDN'T assume he was working with the defense might want to be careful about inheritances from Nigerian princes.

Look, I'm not proud of the public rant while on the air live.

But I'm not ashamed of it either. I wish I had done it differently and done it much earlier, but I would truly be ashamed if I hadn't done it at all.

However, I was wrong to allow someone to come on my show just to deny the truth of rumors (about Karen and previous boyfriends) about something that many people were probably completely unaware of.

I didn't pay a price for allowing Seamus on to discuss the debunked rumors, but I paid a very heavy price for the meltdown with Turtleboy. Dave jumped off the air in the middle of the show. Erica scolded me while still live. I apologized, but it didn't take and produced another scolding. I did truly feel bad about making them uncomfortable. But I also understood that even our close friendship wouldn't be enough to overcome their loyalty to Aidan. That was another cult-like aspect of the Turtle phenomena. For those who truly become absorbed in it, breaking away isn't at all easy.

Months later, I would talk to someone related to one of the witnesses, who were under constant siege by the mob. She told me she happened to be watching that night, and when the meltdown occurred, she started crying tears of joy. Because she felt their families had been completely alone and isolated, stunned into silence, unable to process how their own community had turned on them, shell-shocked as a rabble rouser led neighbors and friends into believing they were part of an utterly absurd murder conspiracy. And now, finally, someone had stood up to him. It wasn't anyone important; just some Bloody Mary maker pretending to live in a yellow cottage, but they felt anything was better than nothing.

Hearing how much relief it gave her would eventually make me feel better about the "meltdown" episode. But for the moment, it was a low point for the channel. Forty percent of the subscribers unsubscribed within a couple of hours.

And an FKR fan created an image of a yellow cottage on fire.

# CONCLUSION

# 1. LIFE IN A YELLOW COTTAGE

Privately, Dave and Erica were both telling me they were now highly skeptical of the conspiracy theory, and Erica even sent an email in which she stated that she was 98% sure the prosecution's case was beyond a reasonable doubt. But both had young kids, and they were very concerned about the wrath of the mob. Erica's husband was an FKR diehard, and though Dave's wife didn't believe in Karen's innocence at all, she too was worried about mob reaction.

People reading these words might not appreciate just how vicious the Turtleboy mob is. In another time and place, they would be parading with torches and roping people up. It's not that this mob is violent... though I have received threats. No, it's more that it draws from the same dark, human impulse that rears its ugly head, maybe in historical times of anxiety, and causes people who are more or less decent to become quite indecent. Aidan, like any cult leader, merely exploits this dark impulse for his own purposes.

A sign of this dark impulse is the absolute glee with which they try to destroy witnesses, or anyone who raises questions or who challenges Turtleboy. The glee is what truly identifies the cruelty. They display joy in hounding people and attempting to ruin lives. It's a party for them. This is why for over a year we've seen them mercilessly booing the O'Keefe family and John's friends. When Turtleboy says the family should "burn in hell" and repeatedly calls John's mother a "cunt," not a single person in his mob breaks ranks.

What is the O'Keefes' crime, you ask?

Merely staying silent and disbelieving the absurd conspiracy theory developed by the defendant.

This is absolutely not a situation where people are viciously crossing the line on both sides. That's false equivalency. Turtleboy threatened to bring a mob to the soccer games of the children of the young Attorney General, a mother in Boston who isn't even involved with the Karen Read case. And this doesn't seem to slow his popularity. The lure of this mob has created a feeding frenzy where people who feel aggrieved in life, including low-level staff within the courts or law enforcement, are eager to contribute.

This is what rightfully worried Dave and Erica. I understood. And in every conversation, I made it clear that I didn't expect them to stick their necks out in any way.

At this time, they were also getting bombarded by FKR fans who suggested they break away from me. They didn't talk about it with me, but I was aware.

And they struggled with it. We worked well together, and we all liked each other. I had never asked them to do anything that would make them uncomfortable. After the meltdown episode, I made clear that I wasn't going to be silent anymore, but I was still going to cover things fairly, from both sides. As always, I would follow the evidence wherever it went. And I didn't expect them to stick their necks out.

In September, a new filing from the State revealed more information, including GPS data from John's phone showing that he never went inside the house. The mob dismissed this evidence without even a moment's thought. They weren't interested in learning about the State's evidence. They had no desire to research the accuracy of GPS. After I did a show that morning, saying it was time to start mending fences because John didn't go in the house, Turtleboy and the other content creators posted on Twitter that I was lying… while oddly admitting they hadn't read the document.

So, believing in the conspiracy theory now required blindly rejecting any evidence, no matter how solid, that they didn't like.

I felt isolated. Convincing people to weigh evidence honestly seemed hopeless. The public temperature hadn't changed at all. Few seemed to be absorbing arguments logically. We were in the midst of a period of hysteria.

Dave and Erica wanted to remain loyal, but the final pressure to go out on their own came not just from fear of the mob. It came from that hardest-to-resist of human motivators: temptation.

Other people with far less talent than Dave and Erica were jumping into the game, launching their own channels, and overnight, their numbers were multiple times that of Yellow Cottage Tales. Conspiracy theories always draw a lot of interest, and the Karen Read one really had legs. It was getting national attention.

The hunt for numbers, whether it's in regular media or small YouTube channels, is insatiable. Whether you're competing in a big lake or a small pond, you need views to survive. It's a Darwinist environment made for grifters, and everyone was jumping on the bandwagon. Dave and Erica felt like they were missing the boat.

I heard that Dave had launched his own channel from Free Karen Readers taking shots at me. I had seen the handwriting on the wall for weeks, but now I could read it. The Discord team folded shop, Erica joined Dave's channel, and all that was left with me was faithful old friend Tom Fleming, who had been by my side breaking up bar fights once upon a time.

In the fall of 2023, now having to rebuild from the ashes, I stopped doing shows for a couple of weeks and took stock. Did I want to go back to doing live shows by myself? Did

I want to start over having to win the trust of a whole new audience?

I did restart, but the live audience had dwindled down to about 20 people, and about half of those were Turtle Riders who showed up to taunt me.

But the thing about life in a cottage is that you don't need much. You don't even need anyone to know you're there. A little light to read by. A table for your coffee.

And time to write.

# 2. AMERICAN EVIL

Everyone knows the famous quote:

> ***"The only thing necessary for the triumph of evil is for good men to do nothing."*** - Edmund Burke.

But there are other ways that evil and good people are inherently linked. There are evil individuals in the world, but they're the exception. Most human beings are essentially decent. However, under certain circumstances, and within the context of a group, they become capable of evil.

Not evil like the days of yesteryear, at least not in most parts of the modern world. There are no lynchings. No burning of witches at the stake. No concentration camps. Now evil is more subtle. Quite cruel and quite destructive, but generally no longer violent.

What remains true both in the more vicious historical past and in the milder present is this: large-scale evil requires the active participation of people who are, on the whole, good people. People who love their families, pay their taxes, and generally don't engage in criminal activity. Regular people.

They're *led* by individuals who are most certainly not good people, individuals who are exploiting them for their own selfish purposes. But those leaders would be powerless without a crowd to follow them.

These followers don't consider themselves evil and, in fact, they believe they're on the side of good, doing the right thing.

I'm not talking about something where people can legitimately disagree about what is right and wrong. Democrats think Republicans are evil and vice versa. People take different sides on the conflict in the Middle East, or whether vaccines should be mandated, or abortion allowed.

What I'm talking about is people engaging in behavior which, were it not for the unusual blinders they put on when their passions are inflamed, they would know is evil. In other words, they're not being themselves.

We've seen this behavior in the Free Karen Read hysteria since Turtleboy first started covering the story and orchestrating a circus to create entertaining content for his channel. Within a few weeks of his coverage, he took his cameraman to the youth lacrosse game of Jen McCabe's daughter and went into the bleachers to harass Jen, who was quietly watching the game. Matt McCabe was there, but he's a very congenial man, not confrontational, and Turtle felt protected by the presence of the cameraman.

Every decent person knows what Turtleboy did was wrong. No one needs me to point it out. They already know it. It's abhorrent behavior. And if you had shown to Turtle's fans some other YouTuber in some other case doing this, they would be horrified.

However, they weren't at all bothered in this case.

When Turtleboy threatened to bring his mob to the Attorney General's kids' soccer game, no one uttered a peep.

But that same crowd regularly and loudly booed John's family and friends when they showed up in court.

If that isn't a mindless mob, what is?

In June of 2023, they organized over a hundred people and dozens of cars to go on a Rolling Rally, which took this angry mob to the homes of each of the witnesses as well as Trooper Proctor. The event was planned and coordinated, so most of the witnesses knew it was coming, and the State Police set up cameras in some of the houses.

But while some residents arranged to not be around, most of these people had large families with young children, and they couldn't really get away. The angry mob, led by Turtle with a bullhorn, lingered at each house, blocking all street traffic, shouting at neighbors that these people were murderers, while small kids were brought into bathrooms in the hopes of protecting them from what was being shouted.

There were two women, who turned out to be hospital nurses, who got out at each spot to spit in the driveways.

At Chris Albert's D&E Pizza, people—some from distant states—come in just to call them murderers, or to throw rubber duckies inside, on the bottom of which is written baseless accusations about his son.

Seamus O'Malley, despite having spent his career in law enforcement, launched his own YouTube channel, which quickly built a following of thousands, and his verbal attacks on the witnesses and John's family grew increasingly bizarre and exceptionally offensive. They can't even be repeated here. But he became a guest on Howie Carr's radio show and was on the front page of the *New York Post*.

Many channels and even several LawTubers sprang up to join the grift. Every content creator understood that there was a tremendous thirst in the public to believe in this conspiracy.

They talked frequently about being champions of free speech, but they were the exact opposite. Anyone… anyone… who tried anywhere in social media to ask questions immediately had a target on their back.

And on the backs of their families.

The methods had been developed by Aidan over years. Aidan understood a couple of things.

Once a social media mob gets big enough and has enough attention, it draws in people who just want to be a part of it. And to stand out in that mob, they try to bring him what he needs most: dirt. So they dig and, as needed, they invent.

He also knew that with the threat of social media smear comes substantial power.

I've talked to multiple lawyers who refused to join the prosecution of Karen Read or Aidan Kearney, who faced multiple charges of witness intimidation. These lawyers feared the impact of social media smear.

Faced with the threat of such smear, most people remain terrified into silence.

But it's more than silence that enables it. Thousands of people are active participants. Thousands find entertainment in the attacks on innocent witnesses.

So, let's finish with a final YCT rule, a spin on the old Burke quote.

**The only thing necessary for the triumph of evil is for good people to trick themselves into thinking that what they're doing is NOT evil.**

*For More News About Kevin Lenihan, Signup For Our Newsletter:*

**http://wbp.bz/newsletter**

*Word-of-mouth is critical to an author's long-term success. If you appreciated this book please leave a review on the Amazon sales page:*

**https://wbp.bz/sosreviews**

ALSO AVAILABLE FROM WILDBLUE PRESS

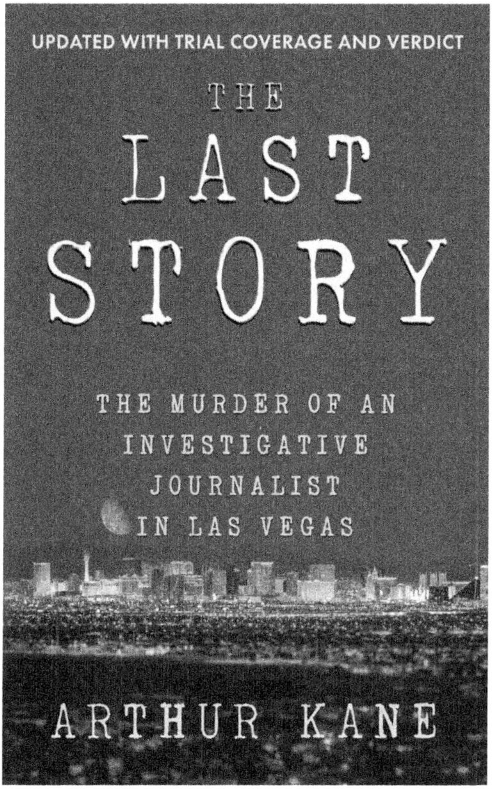


http://wbp.bz/laststory

THE LAST STORY: The Murder of an Investigative Journalist in Las Vegas is an exclusive deep dive into a chilling true tale of sex, ambition, retribution, and homicide.

# ALSO AVAILABLE FROM WILDBLUE PRESS

## CASE SOLVED! THE DELPHI MURDERS

### THE QUEST TO FIND 'THE MAN ON THE BRIDGE'

BY THE HOST OF *TRUE CRIME GARAGE*

**NIC EDWARDS**
WITH BRIAN WHITNEY

http://wbp.bz/delphi

**UPDATED WITH STUNNING INVESTIGATION AND TRIAL COVERAGE!**

"A crime story with heart. Impressively researched and written with passion."--Patrick Quinlan, Los Angeles Times Best Selling author of ALL THOSE MOMENTS

ALSO AVAILABLE FROM WILDBLUE PRESS

BURL BARER
FRANK C. GIRARDOT JR.
KEN EURELL
BETRAYAL IN BLUE
THE SHOCKING MEMOIR OF THE SCANDAL THAT ROCKED THE NYPD
THE STORY BEHIND THE DOCUMENTARY "THE SEVEN FIVE"

http://wbp.bz/biba

The true story of drugs and corruption in Brooklyn's 75th precinct, as told by a cop who lived it, a journalist, and an Edgar Award-winning author.

Printed in Great Britain
by Amazon

61291729R00211